Instructor's Manual with Test Bank for
Hartmann and Impey's

Astronomy
The Cosmic Journey

SIXTH EDITION

John L. Safko
University of South Carolina

BROOKS/COLE

THOMSON LEARNING

Australia • Canada • Mexico • Singapore • Spain • United Kingdom • United States

COPYRIGHT © 2002 Wadsworth Group.
Brooks/Cole is an imprint of the Wadsworth Group, a division of Thomson Learning, Inc.
Thomson Learning™ is a trademark used herein under license.

For more information about this or any other Brooks/Cole products, contact:
BROOKS/COLE
511 Forest Lodge Road
Pacific Grove, CA 93950 USA
www.brookscole.com
1-800-423-0563 (Thomson Learning Academic Resource Center)

For permission to use material from this work, contact us by
www.thomsonrights.com
fax: 1-800-730-2215
phone: 1-800-730-2214

Printed in the United States of America

10   9   8   7   6   5   4   3   2   1

ISBN: 0-534-38251-7

Contents

Preface

Astronomy has evolved rapidly in recent decades. Every few years, it seems, some major discovery has caused reassessment of one theory or another. A recent article on publishing pointed out that astronomy text publishers risk having obsolete books before finishing their first press run! For just this reason, the text takes the long view and states the uncertainties of some current mysteries and controversies rather than endorsing the latest interpretation of research of the last few years. For the same reasons, some of the problems in the text are worded so that there is not necessarily one correct answer; the intention is to get students thinking about the material. Each chapter of this manual has three sections: Answers to Problems in the Text, Sample Test Questions, and Word Practice. The answers provided for some of these problems should be considered only as a guide to possible student responses; instructors will have to decide for themselves what range of answers they will accept.

The Sample Test Questions are of three types: True-False, Multiple Choice, and Essay. The questions attempt to cover most of the points raised in the text; again, instructors will have to select those questions most appropriate to the material emphasized in the classroom. Answers are provided for the True-False and Multiple Choice questions, but no suggested answers are provided for the Essay questions. Some of the questions on material covered in the optional math sections are denoted by an asterisk.

At the end of each chapter is provided some suggested Word Practice (or fill-in-the-blank) exercises. These may be used for exam questions, but they are most useful as a study aid for your students. Most of the terms in the Word Practice are from the Concepts List at the ends of the chapters. The few that are from elsewhere in the chapters are marked by an asterisk (*).

Suggestions and comments from users have resulted in modifications in each of the editions of this manual. We thank those users who have submitted suggestions and also the staff members of the Astronomy Center of the University of South Carolina for helping with the proofing of this material. Since we are trying to develop the most useful form for this supplement, we invite instructors' comments and criticisms. We also welcome corrections for any errors in the answer sections.

William K. Hartmann
Chris Impey
Tucson, Arizona

John L. Safko
Columbia, South Carolina

Invitation to the Cosmic Journey

Answers to Problems in the Text

1. Each student will have his or her own answer to this question. Their answers should be justified. The instructor might want to ask this question again at the end of the course.

Sample Test Questions

True-False

1. The definition of astronomy today is the same as it always was. F
2. This text treats scientific research as being like climbing a tree, starting near the trunk and proceeding to ever more specialized branches of knowledge. F
3. Our galaxy contains open star clusters. T
4. 3×10^7 is the same as 30,000,000. T
5. The unit of length in the SI system is the kilogram. F
6. We are on a cosmic journey, and astronomy is the process of finding out where we are. T
7. Our Sun is a star. T
8. A typical star cluster is bigger than the galaxy. F

Multiple Choice

1. Scientific research can be likened to
   A. climbing up the tree of knowledge
 * B. climbing down the tree of knowledge
   C. riding a sled down a steep hill
   D. climbing stairs
   E. none of the above

2. This text treats astronomy as
   A. a narrow set of academic observations
 * B. a voyage of exploration with practical effects on humanity
   C. the science of casting horoscopes
   D. both B and C
   E. none of the above

3. The _____ is everything that exists.
   A. nebula
   B. Sun
   C. galaxy
 * D. universe
   E. solar system

4. A _____ is a swarm of billions of stars.
   A. universe
 * B. galaxy
   C. solar system
   D. globular star cluster
   E. nebula

5. A globular star cluster is
   A. everything that exists
   B. a swarm of billions of galaxies
   * C. a spheroidial mass of hundreds of thousands of stars
   D. a cloud of dust and gases
   E. none of the above

6. 5000 written in power-of-ten notation is
   A. 5×10^5
   B. 5×10^4
   * C. 5×10^3
   D. 5×10^{-3}
   E. 5×10^{-4}

7. The number 2.9×10^5 is the same as
   * A. 290,000
   B. 2,900,000
   C. 290
   D. 0.000029
   E. 0.0000029

8. Masses are expressed in kilograms in the _____ system.
   A. solar
   B. English
   * C. SI
   D. natural
   E. star

9. Lengths are expressed in _____ in the SI system.
   A. feet
   * B. meters
   C. centimeters
   D. kilometers
   E. inches

Essay

1. Describe how scientific research is analogous to working our way down a tree.
2. Analyze the text's definition of astronomy.
3. Why does the author treat scientific research as analogous to working our way down a tree rather than up a tree?
4. Arrange the following objects in order of increasing size: galaxy, Moon, Sun, Earth, star cluster, universe.
5. Distinguish among galaxies, globular star clusters and open star clusters.
6. Distinguish between science and a collection of facts.

Word Practice

1. A(n) _____ is a cloud of dust and gas.
2. _____ is the process of finding out where we are.
3. A(n) _____ is an enormous ball of gas, mostly hydrogen.
4. The largest grouping of stars is the ___. All of these groupings make the universe.
5. The _____ is everything that exists.
6 A grouping of stars found only in the spiral arms of galaxies is a(n) _____.
7. The _____ is the nearest natural body to the Earth.
8. The planet upon which we live is the _____.
9. A(n) ____ _____ _____ is a spheroidial mass of hundreds of thousands of stars.
10. The nearest star to us is the _____.
11. The _____ _____ is comprised mostly of the planets about our Sun.
12. The _____ notation is a convenient system for expressing large and small
    numbers.
13. The ___ ___ is the set of units that we will use to express physical dimensions.
14. _____ and _____ are small bodies orbiting between the planets.
15. The smaller bodies orbiting planets are called _____.

Answers to Word Practice

1. nebula
2. astronomy
3. star
4. galaxy
5. universe
6. open star cluster
7. Moon
8. Earth
9. globular star cluster
10. Sun
11. solar system
12. powers of ten
13. SI system
14. comets, asteroids
15. satellites

Chapter 1

Prehistoric Astronomy:
Origins of Science and Superstition

Answers to Problems in the Text

1. a. Moves westerly (left). As it continues, it comes closer to the horizon.
    b. Moves easterly (right). As it continues it rises higher above the horizon.
    c. Moves toward the horizon (down). As it continues, it moves toward the east (right).
    d. If initially to the right of the NCP, it moves toward the east (right). As it continues, it will rise (up). If initially to the left of the NCP, it moves toward the east (right). As it moves it will first set (down) and later rise.

All of these motions result from the stars moving counterclockwise in circles about the NCP.

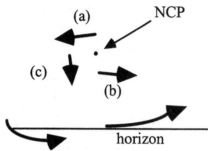

Many students take the *just above* as a literal *at* and say "no motion."

2. a. Moves westerly (right) and comes closer to the horizon.
    b. Moves easterly (left) and rises higher above the horizon.
    c. Moves away from the horizon and toward the west (right).
    d. Moves away from the horizon and toward the east (left).
    All motions are now clockwise as seen by the observer, but east and west are now on different sides of the observer than they were in the Northern Hemisphere.

3. The elevation of Polaris is your latitude.

4. The circumpolar zone is the angular region about the celestial pole (NCP or SCP) of stars that do not set. At the equator the radius of the circumpolar zone is 0°, while at the North Pole it is 90°, so the radius, in general, is equal to your latitude.

5. Again, as in problem 4, at the equator you can see to the SCP, so you see 0°. At the north terrestrial pole you cannot see constellations closer than 90° from the SCP. The radius must be your latitude.

6. At any one point on the Earth, a solar eclipse will last no longer than 7.5 minutes, while a total lunar eclipse might last 1.75 hours. And the actual surface area of the Earth over which a total eclipse of the Moon can be seen is larger than the area over which a total eclipse of the Sun can be seen. The surface area of the Earth on which you can see the Moon during a lunar eclipse is much larger than the area covered by the umbra of the Moon's shadow during a solar eclipse.

7. In general, no, for during an annular eclipse you are in the penumbral shadow. There is the rare possibility of an eclipse starting out total in one region of the Earth and then becoming annular at another point. At no time during the eclipse does the umbra touch that other point.

8. If the Earth had no atmosphere, the Moon would completely disappear during a total lunar eclipse. During totality, light refracted by the Earth's atmosphere reaches the Moon to make a reddish cast. If, during what is a lunar eclipse as seen from Earth, we were on the Moon, there would be a total solar eclipse (as seen from the Moon). If the Earth had no atmosphere, it would appear as a black disk passing in front of the Sun. Because the Earth has an atmosphere, the true appearance is quite different. The atmosphere refracts (bends) light so the Earth appears to be surrounded by a brilliant ring of reddish light—red because that wavelength penetrates the Earth's atmosphere most easily.

9. It is probably easier to describe why either eclipse does not occur once each month. Because the Moon's orbit is tilted 5° to the Earth's orbit about the Sun, the shadow of the Moon usually falls above or below the Earth. Since the separation is 81 times the Earth's radius, 5° is enough for even the penumbra to miss the Earth. Only when the Moon is crossing the Earth's orbit when it is new (or full) can a solar (or lunar) eclipse occur.

10. a. Europeans became able to predict eclipses as early as 580 BC., if not earlier. It would be fair to say that, although the Mayans did not become able to predict eclipses until AD. 200–500, their knowledge was actually superior to that of the Europeans in common awareness.
    b. 600–800 years.
    c. This question can best be answered after Chapter 2. The Greeks understood the cause of eclipses many centuries before the Mayans. However, much of this knowledge was lost before the period under consideration. Both the Europeans and the Mayans were forced to use empirical tables that were corrected as they failed. The Mayan tables were better than the European tables.
    d. The Europeans were ahead in technology (for example, the American cultures did not have the wheel).
    e. No. Many other factors must be considered.

Advanced Problem

11. Referring to the diagram: Zenith–Celestial Equator angle equals the latitude of the observer. Thus, NCP–zenith angle equals 90° – latitude. Horizon–zenith angle is 90°, so λ (Horizon–NCP angle) is $\lambda = 90° - (90° - \text{latitude of observer})$. Hence, λ = latitude of observer.

Sample Test Questions

True-False

1. The NCP is the projection of the Earth's north axis of rotation. T
2. Polaris has always been the North Star. F
3. The ecliptic is the apparent path of the Moon across the sky. F
4. The zodiac is the region of the sky in which the planets are always found. T
5. A heliacal setting of a star is said to occur when a star sets soon after the Sun has set. T
6. The circumpolar zone is the region of the sky in which the stars set only after midnight. F
7. A solar eclipse can occur only when the Sun comes between the Earth and the Moon. F
8. If an eclipse occurs when the Moon's angular diameter appears smaller than the Sun's angular diameter, we have an annular eclipse at best. T
9. The umbra of the Moon is the region of the Moon's shadow in which none of the Sun can be seen. T
10. When the Moon is at the node of its orbit, it is north of the Earth's orbital plane. F
11. The line drawn between the two points where the Moon crosses the Earth's orbital plane is the line of nodes. T
12. The saros cycle is about 18 years, 11 days long. T
13. The circumpolar zone is the region of the sky in which the stars set only after midnight. F

14. If the Moon were much farther from the Earth than it is, there would be no total solar eclipses. T
15. The umbra of the Moon is the region of the Moon's shadow in which none of the Sun can be seen. T

Multiple Choice

1. Some contemporary aborigines make calendar sticks to record
    A. historical events
    B. phases of the Moon
    C. binary star periods
*   D. both A and B
    E. all three: A, B, and C

2. The projections of the Earth's axis on the sky are the
    A. celestial equators
    B. zenith
*   C. celestial poles
    D. ecliptic
    E. none of the above

3. The brightest star nearest the Earth's celestial pole is currently
*   A. Polaris
    B. Vega
    C. Sol
    D. Ecliptus
    E. none of the above

4. The path of the Sun among the stars is called the _____.
    A. celestial equator
    B zodiac
    C. helical path
*   D. ecliptic
    E. none of the above

5. The heliacal rising of a star occurs
    A. on the last day of each year when a star can be seen just before dawn
*   B. on the first day of each year when a star can be seen just before dawn
    C. on the last day when a star can be seen at dusk
    D. on the first day when a star can be seen at dusk
    E. when the Moon eclipses it

6. Many of our familiar constellations probably came from the
    A. Romans
    B. Greeks
    C. Mayans
    D. Chinese
*   E. Minoans

7. The precession of the Earth's axis is caused by
    A. lunar forces
    B. solar forces
    C. the attractions of Polaris
*   D. both A and B
    E. none of the above

8. The precessional period of the Earth's axis takes about
    A. 13 years
    B. 37.5 days
    C. 2,600 years
    D. 26,000 years
    E. 3×10^7 years

9. The Sun crosses the celestial equator going north on or about March 21. This is known as the vernal (or spring)
*   A. equinox
    B. solstice
    C. Stonehenge
    D. zodiac
    E. crossing

10. Ancient buildings oriented east west are said to have _____ orientation.
    A. a solstitial
*   B. an equinoctial
    C. an ecliptical
    D. a precessional
    E. a heliacal

11. Stonehenge is a(n) _____ oriented structure.
*   A. solstitially
    B. equinoctially
    C. ecliptically
    D. precessionally
    E. heliacally

12. If the Moon completely covers the Sun as seen by an earthbound observer, we have a(n) _____ eclipse.
    A. total lunar
*   B. total solar
    C. partial lunar
    D. partial solar
    E. both A and B

13. For a lunar or solar eclipse to occur, we must have
    A. the line of nodes of the Moon's orbit pointing at the Sun
    B. the Moon at or near one node
    C. the Sun between the Earth and the Moon
*   D. both A and B
    E. all three, A, B, and C

14. The eclipse year is about 346.6 days rather than 365 days because
  *   A.   the nodes of the Moon's orbit precess
       B.   the Moon's orbit is not perfectly circular
       C.   misleading: The eclipse year is 365.24 days, as is the regular year.
       D.   the lunar month is about 29 days
       E.   both B and C

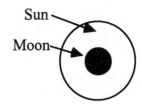

15. Where would you be with respect to the Sun and Moon to be able to see
   the Sun and Moon as shown to the right? What you see: ⇒

   The location is shown below:

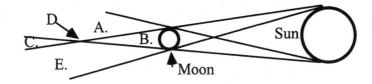

       A.   A
       B.   B
  *   C.   C
       D.   D
       E.   E

16. The saros cycle is completed when which two cycles repeat together again?
       A.   the lunar period of 29.5 days and the year of 365.24 days
  *   B.   the lunar period of 29.5 days and the eclipse year of 346.6 days
       C.   the lunar period of 29.5 days and the precessional period of 5000 years
       D.   the menstrual period and the average month in the year
       E.   none of the above

17. The Mayan Sacred Round of 260 days was chosen so that _____ eclipses could occur in two rounds.
       A.   one
       B.   two
  *   C.   three
       D.   four
       E.   five

18. Even though solar eclipses occur more often than lunar eclipses, why is it more likely that you will
   see a lunar eclipse?
       A.   It is easier to see eclipses at night.
       B.   A lunar eclipse is visible for only a small region of the Earth.
  *   C.   A solar eclipse is visible for only a small region of the Earth.
       D.   misleading: Lunar eclipses occur more often.
       E.   Both B and D.

19. In the northern hemisphere the Sun will set in its most southerly position during the month of _____.
       A.   March
       B.   June
       C.   September
  *   D.   December
       E.   January

Essay

1. Describe some of the probable motivations of early astronomy.
2. Briefly discuss the probable origin of the constellations according to Ovenden's reasoning.
3. Discuss the difference between equinoctial and solstitial orientation of buildings.
4. Describe the basic structure of Stonehenge and its probable use.
5. Compare the structure and possible use of:
   a. Temple of Amon-Re, Karnak, Egypt
   b. Casa Grande, Arizona
6. Distinguish between astrology and astronomy.
7. Describe at least two tests that astrology fails.
8. What is the saros cycle?
9. Make a sketch of the Sun and Moon and show the shadow regions behind the Moon. Label the regions in which only the Moon can be seen as (a), label an annular Sun as (b), and label a partial eclipse as (c).

Word Practice (a few extra words are marked with an *)

1. The slow rotation of the plane of the celestial equator is called __.*
2. Stars that never set throughout the year are said to lie in the _____.
3. The _____ _____ of a star occurs on the first day of each year when the star can be seen just before dawn.
4. The region of the sky that contains stars that rise and set is termed the _ __.
5. Globes that circle the Sun, such as our own Earth, are called _____.
6. An eclipse in which the Sun can be seen all around the edges of the Moon is termed a(n) _____.
7. Groupings of stars used as a memory aid are called _____.
8. The _____ are points where the Moon's orbit crosses the ecliptic.
9. The current North Star (or pole star) is _____.
10. The point directly overhead is the _____.*
11. The region of the Moon's shadow where the Sun cannot be seen is the _____.
12. The line of intersection of the Moon's (or any planet's) orbit with the ecliptic plane is called the ___ ____ _ _____.
13. The plane of the Earth's orbit is the _____. This is the apparent path of the Sun against the stars.
14. The tilt of the Earth's rotation axis to the plane of the ecliptic is the _____.
15. The star nearest to the north celestial pole is the _____ _____.
16. When the Sun or Moon disappears while above the horizon, we have a(n) _____.
17. The projection of the Earth's axis of rotation onto the sky produces the _____.
18. When the Earth's shadow falls on the Moon, we have a(n) _____.
19. When the Sun is completely hidden by the Moon, we have a(n) _____. Thus, we are in the Moon's umbra.
20. The zone 9° on both sides of the ecliptic (18° total width) is called the ____.
21. ____ occur when the Sun crosses the celestial equator going north or south.*
22. A(n) ____ ___ ___ occurs when the Moon hides only part of the Sun.
23. When the Moon passes in front of the Sun, we have a(n) _____ eclipse.
24. A(n) ___ __ occurs on the last day when a star can be seen at dusk.
25. The projection of the Earth's equator on the sky is the ____ _____.
26. The _____ is the region of the Earth's or Moon's shadow where the Sun is only partially covered.
27. An imaginary line passing through the north celestial pole and your zenith is the ___.
28. When the Sun is farthest north or south of the celestial equator, we have a(n) ____.
29. The hour circle through the zenith is the local _____.

30. The local meridian passes through the _____ and the celestial poles.
31. ____ causes the vernal equinox to appear to move along the celestial equator.*
32. A(n) _____ occurs when the Sun is on the celestial equator.*
33. The Moon's position in the sky when it crosses the ecliptic moves backwards. This is called the ____ of the nodes of the lunar orbit.
34. The is the approximate 18 separation between similar eclipses.
35. _____ is a prehistoric English ruin with astronomical alignments.
36. _____ is the superstitious belief that human lives are influenced by the positions of the stars and planets.

Answers to Word Practice

1. precession
2. circumpolar zone (web site)
3. heliacal rising
4. equatorial zone (web site)
5. planets
6. annular solar eclipse
7. constellations
8. nodes
9. Polaris
10. zenith
11. umbra
12. line of nodes
13. ecliptic
14. cause of the seasons
15. North Star
16. eclipse (cause of eclipse)
17. celestial poles
18. lunar eclipse

19. total solar eclipse
20. zodiac
21. equinoxes
22. partial solar eclipse
23. solar
24. heliacal setting
25. celestial equator
26. penumbra
27. meridian
28. solstice
29. meridian
30. zenith
31. precession
32. equinox
33. regression
34. saros cycle
35. Stonehenge
36. astrology

Chapter 2
Historic Advances: Worlds in the Sky

Answers to Problems in the Text

1. Not until the days of space exploration could a theory that placed the Earth at the center of the universe be completely ruled out. Until then, it was always possible that the laws controlling the planets and stars were different from those controlling the Earth, although great simplification and unification were to be gained by assuming these laws were the same. Thus, whereas now that we have sent out spacecraft we cannot support by any scientific means the Earth-centered universe, the early theorists had the opposite problem: There was no direct evidence to show that the Earth moved.
   a. There was no observational basis for not putting the Earth at the center. In fact, theorists could argue that because they felt no motion, the Earth was obviously at rest. Those who asserted that the Earth was in motion were probably in the "lunatic fringe" of their day because they lacked any direct observational support for their ideas.
   b. Either theory could fit the available data. The lack of parallax of the stars when observed by the naked eye supports the Earth-centered universe. Only the invention of the telescope enabled astronomers to see the small motions (parallax) of the stars caused by the Earth's revolving about the Sun.
   c. The Greeks did make good arguments to show that the Moon revolves about the Earth and that the planets and Sun do so as well. But they could neither *prove* nor *disprove* their theories.

2. Remember that the terminator is not the shadow of the Earth. The Sun lights half the Moon at all times. The terminator is the division between the lit and the unlit halves. We see a terminator only because of the angle at which we view the Moon.
   a. The terminator is usually seen as curved because we are not looking straight down on it. That is, if the terminator were imagined as a plane bisecting the Moon, our viewpoint of the Moon is usually at an angle to that plane.
   b. The terminator is a straight line at half phase, that is, when the Sun and Moon form a right angle (90°) when seen from the Earth.
   c. The terminator is not seen when the Moon is new because nothing is seen then (assuming no eclipse). When the Moon is full, the terminator is the edge of the disk of the Moon. During an eclipse, the edge of the occulting disk is the terminator.

3. The Greeks could measure the cyclic motions of the planets, Moon, and Sun using sighting devices similar to the ones described in Chapter 1. They could also rank the stars by apparent relative brightness using only the eye, but they had no information on the relative distances or physical nature of the stars. All observations were limited to visible light. Modern astronomers can use wavelengths from gamma rays up to radio waves. Telescopes are available to collect light so we can see fainter objects and magnify images. We can even reduce light to its various wavelengths. Modern techniques can more accurately measure the relative brightness, distances, sizes, compositions, and motions. The space program allows us to actually visit some of the nearer astronomical objects.

4. Most students will say yes to these questions. Examples can range from such dramatic events as eclipses, meteorite falls, and comets to the less dramatic but more regular seasonal change in the heavens. Astronomical observations suggest that humanity is subject to cosmic forces—forces that affect human behavior and events.

5. Aristotle's belief helped in the sense that raw observations must be structured, to be interpreted. (Indeed, a structure is needed even before observations are made—how else to decide what is worth observing?) Aristotle's faith in symmetry and "perfection" provided such a structure. But his faith hindered him in that it caused him to ignore or explain away observations that did not support his structure. (This is always a danger when the faith is too detailed.) Thus, he placed the Earth at the center of the universe.

6. Looking at Fig. 2-7, which shows the Earth and the Moon, we see the farther away we are from the object casting the shadow, the smaller the shadow is. This is true whenever the object providing the light (the Sun) is physically larger than the object casting the shadow (the Moon). It does not matter how far apart the objects are. In brief, the answer is because the Sun is bigger than the Moon.

7. To have discovered that the north celestial pole (or the stars near the vernal equinox) had moved, he needed records at least 500 to 1000 years old because all observations were by the naked eye.

8. The answer will vary from student to student, but the most common answer should be significant. Because most ancient knowledge was lost, astronomers were forced to start over again. Whether this was good or bad is another question. Some students will argue that such events are insignificant because they only delayed but did not stop the development of astronomy.

9. Remember, the zenith is the point overhead. At the equator, the zenith lies on the celestial equator. On the equator, the Sun passes through the zenith only in late March and September (at the equinoxes).

Advanced Problems

10. The Sun is at most 23.5° north of the celestial equator. Let λ be your latitude. Then the NCP lies λ up from the north, while the celestial equator lies $90° - \lambda$ up from the south $[180° - (90° + \lambda)]$. So the Sun is at most $90° - \lambda + 23.5°$ up from the south. If $\lambda = 40°$, the Sun rises at most 73.5° from the south—the answer is no. If $\lambda = 23.5°$, then the Sun can be at the zenith, and it is so only on the summer solstice (about June 21).

11. a. Use the small angle equation. α must be in seconds of arc so
    $1/2° = 30' = 1800''$, while $D = 150$ million km $= 1.5 \times 10^{11}$ m. The small angle equation
    $$\frac{\alpha''}{206,265} = \frac{d}{D}$$
    becomes $d = \frac{\alpha'' \times D}{206,265} = \frac{(1.8 \times 10^3 \times 1.5 \times 10^{11} \ m)}{206,265} = .d = 1.31 \times 10^9$ m $= 1.31 \times 10^6$ km.
    b. Yes, he could measure α, so $d/D = \alpha''/206,265$.
    c. They had no technique to separately measure either d or D. To get D independently, they would need to measure an angle about 8", whereas without telescopes they could at best measure to a few minutes of arc. The latter comment is extra information probably not known by the students at this point.

12. a.   The eye can resolve 2', so if there are 435 pixels in a 40° angle, then each pixel is 40/435 =.092, which is about 5.5'. We can approximate how close this would be for the human eye by using the small angle equation, although 40° is clearly not a small angle. Converting 40° to seconds of arc and assuming a 21-inch TV, we get 3 inches. At 3 inches we can clearly see pixels. At most viewing distances, the pixels will not be resolved.

    b.   European TVs will look better at close distances, while British TVs will look worse. At usual viewing distances, the choice will not make much difference. If the TV is used for a computer readout, or other close work, the European system will be superior.

13.   Again use the small angle equation.

You are given $\alpha'' = 1''$ and $D = 400{,}000$ km $= 4 \times 10^8$ m, so

$d = (1'' \times 4 \times 10^8$ m$)/206{,}265 = 1.9 \times 10^3$ m $= 1.9$ km.

14.   Remember, on Earth the angle of the NCP is your latitude. If on the satellite 1 km corresponds to a star movement of 1° (and hence the local NCP moves 1°), then 360 km would be a 360° motion. Thus, the circumference would be 360 km. The diameter is the circumference divided by π (3.14), so the diameter is about 115 km.

15.   The "horns" must point away from the Sun. Since we can see the horizon, the Sun must be up, and since the crescent is narrow, we are not too far from new Moon so the Sun is not post noon. Conclusion: In the morning when the Moon is past the third quarter.

Sample Test Questions

True-False

1.   Cosmologies are theories of the origin and nature of the universe. T
2.   The Egyptians did not believe there was a "divine order" to the universe. F
3.   Early Greek astronomy began around 600 BC. T
4.   Thales of Miletus was an early astronomer of the Greek world. T
5.   Anaximander is known for his eclipse predictions. F
6.   The lunar terminator separates the lit side of the Moon from the unlit side. T
7.   Anaxagoras deduced the true cause of eclipses. T
8.   Aristotle believed the Moon was farther away than the Sun. F
9.   Aristarchus deduced the approximate relative sizes and distances of the Sun and Moon. T
10.   Aristotle deduced the relative sizes of the Sun and Moon. F
11.   Eratosthenes discovered the precession of the equinoxes. F
12.   The number of digits known for certain in a quantity is the number of significant figures of that quantity. T
13.   The epicycle theory is especially associated with Ptolemy. T
14.   Al-Battani was an early Indian astronomer. F
15.   Chinese astronomy began much later than Greek astronomy. F
16.   Among other things, Al-Battani is known for his measurement of the mass of the Sun. F
17.   Science is a theory of the origin of the universe. F
18.   The parallax we see in the position of a nearby star is caused by that star's motion. F
19.   The cosmology of Akhenaton was proposed about 350 BC. F
20.   Anaxagoras deduced the true cause of eclipses. T
21.   The lunar terminator separates the lighted side of the Moon from the dark side. T

Multiple Choice

1. The early Greek astronomer who is first recorded as believing that the heavenly bodies are spherical in shape is
    * A. Brahe
      B. Philolaus
      C. Aristotle
      D. Pythagoras
      E. Ptolemy

2. An early Greek who gave a clear and correct explanation of the phases of the Moon was
      A. Ptolemy
      B. Copernicus
      C. Brahe
      D. Kepler
    * E. Aristotle

3. The Ptolemaic cosmology of deferents and epicycles was based on the ideas of Hipparchus.
    * A. Correct
      B. Incorrect — Ptolemy thought it up all by himself.
      C. Incorrect — It was based on the work of Kepler.
      D. Incorrect — It was based on the work of Copernicus.
      E. Incorrect — It was based on the work of Newton.

4. The cosmological scheme in which the Earth is at the center of the universe and the planets, Sun, and Moon are on circles whose centers are moving in circles about the Earth was devised by the Greek astronomer
      A. Copernicus
      B. Aristotle
      C. Hartmann
      D. Philolaus
    * E. Ptolemy

5. In Ptolemy's cosmology, a planet moves on the epicycle and the center of the epicycle moves around the Earth on the deferent circle.
    * A. correct
      B. Incorrect — The planet stays on the deferent circle.
      C. Incorrect — The Earth is at the center of the epicycle.
      D. Incorrect — Ptolemy put the Sun at the center.
      E. Incorrect — Both B and C are correct.

6. One of the first known Greek astronomers was
      A. Brahe
    * B. Thales of Miletus
      C. Aristotle
      D. Pythagoras
      E. Ptolemy

7. Aristarchus of Samos is famous for
   A. his discussion of the Moon's phases
 * B. his calculations of the relative distances of the Sun and Moon
   C. his catalog of nebular objects
   D. finding that the orbits of the planets were ellipses
   E. none of the above

8. Eratosthenes was the first astronomer to correctly measure the Earth's size.
 * A. correct
   B. Incorrect — Eudoxus
   C. Incorrect — Hipparchus
   D. Incorrect — Bernard
   E. none of the above

9. A theory of the origin and nature of the universe is termed
 * A. a cosmology
   B. a constellation
   C. an eclipse
   D. a deferent
   E. an epicycle

10. Thales of Miletus is best known for
    A. discussing a planet
    B. explaining the phases of the Moon
 * C. predicting an eclipse
    D. measuring the size of the Moon
    E. inventing the telescope

11. The line separating the lit side from the unlit side of the Moon is termed the lunar
    A. period
    B. phase
    C. epicycle
 * D. terminator
    E. node

12. The shift in the apparent position of a star due to the Earth's motion about the Sun is termed the star's
    A. terminator
 * B. parallax
    C. deferent
    D. phase
    E. ellipse

13. Precession was discovered by
    A. Eratosthenes
 * B. Hipparchus
    C. Ptolemy
    D. Thales of Miletus
    E. Hartmann

14. The *Almagest* was written by
    A. Eratosthenes
    B. Hipparchus
* C. Ptolemy
    D. Thales of Miletus
    E. Impey

15. The Arab astronomer best known in medieval Europe was
    A. Muhammad Almagest
* B. Muhammad Al-Battani
    C Eratosthenes
    D. Aristotle
    E. none of these

16. The main center of Indian astronomy was at
    A. Almagest
    B. Al-Battani
* C. Benares
    D. Alexandria
    E. London

17. Chinese astronomers believed
    A. the Earth was at rest
* B. the Earth was in motion
    C. the stars were most important for sailing

18. If a building 500 meters away has an angular height of 1°, approximately how tall is it?*
    A. 5 m
* B. 9 m
    C. 12 m
    D. 90 m
    E. 500 m

19. When Mars is closest to the Earth, its angular diameter is about 85" and its distance is about 7.7×10^7 km. The approximate diameter of Mars is*
    A. 6×10^3 km
    B. 300 m
    C. 77×10^3 km
* D. 3.2×10^3 km
    E. 5×10^3 km

20. (easy numbers) A space satellite 1 meter in diameter is circling the Earth. It is observed to have an angular size of 2.06 seconds of arc. The distance to the satellite is*

    A. 10^5 cm

    B. 10^6 cm

    C. $\dfrac{1}{2.06} \times 10^3$ cm

 * D. 10^7 cm

    E. 2.06×10^3 cm

21. (easy numbers) A 2.00-meter-tall man is observed to have an angular height of $0.57° = 2060''$. How far away is he?*

 * A. 200 m

    B. 200 km

    C. 200 cm

    D. 570 cm

    E. 5.7×10^3 m

22. The difference in direction between two points as measured from a specified third point is the*

    A. parallax

    B. linear measure

 * C. angular measure

    D. constant of proportionality

    E. separator

23. If α is the angular size of an object in seconds of arc, d its real size, and D the distance to the object, these quantities are related by*

    A. $\alpha d = D / 206{,}265$

 * B. $\alpha / 206{,}265 = d/D$

    C. $\alpha / 206{,}265 = D/d$

    D. $\alpha / 206{,}265 = d\,D$

    E. $\alpha d\,D = 206{,}265$

24. (Significant figures) What is the product of 2.5×3.95?*

    A. 9.8

 * B. 9.875

    C. 9.9

    D. 10

    E. 98.7

Essay

1. Discuss the effects that early East Indian, Chinese, Polynesian, and American Indian astronomy had on European astronomy.
2. Name and discuss the contributions of three early Greek astronomers.
3. Name and discuss the contributions of two late Greek (Alexandrine) astronomers.
4. What is resolution?
5. Discuss the units of angular measurement.
6. What is an angle?
7. Discuss significant figures.

Word Practice (A few additional words, marked by an *, are listed as an aid to the student.)

1. A shift in apparent position of an object due to your motion is termed _____.
2. Over the course of the year, stars near the ecliptic appear to move in a straight line. This is the _____.*
3. 1/60 of a minute of arc is a(n) _____ _____ _____.
4. _____ _____ is a measure of the difference in direction between two points as seen from a specified third point.
5. _____ was a Greek astronomer who wrote the *Almagest.*
6. One of the first known Greek astronomers was ____ ____ _____. He predicted the eclipse discussed in Chapter 1.*
7. Theories about the origin and nature of the universe are called _____.
8. _____ _____ is a measurement of the distance between two points.
9. The _____ _____ was a famous library in Egypt.
10. The ___ ____ _____ is a drift in the location of the celestial poles with respect to the stars, caused by forces produced by the Sun and Moon.
11. The ___ ___ ___ relates an object's angular size, linear size, and distance.
12. _____ was a Greek who is credited with deducing the true cause of eclipses.*
13. The _____ is a circle whose center moves in a circular orbit centered near the Earth (Ptolemaic cosmology).*
14. _____ was a Greek who proposed that the matter from which things were made was composed of an eternal substance.*
15. The _____ is a measure of the finest detail that can be seen in an image.
16. The _____ is the line separating the light and dark sides of the Moon (or any planet).
17. _____ is a process of learning about nature by formulating questions and answering them through observation and experiment.
18. The _____ is a circle upon which the epicycle moves (Ptolemaic cosmology).*
19. Sixty seconds of arc make up one ____ ____ ____.
20. A famous Arab astronomer was _____.*
21. _____ was an astronomer who proposed that the Sun was farther from the Earth than the Moon and who explained the phases of the Moon.*
22. The digits known for certain in a quantity are the _____.*
23. 1/360 of a circle is a(n) _____.
24. Ptolemy proposed the _____ _____ to predict positions of the Sun, Moon, and planets.
25. _____ was a Greek astronomer who proposed a spherical shape for heavenly bodies.*
26. The name of _____ is associated with determining the size of the Earth.*
27. _____ was a Greek famous for his star catalog and observations.*
28. The first astronomer to propose the heliocentric hypothesis was _____.
29. If an object has an angular size equal to a specified angle it is said to _____ the specified angle.

Answers to Word Practice

1.	parallax	16.	terminator
2.	parallactic shift	17.	science
3.	second of arc	18.	deferent
4.	angular measure	19.	minute of arc
5.	Ptolemy	20.	Al-Battani
6.	Thales of Miletus	21.	Aristotle
7.	cosmologies	22.	significant figures
8.	linear measure	23.	degree
9.	Alexandrian library	24.	epicycle theory
10.	precession of equinoxes	25.	Pythagoras

11. small angle equation
12. Anaxagoras
13. epicycle
14. Anaximander
15. resolution

26. Eratosthenes
27. Hipparchus
28. Aristarchus
29. subtend

Chapter 3
Discovering the Layout of the Solar System

Answers to Problems in the Text

1. Counterclockwise; clockwise.

2. Mercury; Pluto.

3. No. The full Moon must be on the side of the Earth away from the Sun. Ask for justification. Some students will use a Ptolemaic picture.

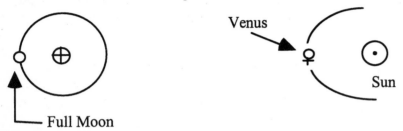

4. Venus can be full phase only when it is on the far side of the Sun from the Earth.

5. Earth.

6. No. The effect is purely one of appearance and occurs when the observation point (Earth) is overtaking Mars.

7. Presumably we are only asking them to be nearly on a straight line—their being exactly on a straight line is extremely rare. If they are nearly on a straight line, we see Venus at sunset on the western horizon (inferior conjunction) and Mars and Jupiter rising in the east nearly together (in conjunction with each other while at opposition). If all are exactly on a straight line, we see Venus pass in front of the Sun (transit) and Mars pass in front of Jupiter (occult Jupiter). If we are on Mars, we see Earth and Venus on the western horizon at sunset (in inferior conjunction) and Jupiter rising on the eastern horizon (in opposition), and if the line is exactly straight, then from Mars we see Earth and Venus transit the Sun. From Jupiter, we see Venus, Earth, and Mars on the western horizon at sunset (in inferior conjunction); if they are on an exact straight line, we see all three transit together as one.

8. Any answer may be acceptable provided it is properly justified. Provided below are several viewpoints and their justifications for the questions involved.

Revolutionaries and Why
   a. Perhaps not: They were only following the evolving scientific knowledge, although they were aware of the strong pressures against their findings.
   b. Definitely: Copernicus would not publish until he was on his deathbed. Galileo recognized that he was undermining the power structure. Both, by their actions, showed they recognized the revolutionary nature of their ideas.

Scientific vs. Political: Similarities and Differences

a. Similarities: There is an established power structure, new ideas about how things should be done, and newcomers who force their ideas to attention. Both scientific and political revolutions have gestation periods of about a generation in length. Many scientific revolutions have succeeded because those in the establishment died of old age, not because they became convinced by the "facts."

b. Differences: A political revolution much more strongly involves opinion, social style, and other factors that do not involve verifiable fact. Scientific revolutions are based on verifiable observations (independent of style or opinion).

Role of Factual Discoveries, Strong Personalities, and so on

Probably all agree that in the long run a scientific revolution is much more dependent upon factual discoveries than is a political revolution. Both revolutions are strongly affected by strong personalities and publicity. A strong personality, by promoting or rejecting new data, may help or hinder a scientific revolution. Koestler, in his book *The Sleepwalker,* argues that Galileo's strong personality actually hardened opposition to the Copernican theory.

a. The long run referred to above may be very long—witness the tenacity of Soviet biology against overwhelming disconfirming "facts." Strong personality and publicity were the weapons of resistance to change.

b. But it must be stressed that in the long run the verifiable facts win out in a scientific revolution, whereas in a political revolution there may, indeed, be no verifiable facts.

Advanced Problems

9. $\dfrac{\alpha"\mathbf{Mars}}{2.06\times10^5} = \dfrac{6.79\times10^6\,m}{6\times10^{10}\,m} = 1.13 \times 10^{-4}$; $\alpha"\mathbf{Mars} = 23"$

$\dfrac{\alpha"\mathbf{Jupiter}}{2.06\times10^5} = \dfrac{1.43\times10^8\,m}{6.3\times10^{11}\,m} = 2.27 \times 10^{-4}$; $\alpha"\mathbf{Jupiter} = 47"$

That is, Jupiter is about 30 times bigger than Mars and 10 times farther away. Jupiter appears larger.

10. We are given that Mars has a diameter of 6787 km = 6.8×10^3 km and that it approaches within 60 million km = 6.0×10^7 km. We are asked the smallest surface feature we can resolve on Mars if our resolution is 1/2". Let $D = 6.0 \times 10^7$ km be the distance to Mars and d be the size of the smallest feature we can resolve. The small angle equation gives

$\dfrac{\alpha}{206,265} = \dfrac{d}{D} = d/D$ or $1/2(2.1 \times 10^5) = d\,(6.0 \times 10^7\ \text{km})$

$d = 1.4 \times 10^2$ km = 140 km.

Sample Test Questions

True-False

1. Jupiter is closer to the Sun than Saturn. T
2. Neptune is closer to the Sun than Uranus. F
3. Superior planets are closer to the Sun than the Earth. F
4. Only superior planets can be in opposition. T

5. A planet in opposition rises at sunset. T
6. The Ptolemaic model had the Sun at the center of the universe. F
7. One way of stating Occam's razor is, "The best explanation is the simplest." T
8. The Copernican theory put the Sun at the center of the solar system. T
9. Copernicus wrote *De Revolutionibus*. T
10. Tycho Brahe was a Czech astronomer. F
11. Tycho Brahe is best known for his observations. T
12. Kepler first studied the planet Mars to develop his laws. T
13. Galileo is the first known astronomer to use the telescope. T
14. Newton deduced the laws of planetary motion from more basic laws of general motion. T
15. Kepler found his laws of motion empirically rather than by deducing them. T
16. Newton's third law may be stated as follows: The force on a body is equal to the product of its mass times its acceleration. F

Multiple Choice

1. The superior planets are, in order of increasing average distance from the Sun:
   A. Mercury, Venus, Mars, Jupiter
   B. Mars, Jupiter, Saturn, Uranus, Pluto, Neptune
   * C. Mars, Jupiter, Saturn, Uranus, Neptune, Pluto
   D. Mars, Jupiter, Saturn, Neptune, Uranus, Pluto
   E. Saturn, Neptune, Jupiter, Pluto, Uranus, Mars

2. Which of the planets is closer to the Sun than the Earth is?
   A. Mars
   * B. Venus
   C. Jupiter
   D. Saturn
   E. both A and B

3. Brahe found that the planets move in ellipses with the Sun at one focus.
   A. Correct
   * B. Wrong — Kepler did this
   C. Wrong — Copernicus did this
   D. Wrong — the planets move in oval orbits
   E. Wrong — eclipses not ellipses

4. Match a description with the astronomer Tycho Brahe _____
   Made the first accurate measurements of the Earth's size using a well at Syrene and observations at Alexandria in Egypt.
   A. First astronomer to use a telescope to observe the phases of Venus.
   * B. 1546–1601—famous for his accurate observations of positions of planets and stars—did not use a telescope.
   C. 571–1630—was the first to discover the orbits of the planets were ellipses.
   D. 1642–1727—first to successfully find physical laws which both explain terrestrial and celestial motion.
   E. Made the first accurate measurements of the Earth's size using a well at Syrene and observations at Alexandria in Egypt

5. Match a description with the astronomer: Isaac Newton
    A. First astronomer to use a telescope to observe the phases of Venus.
    B. 1546-1601—famous for his accurate observations of positions of planets and stars—did not use a telescope.
    C. 1571-1630—was the first to discover the orbits of the planets were ellipses.
 * D. 1642-1727—first to successfully find physical laws which both explain terrestrial and celestial motion.
    E. Made the first accurate measurements of the Earth's size using a well at Syrene and observations at Alexandria in Egypt

6. Match a description with the astronomer: Johannes Kepler
    A. First astronomer to use a telescope to observe the phases of Venus.
    B. 1546-1601—famous for his accurate observations of positions of planets and stars—did not use a telescope.
 * C. 1571-1630—was the first to discover the orbits of the planets were ellipses.
    D. 1642-1727—first to successfully find physical laws which both explain terrestrial and celestial motion.
    E. Made the first accurate measurements of the Earth's size using a well at Syrene and observations at Alexandria in Egypt

7. The first astronomer, after the Greeks, to introduce the idea of the Earth moving around the Sun was
    _____.
    A. Philolaus
    B. Kepler
 * C. Copernicus
    D. Hipparchus
    E. Galileo

8. Kepler's first law says essentially that _____.
    A. For every action there is an equal and opposite reaction
 * B. The orbits of the planets are ellipses with the Sun at one focus
    C. The orbits of the planets are ellipses with the center of mass of the Sun-planet system at one focus
    D. The force equals mass times acceleration
    E. The square of the sidereal period is proportional to the cube of the semi-major axis

9. Kepler's second law says essentially that _____.
    A. The force equals mass times acceleration
    B. The square of the sidereal period is proportional to the cube of the semi-major axis
    C. For every action there is an equal and opposite reaction
    D. The orbits of the planets are ellipses with the Sun at one focus
 * E. The radius vector from the Sun to the planet sweeps out equal areas in equal times

10. Kepler's third law says essentially that _____.
    A. The force equals mass times acceleration
 * B. The square of the sidereal period is proportional to the cube of the semi-major axis
    C. For every action there is an equal and opposite reaction
    D. The orbits of the planets are ellipses with the Sun at one focus
    E. The radius vector from the Sun to the planet sweeps out equal areas in equal times

11. Suppose an asteroid has an average distance of 4 AU from the Sun. Then its sidereal period is about _____ years.
    A. 0.5
    B. 1
    C. 4
    * D. 8
    E. 16

12. The radius vector from the Sun to the planet sweeps out equal areas in equal time is the essential content of _____.
    A. Newton's version of Kepler's 1st law
    B. Kepler's 1st law
    C. Newton's 1st law
    * D. Kepler's 2nd law
    E. Kepler's 3rd law

13. The astronomical unit is about _____ cm. (Note units)
    A. 1.5×10^{11}
    B. 1.5×10^{8}
    C. 3×10^{10}
    D. 186,000
    * E. 1.5×10^{13}

14. There are about _____ kilometers in the astronomical unit. (Note units)
    A. 1.5×10^{13}
    B. 1.5×10^{11}
    * C. 1.5×10^{8}
    D. 3×10^{16}
    E. 3×10^{8}

15. If R is the distance between two gravitating bodies, then the gravitational force produced by one on the other is _____.
    A. Proportional to R
    B. Proportional to R^2
    C. Inversely proportional to R
    * D. Inversely proportional to R^2
    E. Independent of R

16. Assume m_2 is a small mass orbiting m_1, which is a very large mass. The mass m_2 is in a circular orbit of radius r (the distance of separation) with v the velocity of revolution and G a constant. What is the gravitational force between the masses?
    A. $F = m_1 \, v \, r$
    B. $F = m_2 \, v / r^2$
    C. $F = m_1 \, m_2 / r$
    D. $F = G \, m_1 \, m_2 / r$
    * E. $F = G \, m_1 \, m_2 / r^2$

17. Newton's 2nd law relates mass to _____.
    A. Velocity
    B. Size
*   C. Force and acceleration
    D. Period and color
    E. Temperature

18. Newton's first law states, essentially that _____.
    A. Force equals mass times acceleration
    B. The radius vector from the Sun to a planet sweeps equal areas in equal times
    C. Orbits are ellipses with the Sun at one focus
*   D. In the absence of outside forces a body at rest remains at rest
    E. Area equals one-half the base times the height

19. The inverse square law for the gravitational force was first proposed by _____.
    A. Brahe
    B. Kepler
    C. Galileo
*   D. Newton
    E. Hartmann

20. Weight is _____.
    A. The same as mass
    B. The only measure of the amount of matter present
    C. Both A and B
*   D. A force
    E. Not a scientific term

21. The mass of a body is always _____.
    A. The gravitational force by which the Earth pulls a body
    B. Proportional to the mass of the Sun
*   C. A measure of the amount of matter it contains
    D. both A and B
    E. None of the above

Essay

1. Describe why the retrograde motion of Mars occurs according to Ptolemy. Compare this with the description according to Copernicus.
2. What is Occam's razor? How is it used?
3. Decide why the retrograde motion of Mars occurs in the Copernican theory.
4. Give an example of Newton's third law.
5. State Newton's three laws of motion.
6. State Kepler's three laws.
7. State Newton's Universal Law of Gravitation.
8. Compare the empirical versus deductive approaches of Kepler and Newton.

Word Practice (* denotes word not on the concepts list.)

1. _____ _____ _____ _____ relates the masses, the separation, and the mutual gravitational force between two bodies.
2. The apparent westward drift of Mars at certain times is termed the ____ _____ _____ _____.
3. The change in European beliefs from an Earth-centered system to a Sun-centered system is often referred to as the___.
4. The orbit of a planet is a(n) _____.
5. _____ _____ is best known for providing the observational data of the motion of Mars that Kepler used to derive his three laws.
6. The _____ _____ has the Sun going about the Earth.
7. The Sun and its surrounding worlds are called the _____ _____.
8. The average Earth-Sun separation is one _____ _____.
9. According to Kepler, each planet moves in an ellipse with the Sun at one _____.
10. ___ ___ ___ ___ are three laws that are fundamental postulates from which Kepler's three laws can be deduced.
11. _____ _____ tells us to take the physical theory that makes predictions with the fewest assumptions.
12. The _____ _____ of the solar system, perfected by Ptolemy, places the Earth near the center of the solar system.
13. _____ _____ was one of the first astronomers to use a telescope. He wrote his results in Italian.
14. We live on the planet _____.*
15. ____ are the passages of an inferior planet directly between the Earth and the Sun.
16. ___ ___ is helpful for remembering the orbital distances of the planets.
17. _____ _____ empirically developed three laws that fit the motions of Mars to an elliptical orbit.
18. The three laws of planetary motion are called _____ _____.
19. _____ _____ was able to deduce Kepler's three laws.

Answers to Word Practice

1. Newton's law of gravitation
2. retrograde motion of Mars
3. Copernican revolution
4. ellipse
5. Tycho Brahe
6. Ptolemaic model
7. solar system
8. astronomical unit
9. focus
10. Newton's laws of motion
11. Occam's razor
12. epicycle model
13. Galileo Galilei
14. Earth
15. transits
16. Bode's rule
17. Johannes Kepler
18. Kepler's laws
19. Isaac Newton

Chapter 4
Gravity and the Conquest of Space

Answers to Problems in the Text

1. Because the height of the Earth's atmosphere is a minuscule fraction of the Earth's radius, we can consider the spaceship to have a circular velocity about equal to that at the surface (8 km/s). Since escape velocity is 11 km/s, the spaceship needs to add only 3 km/s (11 – 7.91 km/s if carefully done).

2. From problem 1, we see that to change one orbit into another orbit that passes through the first it is only necessary to change the velocity. In problem 1, a change in velocity of 3 km/s changes a circular orbit into a parabolic (escape) orbit. This change in velocity is often called "delta V," or ΔV, by rocket engineers.

3. First note that
    $$1000 \text{ mph} = \frac{1609 \text{ km}}{\text{hour}} = \frac{1609}{60 \times 60} \text{ km/s} = 0.447 \text{ km/s}$$
    so the spacecraft has a velocity of 0.447 km/s west to east before launch. (The stars appear to move east to west because the Earth is rotating the opposite way.) Hence, in west-to-east launch, a circular orbit needs only about 7.5 km/s added velocity (making a total of 8 km/s; see problem 1). An east-to-west launch needs about 8.5 km/s opposite velocity because it must overcome the initial velocity in the west-to-east direction.

4. a   Newton's third law: Action equals reaction. To push yourself toward the dock, you must push the boat in the opposite direction.
    b.   If we take the boat as analogous to the rocket, then as you leave the boat you are performing the same function as the rocket exhaust; that is, the particles depart from the rear of the rocket as you are departing from the rear of the boat.

5. Probably either answer can be justified, but the most common should be no. We are now caught in an energy shortage and an inflationary spiral; adding this expenditure would only fuel inflation. (However, you might argue that it would reduce unemployment.) Although the space program takes only a very small percentage of the national budget, it could serve as an obvious "whipping boy." However, if the USSR were to make its first spectacular space launch now, the public might be aroused.

6. Again, either side may be argued. Realistically, however, manned flights are very expensive as well as energy- and material-consuming, even though at present rates we are using a small percentage of the budget. It is not clear that the economic situation will allow a political decision to undertake such travel. At present, our manned space program is equivalent to building an airplane to fly one passenger from New York to San Francisco and then throwing the airplane away. The space shuttle and other advances may reduce the cost enormously. There is no question from an intellectual point of view that such a development of space travel would be a great advance. It might also lead to revolutionary technologies in space (such as energy-producing satellites). We might ask if our society can exist for the next hundred years without developing manned interplanetary travel. Perhaps in the next hundred years we can solve our problems on the Earth sufficiently that space travel can become a symbol of great social progress.

Advanced Problems

7. Some students may make this a difficult problem if they realize that the form of Newtonian gravitational law given is valid only if we are outside a spherical body. In this problem, we are looking at effects that depend upon the shape of the Earth. The intent is to take the force law and see the effect of distance from the center. Let M be the Earth's mass, m your mass, r the sea level radius of the Earth, and h the altitude above (+) or below (–) sea level. Then if w is the weight,

$w(h) = \dfrac{GMm}{(r+h)^2}$. If we look at the ratio $\dfrac{w(h)}{w_{sea\ level}}$ we get $\dfrac{w(h)}{w_{sea\ level}} = \dfrac{1}{(1+\frac{h}{r})^2}$. In the Dead Sea,

$\dfrac{h}{r}$ = -0.000062, so $w_{(DS)}$ = 1.0001 $w_{(sea\ level)}$. On Mt. Everest, $\dfrac{h}{r}$ = 0.0014, so $w_{(ME)}$ = 0.997 $w_{(sea\ level)}$.

Assuming a weight of 150 lb., this is a gain of about 1/4 oz in the Dead Sea and a loss of 7 oz on Mt. Everest.

8. Use weight = $w = \dfrac{GMm}{r^2}$ and the notations p for the planet and E for the Earth.

a. So $\dfrac{w_p}{w_E} = \dfrac{M_p}{M_E} \times \left(\dfrac{r_E}{r_p}\right)^2 = = 0.11/(1/.53)\,(1/.53) = 0.031$.

b. The mass ratio and size ratio for Mars/Earth from Table 8-1 are the same as used in part a, so the value of weight must be the same.

9. At the Moon's distance, as the text tells us, the velocity for a circular orbit is 1 km/s. Now the escape velocity is $\sqrt{2}$ times the circular velocity, so escape velocity is 1.414 km/s. Hence, he or she would need to increase the velocity by only 0.414 km/s.

10. a. $V_{circ} = \sqrt{\dfrac{GM}{R}}$ $G = 6.67 \times 10^{-11}$ Nm^2/kg^2

M = mass of Earth = 5.98×10^{24} kg

R = 42,500 km = 4.25×10^7 m

$= 6.66 \times R_\oplus = (2.58)^2 R_\oplus$

Putting the numbers into the formula:

$V_{circ} = \left(\dfrac{6.67\times10^{-11} \times 5.98\times10^{24}}{4.25\times10^7}\right)^{0.5}$ m/s = 3.0 km/s.

Alternatively, because $R = (2.58)^2 R$,

$V_{circ} = \sqrt{\dfrac{GM_H}{(2.58)^2 R_H}} = \dfrac{1}{2.58}\sqrt{\dfrac{GM_H}{R_H}} = \dfrac{7.91\times10^3}{2.58}$ m/s = 3.1 km/s.

A circle of radius 42,000 km has a circumference of 2.67×10^5 km. The time for one orbit

$T = \dfrac{\text{circumference}}{V_{circ}}$ so $T = \dfrac{2.67\times10^5\,\text{km}}{3.1\,\text{km/s}} = 8.6 \times 10^4$ s.

In one day there are $24 \times 60 \times 60 = 8.64 \times 10^4$ s. These are nearly the same, so the satellite has almost exactly a 24-hour period. The difference is mostly due to our approximations and round-off error.

b. Suppose the orbit passes over the north and South Pole, then our logic fails. During the time the satellite moves from the equator to a pole the Earth rotates 1/4 turn. The orbit projected on the Earth's surface appears as a curved path. The satellite must appear to move relative to the surface, no matter what the orbital height. A "fixed" position is possible only for an orbit confined to the equatorial plane.

Sample Test Questions

True-False

1. Isaac Newton discovered the principle of gravitational attraction in the 1600s. T
2. The gravitational force follows a square law. F
3. If the distance between two gravitating bodies doubles, the force drops by a factor of four. T
4. If the distance between two gravitating bodies doubles, the force increases by a factor of four. F
5. The circular velocity is the speed an object must move parallel to the surface of a body in order to escape from it. F
6. If a spaceship is launched from the Earth with a higher speed than the escape velocity, it moves on a hyperbola. T
7. Newton's third law of motion states that for every action there is an equal reaction in the same direction. F
8. The first artificial satellite, Sputnik I, was launched in 1958. F
9. The first man in space was an American, Alan Shepard. F
10. The decision by President Kennedy to put a man on the Moon in the 1960s was more a political decision than a scientific decision. T
11. Space flight has had no practical results. F
12. If the distance between two gravitating bodies doubles, the force increases by a factor of two. F
13. The perigee of an Earth satellite occurs when the satellite is closest to the Earth in its orbit. T
14. The apogee of an Earth satellite occurs when the satellite is closest to the Earth in its orbit. F

Multiple Choice

1. An orbiting body's point of closest approach to the Earth is called its _____.
    A. Ellipse
    B. Eclipse
    C. Apogee
*   D. Perigee
    E. Parabola

2. If the circular velocity at the Earth's surface is 7.91×10^5 cm/s, at 16 times the Earth's radius the circular velocity is about _____ $\times 10^5$ cm/s.
    A. 3.96
    B. 7.91
    C. 14.2
    D. 1.0
*   E. 1.98

3. Suppose a body is orbiting the Earth. The point in its orbit when it is most distant from the Earth is the body's __?
   A. Perigee
 * B. Apogee
   C. Aphelion
   D. Thrust
   E. Ellipse

4. The _____ are donut-shaped zones of energetic particles surrounding the Earth.
 * A. Van Allen belts
   B. Von Braun zones
   C. Jules Verne regions
   D. Newtonian hyperbolas
   E. Shepherd zones

5. When you step off a rowboat onto a dock the rowboat moves away from the dock. This motion away from the dock is an example of Newton's _____ law.
   A. Fourth
   B. Planetary
 * C. Third
   D. Gravitational
   E. None of these

6. The first artificial Earth satellite was launched in _____ by _____.
   A. 1887/France
   B. 1957/USA
 * C. 1957/USSR
   D. 1959/USA
   E. 1959/USSR

7. The United States launched its first successful artificial Earth satellite in _____.
   A. 1955
   B. 1956
   C. 1957
 * D. 1958
   E. 1959

8. Newton's third law of motion is _____.
 * A. For every action there is an equal and opposite reaction
   B. The gravitational force is inversely proportional to the distance
   C. A projectile keeps moving forward unless a modifying force acts on it
   D. The gravitational force is proportional to the mass
   E. None of the above

9. The first human being in space was _____ in _____.
   A. Jules Verne/1957
 * B. Yuri Gagarin/1961
   C. Yuri Gagarin/1957
   D. Alan Shepard/1957
   E. Alan Shepard/1961

10. The NASA budget in the years 1959-1969 was 25 percent of the total national budget.
    A. Correct
    B. Wrong — 75 percent
    C. Wrong — 1 percent
  * D. Wrong — 2.5 percent
    E. Wrong — NASA wasn't established until after 1969

11. Which of the following was not given as a major practical result of the space program.
    A. Weather satellite
    B. Communication satellite
    C. Photography for mapping
  * D. Development of a cosmic perspective
    E. Misleading — all of the above are major practical results

12. Newton's law of gravitation for two bodies of masses m_1 and m_2 separated by a distance r with "G" a constant and F the force is _____.
  * A. $F = m_1 m_2 / r^2$
    B. $F = m_1 m_2 r^2$
    C. $F = m_1 m_2 r$
    D. $F = m_1 m_2 / r$
    E. None of the above

13. If the Earth's mass were doubled, the circular velocity would be _____.
    A. Divided by $\sqrt{2}$
    B. Doubled
    C. Halved
  * D. Multiplied by $\sqrt{2}$
    E. None of these

14. If two bodies, which are interacting by the gravitational force have their separation decreased by a factor of 2, their mutual gravitational force will be _____ as large.
  * A. 4 times
    B. 1/4
    C. 16 times
    D. 1/16
    E. None of these

15. If two bodies, which are interacting by the gravitational force have their separation increased to 4 times as large, their mutual gravitational force will be _____ as large.
    A. 4 times
    B. 1/4
    C. 16 times
  * D. 1/16
    E. None of these

16. If the Earth's mass were doubled, the circular velocity would be _____.
    A. Doubled
    B. Halved
    * C. Multiplied by $\sqrt{2}$
    D. Divided by $\sqrt{2}$
    E. None of these

17. The weight of a body is _____.
    A. The same as its mass
    * B. The gravitational force by which the Earth pulls the body
    C. The same on all planets
    D. A measure of the amount of matter it contains
    E. Both A and C

18. The force of gravity on the Earth is 6 times greater than on the Moon; this means that _____.
    A. The Moon has 6 times the mass of the Earth
    * B. The weight of an object will be 6 times greater on the Earth than on the Moon
    C. The Moon has 1/6 the mass of the Earth
    D. The mass of an object will be 6 times greater on the Moon than on the Earth
    E. The mass of an object will be 6 times greater on the Earth than on the Moon

19. The mass of a body is always _____.
    * A. A measure of the amount of matter it contains
    B. The gravitational force by which the Earth pulls a body
    C. Proportional to the mass of the Sun
    D. Both A and B
    E. None of the above

20. Which is a correct statement of Newton's first law of motion?
    A. A body will fall back to Earth unless its speed is above the circular velocity.
    * B. A body at rest or in motion preserves that state unless modified by a force.
    C. The acceleration of a body is proportional to the force acting
    D. A body will fall back to Earth unless its speed is above the escape velocity.
    E. Mass and weight are proportional but equal only at the Earth's surface.

21. If G if Newton's gravitational constant, *m* the mass of the central body and *r* the distance of the orbiter from the center of the central body, the velocity of escape is given by _____.
    A. $G\,m\,/\,r^2$
    B. $G\,m \times r^2$
    * C. $\sqrt{\dfrac{2Gm}{r}}$
    D. $\sqrt{\dfrac{Gm}{r}}$
    E. $2\sqrt{\dfrac{Gm}{r}}$

22. If the radius of Venus is taken equal to the Earth and its mass is 0.82 times that of the Earth, the circular velocity at the surface of Venus is about _____ times that of the Earth.
    - A. 0.82
    - B. 1.22
    - * C. 0.91
    - D. 1.1
    - E. 1.0

Essay

1. Describe two direct practical results of the space program. (Some main points: weather predictions, communications, photography for mapping, strengthened sense of international community.)
2. Describe two intangible results of the space program. (Some main points: cosmic perspective, new frontier, and human survival.)
* 3. A small artificial satellite of 50 cm radius is put in Earth orbit with a perigee 200 kilometers above the Earth's surface. What is its angular diameter at perigee? What if the radius were 500 m? In either case, could the satellite be resolved by the naked eye? (See Chapters 2 and 4. Answers: 0.5"; 500"; yes, the 500 m one should be resolvable.)
4. State Newton's first law of motion.
5. Why is the gravitational force law not considered a law of motion? (Laws of motion tell how bodies behave in general; the gravitational force law gives the force if gravity is involved.)
6. Distinguish between mass and weight.

Word Practice (*denotes words from the reading material not on the Concepts list.)
1. Newton's _____ _____ has action equaling reaction.
2. The first American in space was _____ _____.*
3. The _____ _____ of the Earth is 11 km/s.
4. Newton's _____ _____ _____ gives the force a massive body produces on another body.*
5. The _____ _____ is the speed necessary for circular orbit.
6. The closed orbit of one body about another is called a(n)
7. A(n) _____ is the orbit resulting from speeds above escape velocity.
8. One of the practical results of the space program was _____ satellites.*
9. The _____ _____ are doughnut-shaped zones of energetic atomic particles about the Earth.
10. _____ is the force exerted by exhaust gases of a rocket.
11. The _____ is a satellite's closest approach to the Earth.
12. The first Russian satellites were named _____.*
13. _____ was responsible for formulating the law of gravitation.*
14. The first man in space was _____ _____.*
15. NASA's budget was ____ % of the US. national budget during 1959–1969.*
16. A satellite's farthest departure from the Earth is its _____.
17. _____ is a measure of the amount of matter in a body.
18. An orbit with exact escape velocity is a(n) _____.
19. The law of gravitation is a(n) ____ _____ _____.
20. _____ from satellites can help with mapping.*
21. Newton's _____ law of motion states that an object continues in constant motion unless acted upon by an outside force.

Answers to Word Practice

1. third law of motion
2. Alan Shepard
3. escape velocity
4. law of gravitation
5. circular velocity
6. ellipse
7. hyperbola
8. communications
9. Van Allen belts
10. thrust
11. perigee
12. Sputnik
13. Newton
14. Yuri Gagarin
15. 2.5
16. apogee
17. mass
18. parabola
19. inverse square law
20. photography
21. first

Chapter 5
Light and the Spectrum: Messages from Space

Answers to Problems in the Text

1. Since the energy per photon is larger for shorter wavelengths, we would expect it to be easiest to measure blue light and hardest to measure infrared light.

2. Water vapor and clouds tend to absorb and radiate or to reflect heat. Thus, on a warm, cloudy night, less heat escapes than on a dry, clear night.

3. Since only the absorption bands of CO_2 produce featureless photos, we expect the atmosphere of the planet to be nearly pure CO_2.

4. Our atmosphere absorbs most of the ultraviolet and infrared radiation hitting it, while most of the radio waves pass through. Thus, on the Earth's surface most of the radio waves can be detected, while UV and IR telescopes receive little radiation. To study UV and IR, we need to get the telescopes above the Earth's atmosphere.

5. Two binoculars of 50-mm aperture, but one of 7× and the other of 20× magnification.
    a. Magnifying power = (angular size with aid)/(angular size without aid), so the 20× gives a larger apparent image size.
    b. Two cases—for stars, since both binoculars have the same aperture, the images will be equally bright. If we look at extended objects (Moon, planets), then since the 20× pair produces a bigger image, that image must be dimmer than the image produced by the 7× (that is, the same amount of light is spread over a larger area with the 20×).
    c. The lower power will be easier to hold still. The 120× is at the limit for hand-held instruments.

6. For a camera, the lens is the objective and there is no eyepiece. The farther an image forms from a lens, the larger the image. For an astronomical object, the image forms at the focal length. We also expect that the larger the magnifying power the smaller the field of view, so
    a. the 90-mm lens
    b. the 24-mm lens
    c. the 90-mm lens

7. Emission lines are produced when an electron emits a photon and goes to a lower energy level.
    a. The ground state is the lowest energy level, so no photon can be emitted.
    b. Near hot stars, the atoms in a nebula are in high energy levels (the atom is excited). This occurs because the hot atoms often collide very hard and some of this energy of motion is transferred to the electronic structure. Thus, emission can occur as electrons are in their lowest states, and no emission can occur from electronic excitation.

Advanced Problems

8. The curve in Fig. 5-14 peaks at about 2×10^{-5} m. Use Wien's law $T = \dfrac{0.0029}{L}$, where T is the Kelvin temperature and L is the wavelength of the peak of the curve.
    So $T = \dfrac{0.0029}{2 \times 10^{-5}} = \dfrac{2.9}{2} \times 10^{-3+5} = 1.45 \times 10^2 = 145$ K.

9. Use Wien's law. The peak is at $L > 10 \times 10^{-6}$ m. If the peak were at $10 \times 10^{-6} = 10^{-5}$ m, the temperature would be $T = \dfrac{0.0029}{10^{-5}} = 200$ K.
    The true L is larger, so $T < 200$ K.

10. The book is at a temperature of about $27°$ C = 300 K. (A good rule of thumb is room temperature = 300 K.) Use Wien's law,
    $L = \dfrac{0.0029}{300}$ m $= 9.7 \times 10^{-6}$ m.

11. a. Magnification $= \dfrac{\text{focal length of objective}}{\text{focal length of eyepiece}}$. This is a ratio, so we can leave both in inches and get
    $M = \dfrac{70}{0.5} = 140$.
    b. The image brightness depends upon the aperture, which is information that was not given, so we cannot tell.
    c. Use the other definition of magnifying power:
    magnifying power $= \dfrac{\text{angular size with aid}}{\text{angular size without aid}}$
    $140 = \dfrac{\text{apparent size}}{0.5}$ so size $= 70°$.
    d. If the friend wants the aperture size, we do not have enough information. If what the friend wants is the magnifying power, we can give the answer, 140×.

12. The larger the magnifying power the smaller the field of view and the fainter an extended object appears.
    a. The 150× since Mars is small (20"). Thus, $20" \times 150 = 3000" = 50' = .83°$, while for the 30×, $20" \times 30 = 10'$, which is too small to be useful.
    b. The 30× since the image with the 150× would be extremely large and hence too faint (also, so large that only a small portion would be visible in the field of view).
    image size (30×) $= 3 \times 30 = 90°$
    image size (150×) $= 3 \times 150 = 450°$.

Sample Test Questions

True-False

1. In a reflecting telescope, the objective is a mirror. T
2. All radio telescopes are refractors. F
3. One reason useful magnification is limited is that at too high a magnification the image is too bright. F

4. The maximum useful magnifying power for most telescopes is about 20. F
5. The light-gathering power of a telescope increases as the aperture is enlarged. T
6. Faint objects can be seen better on photographs than with the eye. T
7. The hotter an object, the bluer the radiation it emits. T
8. The shortest wavelength of radiation that can be detected by the normal eye is about 4×10^{-7} m. T
9. The shortest wavelength of radiation that can be detected by the normal eye is about 6.5×10^{-7} m. F
10. Radiation with a wavelength longer than visible light is termed ultraviolet. F
11. The study of the colors of light emitted by objects is called spectroscopy. T
12. The shortest wavelength of visible radiation is violet. T
13. The discrete units of light are called photons. T
14. The array of colors in a light beam, ordered according to wavelength, is called white light. F
15. A glow consisting of a mixture of all colors is called an emission line. F
16. A molecule emits an absorption line. F

Multiple Choice

1. The visible light we see from the Sun is mostly ___ radiation.
    A. Reflected
*   B. Emitted
    C. Ultraviolet
    D. Radio
    E. None of these

2. The Kelvin degree is _____ the Celsius degree.
    A. Smaller than
*   B. Equal to
    C. Larger than
    D. Depends on the air pressure
    E. Depends on the temperature

3. The term aperture is shorthand for the _____.
    A. Focal length of the objective
    B. Area of the eyepiece
*   C. Area of the objective
    D. Ratio of the focal length of the objective to the focal length of the eyepiece
    E. Focal length of the eyepiece

4. Radio telescopes are _____ telescopes
*   A. Reflecting
    B. Refracting
*   C. Deflecting
    D. Compound
    E. Schmidt

5. The Newtonian focus telescope is an example of a _____ telescope.
    A. Schmidt
    B. Refracting
    C. Deflecting
*   D. Reflecting
    E. Defracting

6. A telescope whose objective is a lens and which contains no mirrors is a(n) _____ telescope.
*   A. Refracting
    B. Reflecting
    C. Compound
    D. Deflecting
    E. Achromatic

7. In a reflecting telescope the objective is a ____.
    A. Lens
*   B. Mirror
    C. Prism
    D. Grating
    E. None of the above

8. In the following diagram, which of these is (are) a refracting telescope?
    A. A
    B. B
*   C. C
    D. both A and B
    E. none of these

9. In the following diagram, which of these is (are) a reflecting telescope?
    A. A
    B. B
    C. C
*   D. both A and B
    E. none of these

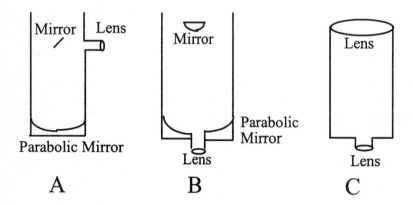

10. In the preceding diagram, which of these is a compound telescope?
    A. A
    B. B
    C. C
    D. both A and B
*   E. none of these

11. Light from a distant source passing through a simple convex lens is brought to an image at a distance L from the lens. L is termed the ___ .
* A. Focal length
  B. Objective
  C. Eyepiece
  D. Ellipse
  E. Hyperbola

12. The light-gathering power of a telescope increases as the aperture of the telescope is enlarged.
* A. Correct
  B. Incorrect
  C. Misleading — Light gathering power is independent of the aperture

13. The magnifying power of a telescope is _____ .
* A. The ratio of the angular size of an object when viewed with the telescope to the angular size without the telescope
  B. The smallest angular separation in which two stars still appear as two
  C. The ratio of the speed of light in a vacuum to that in the telescope
  D. The ratio of the angular size of an object when viewed without the telescope to the angular size with the telescope
  E. Misleading — term does not apply to telescopes

14. For bright planetary objects the eye usually sees more details than a photograph made with the same telescope since _____ .
  A. The eye is smaller than a camera
  B. Most telescopes are designed for eyes, not cameras
* C. The eye can wait for moments of good seeing
  D. Film is grainy
  E. None of these

15. Which has the larger light gathering power?
  A. A telescope of 3 cm diameter and focal length of 100 cm.
  B. A telescope of 3 cm diameter and focal length of 150 cm.
  C. A telescope of 2 cm diameter and focal length of 50 cm.
  D. A telescope of 2 cm diameter and focal length of 75 cm.
* E. Both A and B have the largest and the same light gathering power

16. The minimum angular separation of two stars that can be seen be a particular telescope is called the ____ power of that telescope.
  A. Magnifying
* B. Resolving
  C. F-ratio
  D. Focal
  E. None of these

17. The resolving power of a telescope is _____ .
  A. A measure of the amount of light gathered by the telescope.
  B. The separation between the objective and the image.
* C. A measure of the minimum separation of two stars that can be detected with the telescope.
  D. A measure of the maximum separation of two stars that can be detected with the telescope.
  E. The maximum angle that can be seen with the telescope.

18. What is the normal maximum usable magnifying power of a 30-cm aperture telescope with a focal length of 200 cm?
    A. 10 ×
    B. 300 ×
    C. 4,000 ×
    D. 500 ×
    * E. 600 ×

19. The main purpose(s) of the correcting lens on a compound telescope is(are) to _____.
    A. Collect light from a large area
    B. Produce a real image
    C. Redirect the light beam to a convenient location
    * D. Improve the image
    E. Both A and B

20. The main purpose(s) of the objective of a telescope is(are) to _____.
    A. Collect light from a large area
    B. Produce a real image
    C. Redirect the light beam to a convenient location
    D. Improve the image
    * E. Both A and B

21. A spectrum is _____.
    A. The set of all colors
    * B. An array of colors in order of wavelength
    C. A discrete unit of energy
    D. The limb of the Sun
    E. The cause of limb darkening

22. The dark lines on the solar spectrum are known as _____ lines.
    * A. Absorption
    B. Continuous
    C. Missing
    D. Hot
    E. None of the above

23. A substance emits light as a mixture of all colors. This is called a(n) ____.
    A. Bright line spectrum
    B. Dark line spectrum
    * C. Continuous spectrum
    D. Photon
    E. Photosphere

24. The study of the colors of light emitted by objects is called _____.
    * A. Spectroscopy
    B. Spectrum
    C. Photosphere
    D. Kirchhoff's analysis
    E. Spectroheliograph

25. Wien's law states: _____.
    A. The cooler an object, the bluer the radiation it emits.
*   B. The hotter an object, the bluer the radiation it emits.
    C. The hotter an object, the redder the radiation it emits.
    D. Temperature is proportional to emitted energy.
    E. Force is equal to mass times acceleration.

26. If the constant in Wien's law is about 0.003 and the most energy of a star's emission is observed to be emitted at 4×10^{-7} m, then the star's temperature is _____ degrees Kelvin.
    A. 12,000
    B. 8,000
*   C. 7,500
    D. 3
    E. 75,000

27. The peak in the continuum emission spectrum of a body occurs at a wavelength which is inversely proportional to the _____.
    A. Color
    B. Size of the body
*   C. Kelvin temperature
    D. Fahrenheit temperature
    E. None of the above

28. Given your eye and a camera and using either an optical or a radio telescope (of the same size), which of the following would give a sharper image of Mars?
    A. The eye alone
*   B. Using the telescope to view (telescope + eye)
    C. Using the telescope to photograph (telescope + camera).
    D. The radio telescope
    E. A crystal ball

29. You are using a 30-cm diameter telescope with a 100-cm focal length and an eyepiece with a focal length of 6 mm. What is the magnifying power?
    A. 40 ×
    B. 50 ×
    C. 200 ×
    D. 3600 ×
*   E. None of these

30. As a practical matter, resolution is normally limited by _____.
    A. Diffraction
*   B. The atmosphere
    C. The Sun
    D. Present quality of lens grinding
    E. Spectroscopy

31. A 60 cm aperture telescope of focal length 600 cm would have an ideal resolution of _____ seconds of arc.
  * A. 0.20
    B. 2.0
    C. 10
    D. 3.6×10^2
    E. 0.10

Essay

1. What are the three effects that limit the usable magnifying power of a telescope?
2. Discuss the advantages of the eye versus a camera when using a telescope.
3. Distinguish between an absorption line and an absorption band. Under what conditions does each occur?
4. Discuss the differences in the wave behavior of light and its particle aspect.
5. Give three ways that telescopic images can be stored and modified.
6. Describe interferometry.
7. Discuss light pollution and how it affects astronomical observation.

Word Practice (* denotes questions using words from the chapter that are not on the Concepts list.)

1. The _____ is a small lens system used to magnify the image formed by the objective.*
2. The eyepiece is used to magnify the _____ formed by the objective.*
3. The _____ of a telescope is the diameter of the objective.
4. The ___ ___ of a telescope is determined solely by the aperture size.
5. The main lens or mirror of a telescope is called the _____.
6. _____ telescopes use lenses and mirrors together for their objective.
7. A(n) _____ uses a mirror as its objective.
8. The _____ mirror present in some telescopes is primarily to beam the light rays to a location for easier access.*
9. A telescope with a long-focal-length eyepiece will have a(n) _____ power compared to the same telescope with a short-focal-length eyepiece.*
10. The shorter the focal length of the _____,the larger the magnifying power.*
11. There is a limit to a normal useful _____ of a telescope. This limit is about 20 power per cm of aperture.*
12. The _____ _____ of a telescope is the angular size of the object as seen through the telescope divided by its angular size without the telescope.*
13. A(n) _____ uses a lens as its objective.
14. A(n) _____ reflector is a telescope that uses a secondary mirror to direct the light out the side of the telescope.*
15. A(n) _____ telescope is designed to be looked through.*
16. A(n) _____ is a small telescope attached to a larger telescope. It is used to guide the larger telescope when making photographs.*
17. The _____ length of a lens or mirror is the distance from it that the image of a distant object forms.
18. The _____ is a measure of the clarity of the atmosphere.
19. The process of splitting light into wavelengths so a photomultiplier tube can measure the intensity of each wavelength is _____.

20. The process of measuring the amount of light from an object, usually with electronic devices, is called _____.
21. The spacing between crests of a wave is the _____.
22. One of the _____-like properties of light is its localization.
23. The period between pulsations of a light wave is its _____.
24. The spreading of light in all directions from a source is one of the _____-like properties of light.
25. _____ radiation has a wavelength shorter than visible radiation.
26. _____ radiation has a wavelength longer than visible radiation.
27. The bending of light as it passes an edge is called _____.
28. The arrangement of light by colors is called the _____.
29. ____ is the measure of the average motions of the molecules of a substance.
30. The process of an atom emitting a photon is called _____.
31. The broad emission feature from a molecule is called a(n) __ ____.
32. Radiation not related to the thermal motions of atomic particles is called _____ radiation.*
33. The _____ is a measure of how many times bigger the angular size of an object appears through a telescope.
34. _____ astronomy is free from the blurring effects of the Earth's atmosphere.
35. The _____ of a telescope is a measure of the detail that can be seen through the telescope.
36. The larger the ____ ____of a telescope, the brighter the image it produces.
37. The process of combining signals from separate telescopes to improve resolution is called _____.
38. The _____ temperature scale has a zero chosen to be the temperature at which thermal motion ceases.
39. _____ light is that portion of _____ radiation that can be seen by the human eye.
40. A electromagnetic radiation travels in a vacuum at about 3×10^5 km/s which is the ____ __ ____.
41. A hot low-pressure gas produces ____ lines.
42. When the electrons in an atom are in their lowest possible levels, the atom is said to be in its _____ state.
43. If an electron in an atom absorbs energy and moves to at higher energy level, it is said to be in an ____ state
44. A cool low-density gas between us and a bright star will produce _____ lines.
45. A dust cloud between us an a star will produce absorption _____.
46. The Earth's ____ layer protects the surface from ultraviolet radiation.
47. The particle aspect of light is called the _____.
48. Electrons, which are completely removed from an atom, produce _____ radiation when they return.
49. A hot solid or high-density gas produces a ____ spectrum.
50. Radiation dependent on the temperature of the radiating material is called _____ radiation.
51. _____ radiation depends of the temperature of the light source, not upon the temperature of the reflector.
52. _____ law relates the temperature of a body to the wavelength at which it emits the most radiation.
53. A modern way of recording astronomical images is the ____ camera, which directly produces digital information.
54. A ____ telescope detects radiation with a much longer wavelength than an optical telescope.

Answers to Word Practice

1. eyepiece
2. image
3. aperture
4. light-gathering power
5. objective
6. compound
7. reflector
8. secondary
9. smaller
10. eyepiece
11. power or magnifying power or magnification
12. magnifying power
13. refractor
14. Newtonian
15. visual
16. finder
17. focal
18. seeing (Web site)
19. spectrophotometry
20. photometry
21. wavelength
22. particle
23. frequency
24. wave
25. ultraviolet
26. infrared
27. diffraction
28. spectrum
29. temperature
30. emission
31. emission band
32. non-thermal
33. magnification
34. Space
35. resolution
36. light-gathering power
37. interferometry (Web site)
38. absolute
39. visible, electromagnetic
40. Speed of light
41. emission
42. state
43. excited
44. absorption
45. absorption
46. bands
47. ozone
48. telescope
49. photon
50. fields
51. continuum
52. continuous
53. thermal
54. thermal radiation
55. reflected
56. Wein's
57. energy
58. CCD
59. radio

Chapter 6
Earth as a Planet

Answers to Problems in the Text

1. The answer depends on the student's home location, which each student might discuss. Sources of information are local geologists and insurance agents. Insurance underwriters have an overly pessimistic map, but it is useful.

2. The half-life of U-235 is 7.1×10^8 years. (This figure is not in the text.) With each half-life, the amount of U-235 left decreases by half. In other words, after one half-life there is half as much. After two half-lives there is $1/2 \times 1/2 = 1/4$ as much. After three half-lives there is $1/2 \times 1/2 \times 1/2 = 1/8$ as much. So the rock sample is 2.1×10^9 years old.

3. The indicated surface features show that the Moon is much less active than the Earth, so there is much less "earthquake" activity on the Moon than on the Earth. On the Earth, earthquakes are usually the result of plate tectonics, a process that has not occurred on the Moon.

4. We take the Earth's age as 4.6×10^9 years. Then if the genus *Homo* is 3 million years = 3×10^6 years old, the fractional duration of its existence so far is

$$\frac{3\times10^6}{4.6\times10^9} = \frac{3}{4.6} \times \frac{10^6}{10^9} = (0.65) \times 10^{-3} = 6.5 \times 10^{-4}.$$

Multiply this by 100 to get percent, which gives $6.5 \times 10^{-2}\% = 0.065\%$—that is, much less than 1/10 of a percent.

5. The half-life of U-238 is 4.51 eons. The Earth is 4.6 eons old, so about one-half of the original U-238 is left. Because heat production from U-238 decay depends upon the total number of atoms decaying, the original heat output was higher than now.

6. a. Most of the hydrogen was lost to outer space. If the Earth had been much more massive, such as Jupiter is, the hydrogen would have been retained.
   b. The nitrogen released by the breakup of NH_3 provided much of the nitrogen in our atmosphere.

   c. Volcanoes added carbon dioxide and water vapor. The water vapor produced the oceans, while the carbon dioxide dissolved in the water and reacted with the Earth's surface to form carbonate rocks.

7. This question asks, in effect: What would happen to the Earth as it is now if it were suddenly placed at either the orbital distance of Venus from the Sun or the orbital distance of Mars from the Sun?

   Case 1 (if the Earth were closer to the Sun): Temperature would be above 100° C; most of the oceans would evaporate, and life would cease.

   Case 2 (if the Earth were farther from the Sun): Temperature of the Earth's surface would be below 0° C; the oceans would freeze over, eventually destroying all life in them.

   As extra information (beyond what the question asked), we note that in either case, since life has ceased, the free oxygen and nitrogen in the atmosphere would eventually disappear, leaving the Earth with a carbon dioxide atmosphere (and water vapor in Case 1).

Advanced Problems

8. a.   Surface temperature is 20° C, boiling water is 100° C, so we want an 80° C temperature change. At 20° C/cm, we would need to go 80° C/(20° C/km) = 4 km. This is roughly the depth of the deepest mines. In reality, this calculation fails because within a kilometer of the surface the gradient falls from 20° C/km to a lower figure. The actual depth would be greater than 10 km; however, deep mines are notably hot.
    b.   *Economic consequences*
         1) reduction—although not elimination—of energy crisis
         2) elimination of most coal mining or its conversion to a hydrocarbon source in industry
         3) probable reduced air pollution, but increased thermal pollution
         4) shift in economic power of various industries
    c. *Political consequences*
         1) reduction of political power of OPEC countries
         2) possible rapid industrial development of Third World countries because all countries would be independent of foreign energy sources

9. a.   We need the angular size of the Earth as seen from Mars.
    Use $\dfrac{\alpha''}{206,265} = d/D$ where $d = 1.28 \times 10^4$ km $= 1.28 \times 10^7$ m and $D = 6 \times 10^7$ km $= 6 \times 10^{10}$ m

    so $\alpha_\oplus'' = \dfrac{2.06 \times 10^5 \times d}{D} = \dfrac{2.06 \times 1.28}{6} \times \dfrac{10^5 \times 10^7}{10^{10}}$ while the Sun is $\alpha_\odot = \dfrac{1}{3}^\circ \times \dfrac{60'}{1^\circ} \times \dfrac{60''}{1'} = 1200''$

    b.   No. The disk of Earth is 43", which is smaller than the resolution of the naked eye (120").

Sample Test Questions

True-False

1.   The Earth is perfectly regular in its rotation. F
2.   An eastward or westward deflection of moving air is called a Newtonian drift. F
3.   The Earth is estimated to be 4.6×10^8 years old. F
4.   A radioactive atom is a stable atom that does not change. F
5.   Ages of rocks can be dated by counting relative amounts of radioactive decay products. T
6.   The oldest known Earth rocks are found on circular regions called continental plates. F
7.   The Earth is much younger than the Moon and most of the other planets. F
8.   The center of the Earth's core is liquid. F
9.   Earthquakes occur in the Earth's core. F
10. The crust is the outermost shell of the Earth. T
11. The process that separates the elements in the Earth is termed differentiation. T
12. Melting of the Earth that causes gases to be released is termed convection. F
13. Heat transmission by the motion of materials is termed convection. T
14. The process of crustal disruption by flow of materials is termed plate tectonics. T
15. Mountains are caused by the Earth's shriveling. F

Multiple Choice

1. The outermost layer of Earth is the
    A.   Core
*   B.   Crust
    C.   Asthenosphere
    D.   Mantle
    E.   Epicycle

2. A body moving north in the Northern Hemisphere is deflected to the ___ by the ___ drift.
    A.   East, Foucault
    B.   West, Coriolis
*   C.   East, Coriolis
    D.   West, Foucault
    E.   North, Smith

3. On the Earth, the effect that causes a deflection in the path of a moving body is the _____effect.
*   A.   Coriolis
    B.   Newtonian
    C.   Hartmann
    D.   Foucault
    E.   Deflecting

4. The best current estimate of the Earth's age is _____years.
    A.   5,982
    B. 4.6×10^3
    C. 4.6×10^6
*   D. 4.6×10^9
    E. 1.8×10^{10}

5. When an original radioactive element decays, the new element formed is termed the ____.
    A.   Radioactive atom
    B.   Parent isotope
*   C.   Daughter isotope
    D.   Residue
    E.   Half-life

6. Suppose a radioactive element has a half-life of 300 years. After 600 years, how much of the original amount will be left?
    A.   ½
*   B.   ¼
    C.   1/8
    D.   1/16
    E.   Twice

7. Sound waves traveling through the Earth are termed _____ waves.
   A.   Earth traveling
   B.   Magnetic
   C.   Fault
 * D.   Seismic
   E.   Geologic

8. The technique of radioisotopic dating measures the time since the rocks being studied were ___.
   A.   Formed from a dust and gas cloud
   B.   Dug up
   C.   Last exposed to Sunlight
 * D.   Solidified from an earlier molten material
   E.   None of these

9. Flat, circular regions, found on several continents, that yield the oldest known rocks are the ____.
   A.   Circular field
   B.   Massive crumplings
   C.   Continental disks
   D.   Old schliefs
 * E.   Continental shields

Consider the sketch of the Earth:

10. In this diagram, the core is
    denoted by the letter _A_.

11. In this diagram, the mantle is
    denoted by the letter _B_.

12. In this diagram, the crust is
    denoted by the letter _C_.

13. The Earth's core is primarily composed of ____.
    A.   Lead
    B.   Silicates
    C.   Copper
  * D.   Nickel-iron
    E.   Iron

14. The Earth's magnetic field is believed to be produced by liquid metal circulating in the Earth's ___.
    A.   Crust
    B.   Mantle
  * C.   Outer core
    D.   Inner core
    E.   Misleading: This is not the cause of the Earth's magnetic field.

15. The outermost shell of Earth is the _____.
* A.   Crust
  B.   Mantle
  C.   Core
  D.   Declination
  E.   Sky

16. Mixtures of crystalline compounds called ___combine into groups to form various kinds of ____.
  A.   Elements — compounds
  B.   Atoms — molecules
  C.   Rocks — minerals
* D.   Minerals — rocks
  E.   Plates — continents

17. A dark gray volcanic rock is called _____.
  A.   Silicate
  B.   Granite
* C.   Basaltic
  D.   Stony-iron
  E. Mud

18. The group of processes that have separated some groups of chemical elements from others is termed
    _____.
  A.   Separation
  B.   Drift
  C.   Isotope
  D.   Conduction
* E.   None of these

19. When gases are released by heating, melting, or partial melting of a material, the process is termed
    ___.
  A.   Differentiation
  B.   Conduction
  C.   Radiation
  D.   Radioactive decay
* E.   Outgassing

20. _____ Is the flow of heat through a material by the mechanical agitation of adjacent molecules in the material.
  A.   Outgassing
* B.   Conduction
  C.   Convection
  D.   Radiation
  E.   None of these

21. The eruption of molten materials from a planet's interior onto its surface is ____
  A.   Radiation
  B.   Faulting
  C.   Impact cratering
  D.   None of these
* E.   Volcanism

22. Which of these processes affect(s) the Earth's surface?
    - A.   Impact cratering
    - B.   B and C, but not A
    - C.   Volcanism
  * - D.   A, B, and C
    - E.   Erosion

23. All processes of fracturing and movement of the Earth's crust are called ___, but _____ refers to the effects of a sudden cracking.
    - A.   Motion — sudden
    - B.   Earthquake — tectonics
    - C.   Motion — earthquake
    - D.   None of the above
  * - E.   Tectonics — earthquake

24. The continents were all part of a single massive continent called Pangaea about 7 billion years ago. Convection currents caused the continent to break up into pieces, setting off continental drifts.
    - A.   Correct in all aspects
    - B.   Wrong: The continents never were together.
  * - C.   Wrong: It was 300 million years ago.
    - D.   Wrong: The breakup was caused by radiation, not convection.
    - E.   Wrong: Both changes C and D are needed to correct the statement.

Essay

1. Describe the evolution of scientific thought about the Earth's age. Some main points that might be considered:
    Archbishop Usher, in 1650, estimated 4004 BC.

late 1600s:	Recognition that sediments gave earlier dates.
1700s:	Fossils and strata give earlier dates.
1500s–1800s:	Belief that mountains form by shriveling.
1900s:	Development of radioactive dating; ages of the Earth's surface rocks estimated.

    mid-twentieth century: Dating of meteorites and Moon samples; age of solar system.
2. Describe how earthquakes are used to determine the Earth's structure. A drawing might help. Some main points: Earthquakes produce seismic waves that are bent and reflected by structure. Use a figure similar to Fig. 6-4 to show delay of waves.
3. Discuss the evidence for continental drift. Some main points:
    1620: Francis Bacon noticed fit.
    1922: A. L. Wegener proposed drifting earthquake patterns and mountain building; lowering sea floor at spreading lines.)
4. Let the history of the Earth be one day long. When did fish appear? Mammals? Human beings?
5. Discuss the evidence supporting the asteroidal cause of the Cretaceous-Tertiary extinctions.
6. Discuss the "greenhouse" effect and its relation to our civilization.

Word Practice (* denotes additional words from the chapter.)

1. A(n) _____ atom is an unstable atom that decays into simpler atom(s).
2. The time it takes half of a radioactive sample to decay is that element's _____.
3. The _____ impact probably caused mass extinctions.
4. _____ is a group of processes separating chemical elements.
5. A(n) ____ ____ is a new atom formed by radioactive decay.
6 4.6 billion years is the estimated __ ____ __.
7. _____ _____ travel through the Earth.
8. The materials in the Earth and the way they are arranged are the Earth's _____.*
9. Dark gray volcanic rock is called _____.
10. The Earth's outer core is _____ nickel-iron.*
11. _____ is a release of gases by melting of underground material.*
12. Different _____ of an element have the same number of protons but a different number of neutrons.*
13. The part of the Earth directly beneath the crust is the _____.
14. The crust of the Earth is composed of distinct _____.
15. _____ is the process of fracturing and movement of the Earth's crust.
16. Molten rock that reaches the surface is called _____.
17. The original atom before radioactive decay is called the ____ isotope.
18. The eruption of molten materials from a planet's interior is called _____.
19. _____ is a heat transport process by motions of materials.*
20. A(n) _____ is the result of motion of rock units with respect to each other.
21. If all minerals are melted, we have _____.*
22. _____ is energy carried by electromagnetic waves.*
23. _____ is a process removing and transporting materials across a planet's surface.
24. Liquid metal circulating in the outer part of the Earth's core sets up electric currents that create the Earth's _____ .
25. _____ is the eastward and westward deflection of a moving object due to the Earth's rotation.
26. _____ is a silicate-rich rock of lower density than basalt.
27. _____ _____ involves estimating ages of rocks from relative amounts of radioactive materials.
28. _____ are crystalline compounds formed from elements.*
29. _____ are mixtures of minerals.*
30. Processes that deposit and accumulate materials on a planet's surface are called _____.*
31. A sudden cracking of the Earth's crust is called a(n) _____.*
32. When __ occurs, part of the material flows away, leaving solids behind.*
33. __ is the flow of heat through a material by molecular vibrations.*
34. _____ are circular depressions created by interplanetary debris colliding with the Earth.
35. Convection currents in the mantle cause the crustal plates to move, producing _____.*
36. The theory of _____ _____ accounts for changing plant and animal life on the Earth's surface.
37. The center part of the Earth is its _____.
38. The _____ is the most rigid part of the Earth.
39. The _____ is a fluid and plastic like zone.
40. A physical property associated with a region of space is a(n) ____.
41. The idea that mountains were built in a relatively brief period of time is called _____.
42. The idea that mountains were built by slow geological processes is called _____.
43. The Earth's ____ ____ ____ are about 3.96 billion years old.
44. The oldest, most stable regions on the Earth's surface are called ___ _____.
45. The thin outer layer of the Earth's surface is called the ____.
46. Underground molten rock is called ____.
47. _____ is the process by which materials are accumulated.
48. The ____ _____ atmosphere came from volcanic outgassing.

49. _____ atmosphere is a result of chemical reactions and the effects of life on Earth.
50. The ____ ____ on the Earth are caused partially by changes in the Earth's orbit.
51. Many episodes of ____ extinctions have occurred in the flora and fauna of the Earth.
52. The _____ effect is a warming of the Earth caused by CO_2 blocking radiation of the surface.

Answers to Word Practice

1. radioactive
2. half-life
3. Cretaceous-Tertiary
4. differentiation
5. daughter isotope
6. age of the Earth
7. seismic waves
8. structure
9. basalt
10. liquid
11. outgassing
12. isotopes
13. mantle
14. plates
15. tectonics
16. lava
17. parent
18. volcanism
19. convection
20. fault
21. complete melting
22. radiation
23. erosion
24. magnetic field
25. Coriolis drift
26. granite
27. radioisotopic dating
28. minerals
29. rocks
30. deposition
31. earthquake
32. partial melting
33. conduction
34. impact craters
35. continental drift
36. natural selection
37. core
38. lithosphere
39. asthenosphere
40. field
41. catastrophism
42. uniformitarianism
43. oldest known rocks
44. continental shields
45. crust
46. magma
47. deposition
48. early dense
49. today's
50. ice ages
51. mass
52. greenhouse

Chapter 7
The Moon

Answers to Problems in the Text

1. Use Fig. 7-2 plus a straightedge. Ask where are you on the Earth if it is sunrise, sunset, noon, etc. Students must remember that the Earth should be much smaller if this figure were to scale.
   a. noon
   b. sunset
   c. midnight
   d. sunrise

2. Full

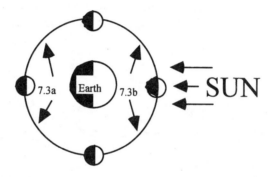

3. There are two possible answers since we could be in the Northern or Southern Hemisphere. If we are in the Northern Hemisphere, then picture 7.3a is correct, and we are seeing a third-quarter Earth. See Fig. 7-1.

4. The Moon rotates once about its axis for each revolution about the Earth. Because the Moon is not exactly spherical, the gravitational forces of the Earth have, over the eons, locked the Moon into synchronous rotation. These tidal forces slowed or sped up the Moon until it had synchronous rotation.

5. We would expect the tidal bulges to be under the Moon and on the far side of the Earth from the Moon (diametrically opposed). Because the Moon is overhead and in line with the Sun at noon when the Moon is new, the ideal tides would be at a maximum then and at midnight. But the real tides are unable to keep up with the Moon (they could if the oceans covered the world to a depth of 2–3 miles). In addition, the seacoasts cause resonance effects that also put the high tide out of phase with the Moon.

6. No. The orbit is inside the Roche limit, so we would expect the tidal forces of the Earth to separate them by overcoming their self-gravitation.

7. a. The inside edges of young craters, where no lava flow has occurred.
   b. Rougher because fresh rock surfaces are exposed. So many small impacts have occurred on older craters that the surface is covered with a smooth regolith.
   c. The crater Aristarchus.

8. a. No. The magnetic field is too weak for an ordinary compass.
   b. The Earth.
   c. It stays roughly fixed over the center of the front side, so it would appear to move very little. For an observer on the Moon, the angle between the observer's zenith and the Earth would be a measure of the distance of the observer from the point where the Earth is overhead.

9. The Moon is less geologically active. No weathering or continental drift occurs on the Moon. No continental drifting is re-circulating the surface material.

10. Sedimentary rocks are formed by air depositing dust or by running water depositing mud. These deposits turn into rock under pressure. For this to happen, there must be appreciable free water and an atmosphere.

11. The uplands are about 25% older than the maria. If the meteoritic cratering rate were constant, we would expect about 25% more craters on the uplands than on the maria and about the same distribution of sizes. Examination of photos shows that there are many more than 25% additional craters on the uplands.

Advanced Problems

12. a. Newton's law of gravity is that the gravitational force is proportional to Mm/r^2; that is,
$$F = G\frac{Mm}{r^2}.$$
Let M be the mass of a test body, $M_\oplus$ the mass of the Earth, and $r_\oplus$ the Earth's radius. Then $F_\oplus$, the weight on the Earth, is
$$F_\oplus = \frac{GM_\oplus m}{r^2_\oplus}.$$
If M is the mass of the Moon and r_m the Moon's radius, then the weight on the Moon, F_m, is given by
$$F_m = \frac{GM_m m}{r^2_m}.$$
If we divide one by the other, we get
$$\frac{F_m}{F_\oplus} = \frac{GM_m m}{r^2_m} \times \frac{r_\oplus^2}{GM_\oplus m} = \frac{M_m}{M_\oplus} \times \frac{r_\oplus^2}{r_m^2}$$
$$= (0.012) \times \left(\frac{1}{0.27}\right)^2 = 0.165 = \frac{1}{6}.$$
   b. Weight on Moon = 0.165 × weight on Earth = 0.165 × 180 = 29.7 lb. (30 lb. if 1/6 is used).

13. Use the small angle equation $\frac{\alpha''}{2.1\times10^5} = \frac{d}{D}$, where α'' is the angular diameter of the Moon in seconds of arc, d is the lunar diameter, and D is the distance to the Moon. So $\frac{\alpha''}{2.1\times10^5} = \frac{3476 \text{ km}}{384,000 \text{ km}} = 0.0091$.

So $\alpha'' = 1.9 \times 10^3$ seconds of arc. To convert this to degrees, remember $60'' = 1'$ and $60' = 1°$, so $1° = 3600''$.
$$\alpha(°) = \frac{\alpha''}{3600} = 0°.51.$$

14. Escape velocity $= \sqrt{2V_{circ}}$; $V_{circ} = \sqrt{\dfrac{GM}{R}}$.

Method 1

$$V_{circ_m} = V_{circ_\oplus}\sqrt{\frac{M_{Moon}}{M_\oplus}}\sqrt{\frac{R_\oplus}{R_{Moon}}}$$

$$V_{circ_m} = 8 \text{ km/s} \times \sqrt{0.012} \times \sqrt{\frac{1}{0.27}} = 8 \text{ km/s} \times \sqrt{\frac{0.012}{0.27}}$$

$$= 8 \text{ km/s} \times \sqrt{4.44 \times 10^{-2}} = (8 \times 0.21) \text{ km/s} = 1.68 \text{ km/s}$$

So escape velocity $V_{esc} = \sqrt{2}\, V_{circ} = 2.38$ km/s.

Method 2

$$V_{circ_m} = \sqrt{\frac{GM_m}{R_m}} \qquad G \qquad = \qquad 6.67 \times 10^{-11}$$

$M = 7.35 \times 10^{22}$ kg; $R = 1.74 \times 10^6$ m

$$V_{circ} = \sqrt{\frac{6.67 \times 7.53}{1.74} \times \frac{10^{-11} \times 10^{22}}{10^6}}^{1/2} \text{ m/s}$$

$$= (2.86 \times 10^6)^{1/2} \text{ m/s} = 1.64 \times 10^3 \text{ m/s} = 1.64 \text{ km/s}$$

Then escape velocity $= \sqrt{2} \times 1.64$ km/s $= 2.38$ km/s.

15. Mean density = mass/volume = $3M \div (4\pi R^3)$. For Earth,

$M = 5.98 \times 10^{24}$ kg,; radius $= \dfrac{\text{diameter}}{2} = 6.38 \times 10^6$ m.

So mean density $= 5.5 \times 10^3$ kg/m^3.
For the Moon,
$M = 7.35 \times 10^{22}$ kg,; radius $= 1.74 \times 10^6$ m.
So mean density $= 3.3 \times 10^3$ kg/m^3.
Since iron is denser than either of these numbers indicates, this implies the Moon has less iron than the Earth.

16. Use small angle $\dfrac{\alpha''}{206,265} = d/D = \dfrac{\text{diameter of crater}}{\text{distance to the Moon}}$ so $d = \dfrac{D \times 2}{206,265}$,where D is the distance to the

Moon from Earth's surface; distance to Moon $= 3.48 \times 10^5$ km $= 3.48 \times 10^8$ m (less 0.06×10^8 m if

you consider that you are on the surface of the Earth. Thus $d = \dfrac{2 \times 3.48 \times 10^8}{2.06 \times 10^5} = 3.38 \times 10^3$ m $= 3.38$

km (1.66 km at best by subtracting Earth's radius).

Sample Test Questions

True -False

1. The visible surface of the Moon has changed dramatically over the past million years. F
2. Because the same side of the Moon is always visible from the Earth, it is obvious that the Moon does not rotate. F
3. A full Moon rises at noon. F
4. The far side of the Moon is always dark. F

5. The sidereal period of the Moon is about 27-1/3 days. T
6. Most of the craters on the Moon were formed by recent impact. F
7. The tidal effects of the Earth on the Moon are causing the Moon to move away from the Earth. T
8. The Moon's tides are causing the Earth to rotate faster. F
9. The Roche limit is the distance from a planet within which a natural, large satellite will be disrupted by tidal forces. T
10. The smoother, gray, flat areas of the Moon are called maria. T
11. The lunar craters were formed by volcanoes. F
12. The first spacecraft reached the Moon in 1957. F
13. The lunar regolith is made primarily of debris blasted out of lunar craters as the craters formed. T
14. The oldest rock sample from the Moon has been dated at 4.5 billion years old. T
15. The bulk density of the Moon is less than that of the Earth. T

Multiple Choice

Use the following diagram to answer questions 1-4:

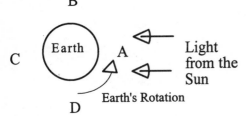

1. When the Moon is full it is in position
   A. A
   B. B
* C. C
   D. D
   E. none of these

2. When the Moon is new it is in position
* A. A
   B. B
   C. C
   D. D
   E. none of these

3. When the Moon is in first quarter it is in position
   A. A
* B. B
   C. C
   D. D
   E. none of these

4. When the Moon is in third quarter it is in position
   A. A
   B. B
   C. C
* D. D
   E. none of these

5. Because the Moon rotates on its axis with a period equal to its orbital revolution about the Earth, it is said to be in _____ rotation.
   A. Harmonic
   B. Synodic
 * C. Synchronous
   D. Elliptical
   E. Sporadic

6. The interval from new Moon to new Moon is not the sidereal period of the Moon because the
   A. Moon is in synchronous rotation
 * B. Earth goes about the Sun
   C. Earth goes about the Moon
   D. Earth produces tides on the Moon
   E. Mean density of the Moon is less than that of the Earth

7. The sidereal period of the Moon is about _____ days.
   A. 13
 * B. 27
   C. 29 ½
   D. 37
   E. 365

8. The period of lunar phases is about _____ days.
   A. 13
   B. 27
 * C. 29 ½
   D. 37
   E. 365

9. Suppose you lived on the rim of the crater Copernicus on the Moon. The Earth would set below your horizon
   A. Once in 12 hours
   B. Once in 24 hours
   C. Every 27 days
   D. Every 29 ½ days
 * E. Never

10. Ideally, the ocean tides should be only a bulge of water directly beneath the Moon.
    A. Correct
    B. Wrong: bulge at 90° to Moon position
 * C. Wrong: also a bulge diametrically opposed to the Moon
    D. Wrong: only a bulge diametrically opposed to the Moon
    E. Misleading: Ideally, there would be no ocean tides. The Earth's rapid rotation produces the tides.

11. The Moon keeps the same side of its surface toward the Earth as the Moon revolves about the Earth. This behavior is caused by the
    A. Tides produced by the Moon
 * B. Tides produced by the Earth
    C. Tides produced by the Sun
    D. Sporadic impact of meteorites on the Moon
    E. None of these

12. Tidal effects are causing the Moon to _____ the Earth.
    A. Approach
    B. Slow down the rotation of
    C. Recede from
 * D. Both B and C
    E. Speed up the rotation of

13. The Roche limit for the Earth is about _____ km.
    A. 6000
    B. 8000
 * C. 18,000
    D. 384,000
    E. 971,000

14. The Roche limit is
    A. the closest distance that an artificial satellite can approach the Earth without being burned up by the atmosphere.
    B. the maximum size a planet can be before its own tidal forces would destroy it.
 * C. the closest distance a natural satellite of any size can be from a planet without being destroyed by tidal forces.
    D. the minimal precessional period a planet can have.
    E. none of these

15. The Moon has a heavy atmosphere and much free water.
    A. Correct
    B. Wrong: little or no atmosphere
    C. Wrong: little or no free water
 * D. Both B and C
    E. Astronomers cannot yet answer this question.

16. The surface of the Moon is very cold even in the daylight.
    A. Correct
    B. Wrong: It is always hot.
    C. Wrong: It is cold in daylight, hot at night or in the shade.
 * D. Wrong: It is hot in the daylight, cold in the shade at night.
    E. We do not know.

17. The circular depressions on the lunar surface are called
    A. Maria
 * B. Craters
    C. Rilles
    D. Rays
    E. Mountains

18. The lunar maria are _____.
    A. Cracks on the lunar surface
 * B. Flat areas on the lunar surface
    C. Bright streaks on the lunar surface radiating from the craters
    D. Mountains on the Moon
    E. Bodies of water on the Moon

19. The lunar craters were apparently caused by
    A. Bursting bubbles of gas from the interior
    B. Spacecraft landings
 * C. Meteoritic collisions
    D. Nothing. There are in fact no craters on the Moon.
    E. Scientists have no good ideas of their cause.

20. The first Apollo mission to land on the Moon was Apollo _____.
    A. 1
    B. 5
    C. 8
 * D. 11
    E. 17

21. The Apollo 16 mission landed on the Moon near
 * A. The crater Descartes
    B. Fra Mauro
    C. Mare Tranquillitatis
    D. Mare Imbrium
    E. The Taurus Mountains

22. The first Apollo to use the lunar roving vehicle was Apollo _____.
    A. 8
    B. 11
    C. 13
 * D. 15
    E. 17

23. Most lunar rocks are _____.
 * A. Igneous
    B. Sedimentary
    C. Tidal
    D. Volatile
    E. None of these

24. The mean density of an object is defined as
    A. Total mass times total volume
 * B. Total mass divided by total volume
    C. Total volume divided by total mass
    D. Total mass divided by total surface area
    E. None of these

25. The _____ elements are those that would evaporate if the rocks containing them were strongly heated.
    A. Sedimentary
    B. Igneous
    C. Refractory
 * D. Volatile
    E. Basaltic

26. Studying the Moon's surface show us that the cratering rate has been roughly constant for the last 4.6 billion years.
    A. Correct
*   B. Wrong: There was early intense bombardment.
    C. Wrong: There has been recent intense bombardment.
    D. Wrong: There was a break in bombardment about 500 million years ago.
    E. Misleading: We can learn nothing about the cratering rate by studying the present surface.

27. The layer of rocky soil covering much of the uplands of the Moon is sometimes called a _____. It was produced by ___.
    A. Tsunamis — neap tides
    B. Sediment — erosion
    C. Lithosphere — meteoritic cratering
    D. Megaregolith — volcanic action
*   E. Megaregolith — meteoritic cratering

28. Which of the following is NOT a clue to the Moon's origin?
    A. The Moon has much less iron than the Earth
    B. The Moon has almost no water
*   C. The Moon is slowing the Earth's rotation
    D. The composition of the Moon resembles the Earth mantle
    E. None of these

Mathematical Multiple Choice

29. Given that the Moon is 3.48×10^5 km from the Earth, assume that you are on a spaceship halfway to the Moon and are using a telescope that enables you to resolve 0.1" of arc. What is the size of the smallest crater you can resolve?*
*   A. 82 m
    B. 17 km
    C. 1.7 km
    D. 32 km
    E. 3.4 km

30. If the command module of an Apollo mission is 1½ times the lunar radius from the surface, how much must the speed be increased to reach escape velocity?*
    A. 0.5 km/s
*   B. 0.8 km/s
    C. 2.38 km/s
    D. 8 km/s
    E. 1.94 km/s

31. If a ball has a mass of 20 kg and a radius of 10 cm, then its density is about _____ kg/m^3.*
    A. 2000
    B. 4.8
    C. 480
*   D. 4800
    E. 4,800,000
    (Note: Students may miss the *cm* and take it as *m* or they may not understand the importance of units)

Essay

1. Describe how the Moon produces tides on the Earth. Use a diagram to clarify your explanation. (Expect figure similar to Fig. 7-4 and discussion similar to that in the text.)
2. Describe how the Moon's orbit is affected by Earth tides and what will happen to the Earth's rotation. Describe how the Sun will affect the Earth-Moon system. (Some main points: Moon moves out and Earth's rotation slows down. When the Moon is far enough away, the Sun slows the Earth enough so that the Earth comes into synchronous rotation with the Moon. Finally, the Sun slows the Earth even further so that the Moon moves back in closer to the Earth.)
3. On a photograph of the Moon (similar to Fig. 7-9), point out the terminator, limb, an impact crater, mare, terra, basin, ray, and rille. (See an identified photo or drawing.)
4. List the four ways of analyzing a rock.
5. Briefly describe the current theory of the Moon's origin.

Word Practice

1. _____ is mass divided by volume.
2. The ____ _____ _____ pulverized the Moon's surface.
3. The _____ theory states that the Moon formed from particles produced from an impact that occurred after the Earth formed.
4. The different shapes that the Moon can appear to have are called the ____ of the Moon.
5. The ____ is the line separating the light and dark sides of the Moon.
6. The _____ were mostly formed on the Moon by impacts.
7. _____ would evaporate if the rocks they were in were strongly heated.
8. The _____ _____ of the Moon is a result of tidal forces.
9. _____ of interplanetary debris formed craters.
10. The gently rolling soil of powdery material that covers most of the Moon is called the _____.
11. _____ are large sea waves produced by earthquakes at sea.
12. The _____ Moon rises at midnight.
13. The _____ _____ is the lunar rotation about the Earth with respect to the stars.
14. _____ _____ have high boiling temperatures.
15. _____ _____ is movement of the Moon away from the Earth caused by the Earth's relatively rapid rotation.
16. The _____ are bright streaks radiating from craters.
17. The ____ _____ is a bulge in the ocean on the front and back sides of the Earth.
18. A(n) ____ Moon occurs between a quarter and a full Moon.
19. _____ _____ is the minimum distance between two bodies such that the larger is able to tidally disrupt the smaller.
20. The _____ _____ Moon occurs seven days after the new Moon.
21. The _____ Moon rises at sunset.
22. The _____ Moon is invisible at any time.
23. The stretching of the Earth produced by the Moon is called___ __ .
24. A(n) _____ is a smooth, gray patch on the Moon's surface.
25. _____ are distortions in shape caused by gravitational forces.
26. The edge of the Moon as seen from Earth is the _____.
27. _____ are vast craters of the Moon.
28. _____ are rocks composed of cemented rock chips.
29. A body that rotates about a larger body is often called a(n) ___ of the larger body.
30. The sheet of debris surrounding a lunar crater is called the ____. ____.
31. About 4.5 billion years ago the Moons surface was molten forming what is called the ____ _____.

Answers to Word Practice

1. mean density
2. early intense bombardment
3. giant impact
4. phases
5. terminator
6. craters
7. volatile elements
8. synchronous rotation
9. impact
10. regolith
11. tsunamis
12. third-quarter
13. sidereal period
14. refractory elements
15. tidal recession
16. rays
17. ocean tide
18. gibbous
19. Roche's limit
20. first-quarter
21. full
22. new Moon
23. body tide
24. mare
25. tides
26. limb
27. basins
28. breccias
29. satellite
30. ejecta blanket
31. magma ocean

Chapter 8
Introducing the Planets—Mercury

Answers to Problems in the Text

1. Venus

2. 11.2; 318

3. See Table 8-1, satellite Titan of Saturn

4. Charon of Pluto—next is the moon of our Earth

5. Pluto, but only because of its large eccentricity. On the average the Earth comes closer.

6.

Property	Terrestrial Planets	Gas Giant Planets
Size	small	large
Temperature	warm	cold
Density	moderate	low
Number of satellites	few or none	many
Orbital properties	near Sun	far from Sun
Composition (surface)	silicates, metals	ices, gas
Atmosphere	hydrogen-poor	hydrogen-rich
Surface	solid, rocky	icy, liquids

7. *Common to Mercury and the Moon:* cratering, pulverization of the surface layers, and lava flows. *Unique to Mercury:* a definite core and a magnetic field generated by currents flowing in the core, no indication of present or past plate tectonic activity. The lack of tectonic activity on Mercury indicates that the heat flow and mantle convection must be smaller than the Earth's.

8. These two planets are above the horizon only during the daytime or near the horizon after sunset or before sunrise. When the planets are near the horizon, the Earth's atmosphere makes observation difficult. Thus, daytime observation may be best. At midnight they are both below the horizon.

9. Both the Moon and Mercury are low-pressure environments, so the suits will need to be airtight. The temperature extremes on Mercury are much greater and the ultraviolet radiation is much more intense, so the Apollo suits would need extra shielding for radiation and against thermal losses.

Advanced Problems

10. Assume orbital velocities are circular velocities:
    $V_{circ} = \sqrt{GM/R}$.
    For planet orbiting Sun, use solar mass $= 2.0 \times 10^{30}$ kg, $G = 6.67 \times 10^{-11}$ SI units.
    $V_{circ} = (6.67 \times 10^{-11} \times 2.0 \times 10^{30})^{1/2}/R^{1/2}$
    $= 1.19 \times 10^{10}/\sqrt{R}$,
    so $V_{\oplus} = 1.19 \times 10^{10}/\sqrt{1.5 \times 10^{11}} = 3.08 \times 10^4$ m/s $= 31$ km/s
    $V_p = 1.19 \times 10^{10}/\sqrt{5.9 \times 10^{12}} = 4.9 \times 10^3$ m/s $= 4.9$ km/s.

11. Use $F = \dfrac{GM_{\oplus}M_*}{R_*^2}$, where $R_* = 1$ AU $=$ Earth-Sun distance; replace $M_{\oplus}$ by $4M_{\oplus}$ and R_* by $2R_*$—no change in result.

12. a. We want d in $\alpha''/206,265 = d/D$ if $\alpha'' = 1''$ and $D = 135 \times 10^6$ km. $d = (\alpha''D)/206,265 = (1 \times 1.35 \times 10^{11})/(2.06 \times 10^5) = 6.55 \times 10^5$ m. We can resolve 655 km.
    b. The side toward us is unlit; that is, Mercury is in new phase. Also, we would be looking almost directly at the Sun.
    c. Assume what is wanted is d in $\alpha''/206,265 = d/D$ with $\alpha'' = 1''$ and $D = 0.277$ AU $= 4.2 \times 10^{10}$ m. Then $d = (1 \times 4.2 \times 10^{10})/(2.06 \times 10^5) = 2.04 \times 10^5$ m. A thickness of 209 km could be resolved.

13. The relevant densities are 5500 kg/m^3 for the Earth and 3300 kg/m^3 for the Moon. Either look these up or use formula below. Use Table 8-1: density of Mercury $= 3M/4\pi r^3 = 5400$ kg/m^2, which is closer to Earth's value than the Moon's, but Mercury is closer to the Moon in size.

14. a. Mass of Mercury = density of core × volume of core + density of mantle × [volume of Mercury – volume of core] but the mass of Mercury is: mean density × volume of Mercury. Equate and divide by volume of Mercury, giving

    mean density = core density $\times \left[\dfrac{\text{volume of core}}{\text{volume of Mercury}} \right]$

    + mantle density $\times \left[1 - \dfrac{\text{volume of core}}{\text{volume of Mercury}} \right]$.

    b. Let ρ be the mean density, ρ_c the core density, ρ_m the mantle density, R_c be the core radius, and R_M be the radius of Mercury. Then, $\dfrac{\text{volume of core}}{\text{volume of Mercury}} = \dfrac{\frac{4}{3}\pi R_c^3}{\frac{4}{3}\pi R_M^3} = \left(\dfrac{R_c}{R_M} \right)^3$ and

    $\rho = \rho_c \left(\dfrac{R_c}{R_M} \right)^3 + \rho_m \left[1 - \left(\dfrac{R_c}{R_m} \right)^3 \right]$. Solving for R_C

    $R_C = R_m \sqrt[3]{\dfrac{\rho - \rho_m}{\rho_c - \rho_m}} = \sqrt[3]{\dfrac{5500 - 3300}{8000 - 3300}} = 0.78 R_M$. The radius of Mercury's core is 0.78 the radius of Mercury, a much larger fraction than for the Earth.

Sample Test Questions

True-False

1. The symbol for the Sun is ☉. T
2. The symbol for Saturn is ⊕. F
3. The four inner planets are called terrestrial planets. T
4. The diameter of Jupiter is about 10 times the Earth's diameter. T
5. The terrestrial planets have more methane (CH_4) than the giant planets. F
6. Superior planets are closer to the Sun than the Earth is. F
7. Only superior planets can be in opposition. T
8. A planet in opposition rises at sunset. T
9. The Ptolemaic model had the Sun at the center of the universe. F
10. Jupiter is slightly more than five times as far away from the Sun as the Earth is. T
11. The orbit of Mercury is closer to lying in the ecliptic plane than is that of any other planet. F
12. The orbital precession of Mercury is about 43 seconds of arc per century. F
13. The orbital precession of Mercury beyond that predicted by Newton's laws is about 43 seconds of arc per century. T
14. The daytime temperature of the surface of Mercury is above 400 K. T
15. The temperatures on the surface of Mercury are so high in the daytime that scientists expect there to be pools of molten metal. F
16. There is no indication that Mercury ever suffered melting. F
17. Jupiter is closer to the Sun than Saturn. T
18. Neptune is closer to the Sun than Uranus. F

Multiple Choice

1. The terrestrial planets are, in order of increasing distance from the Sun:
   A. Mars, Venus, Earth, Mercury
   * B. Mercury, Venus, Earth, Mars
   C. Mercury, Mars, Venus, Earth
   D. Earth, Mercury, Mars, Venus
   E. Venus, Mercury, Earth, Mars

2. Which planet on this list has no satellites?
   A. Mars
   B. Earth
   C. Jupiter
   * D. Venus
   E. Uranus

3. The radius of Saturn is about _____ times the Earth's radius.
   A. 1
   B. 10
   C. 318
   * D. 9
   E. 4

4. Venus is about _____ AUs from the Sun.
   A. 10
   B. 1.5
   C. 1
* D. ¾ n bb
   E. ½

5. Which of the following is a satellite of a planet?
   A. Venus
   B. Ceres
   C. none of these
   D. Uranus
* E. Phobos

6. As Mercury revolves about the Sun, it
   A. keeps the same side toward the Sun
   B. rotates retrograde
* C. keeps similar sides to the Earth and Sun during every third apparition
   D. emits radar waves
   E. does not rotate

7. The solar day on Mercury is about _____ Earth days.
   A. 1
   B. 59
   C. 88
* D. 159
   E. Mercury always keeps the same side toward the Sun

8. The first spacecraft to pass near Mercury was _____ in 1974.
   A. Apollo II
   B. Venera 9
   C. Mercury V
* D. Mariner 10
   E. Sun Probe 7A

9. The orbit of Mercury was puzzling because _____. This effect was explained by general relativity.
   A. it was highly inclined
   B. it was the least circular of the planetary orbits
   C. it regressed
* D. the orbital precession was larger than Newton's laws predicted
   E. the orbital precession was smaller than Newton's laws predicted

10. The larger the planet, the _____ its surface features are likely to be.
    A. larger
    B. smaller
    C. redder
    D. older
* E. younger

11. The _____ the planet, the more likely there will be internal geological activity.
    A. faster
    B. slower
*   C. larger
    D. closer to the Sun
    E. smaller

12. The sidereal day on Mercury is _____ Earth days.
    A. 5
*   B. 59
    C. 88
    D. 159
    E. Mercury always keeps the same side toward the Sun.

13. Since Mercury is smaller than the moon, we would expect it to show signs of _____ tectonic activity,
    A. less
    B. about the same
*   C. more
    D. greener
    E. no prediction suggested

14. Mercury is believed to have a larger iron core than the Moon since _____.
    A. Mercury is closer to the Sun than the Moon
    B. Mercury has a weaker magnetic field than the Moon
*   C. Mercury has a stronger magnetic field than the Moon
    D. Mercury rotates about its axis as it revolves about the Sun
    E. General relativity is needed to properly calculate the orbit of Mercury

Essay

1. Describe the difference between terrestrial and giant planets. (Instructor: See Problem 8-6.)
2. Discuss the idea of comparative planetology.
3. Discuss how surface features and planet size are related.

Word Practice (* denotes additional words from the chapter

1. The closest planet to the Sun is _____.*
2. _____ is the next planet farther away from the Sun than the Earth.*
3. _____ has an orbit between the Earth and Jupiter.*
4. The third planet out from Jupiter is _____.*
5. The planet _____ has rings easily visible with a small telescope.*
6. The four large outer planets of the solar system are often called the _____.
7. _____ is the second planet from the Sun.*
8. _____ is the seventh planet from the Sun.*
9. _____ are solid bodies orbiting around planets.
10. _____ is the largest planet in the solar system.*
11. The farthest known planet from the Sun on the average (in the solar system) is _____.*
12. Our Sun is a(n) _____.

13. About 4 billion years ago there was a(n) _____ that left the planets heavily cratered.
14. The small shift in Mercury's perihelion position left after classical effects are removed is a non-Newtonian ____ ____.
15. The study of the origins and development of planets is called ____.
16. ___ ____ is a process of comparing different planets to try to understand why they are different.
17. The Sun with its family of planets is called the ____ ____.
18. A _____ is a body, at least partially solid and sufficiently large that is orbiting the Sun.
19. The _____ planets are the four inner planets that resemble the Earth.

Answers to Word Practice

1. Mercury
2. Mars
3. Mars
4. Neptune or Pluto
5. Saturn
6. giant planets or gas giants
7. Venus
8. Uranus
9. satellites
10. Jupiter
11. Pluto
12. star
13. intense early bombardment
14. orbital precession
15. planetology
16. comparative planetology
17. solar system
18. planet
19. terrestrial

Chapter 9
Venus

Answers to Problems in the Text

1. Although Mercury is closer to the Sun, Venus is hotter because of the greenhouse effect (trapped infrared rays).

2. Early in its history, Venus probably reached a temperature high enough that most of the H_2O was broken up into H_2 and O_2. The H_2 was lost and much of the oxygen absorbed by the hot surface (oxidation), so H_2O could not reform. On Earth the temperature was low enough that the H_2O remained. When the Earth cooled, the H_2O condensed into a liquid, removing most of it from the atmosphere. On Earth the H_2O could dissolve the CO_2; without water, Venus kept its primordial CO_2 in its atmosphere.

3. A space suit on Venus must keep the atmosphere out and keep the pressure from crushing the wearer. Present astronaut suits would not work on Venus. We would need a rigid suit to withstand the atmospheric pressure.

4. a. On Venus, the flow patterns are roughly parallel to the rotation axis, while on Earth they are more curled.
    b. How the wind patterns are affected by the rotation of the planet. Also, consider the effects of density.
    c. Coriolis force is smaller on Venus. We would expect less spiraling of the wind patterns.

5. Without intervening clouds of water vapor, most of the Sun's radiation can reach the surface of the desert in the daytime, causing the temperature to be high. At night the heat can radiate away more rapidly because there is no water vapor to absorb and return (by re-radiation) the infrared radiation that leaves the surface. In other climates where the air is moist or cloudy, the clouds absorb the Earth's nighttime infrared radiation, thus keeping the air from cooling so rapidly.

6. Primitive features are (a) and (c); evolved features are (b), (d), and (e). In order of increasing geologic evolution: Moon, Mercury, Venus, and Earth.

7. In general, the more massive a planetary body, the more rapidly its surface geologically evolves.

8. There is little chance of life on Venus. There is nothing of any density to serve as a solvent medium (as water does on Earth). Also, the temperature is too high for life as we know it.
    a. If these conditions existed, chances would be good. (See discussion of the origin of life in Chapter 28.)
    b. No, but current beliefs about evolution make the existence of life under Earth like conditions very likely.

9. Closest approach: 0.277 AU $= 4.2 \times 10^{10}$ m. Moon's distance: 3.48×10^8 m. Venus is about 110 times as far away as the Moon.

10. Venus must be near inferior conjunction; that is, it appears very close to the Sun. So Venus is almost between the Earth and Sun. It cannot be near superior conjunction because then its phase would be nearly full.

Advanced Problems

11. Use small angle formula with $\alpha'' = \dfrac{1}{2}$; that is, $\dfrac{\alpha''}{2.1\times10^5} = \dfrac{d}{D}$ where d is cloud thickness and D is distance. From Table 8-1, distance = 1 AU–.723 AU = 0.28 AU = $0.28 \times 1.5 \times 10^{11}$ m = 4.2×10^{10} m.

$$\text{So } d = \frac{\alpha''D}{2.1\times10^5} = \frac{1}{2} \times 4.2 \times 10^{10} \text{ m}\frac{1}{2.1\times10^5} = 1.0 \times 10^5 \text{ m.}$$

Clouds must be more than 100,000 m = 100 km thick.

12. Use Wien's law.

$$W = \frac{0.00290}{T}, \; T = 750 \text{ K},$$

so $W = (2.90 \times 10^{-3})/(7.5 \times 10^2 \text{ K}) = 3.9 \times 10^{-6}$ m.

This wavelength corresponds to infrared radiation.

13. Mean density = $\dfrac{\text{mass}}{\text{volume}} = \dfrac{\text{mass}}{\dfrac{4}{3}\pi r^3} = \dfrac{6 \times \text{mass}}{\pi d^3}$.

(Get mass and radius from Table 8-1.)

Density = $4.87 \times \dfrac{10^{24}\text{kg}}{(1.2\times10^7 \text{ m})^3} \times \dfrac{6}{\pi} = 5.4 \times 10^3$ kg/m^3. Since this is slightly lower than the Earth's mean density, we might expect less than the Earth's amount of iron.

Sample Test Questions

True-False

1. A planet with a prograde rotation rotates east to west. F
2. Venus has a retrograde rotation. T
3. The atmosphere of Venus is mostly nitrogen. F
4. The surface of Venus is hot and wet. F
5. Venus has a surface atmospheric pressure about 90 times that of the Earth's atmosphere. T
6. The clouds of Venus are water clouds like the Earth's. F
7. The surface of Venus is heated by the greenhouse effect. T
8. The study of the origins and development of the planets is termed planetology. T
9. The smaller the planet the younger its surface features are likely to be. F
10. The larger a planet, the more likely it will have an atmosphere. T
11. The larger the planet, the more probable its surface is younger. T
12. The larger a planet the less likely it is to have any surface activity. F
13. The atmosphere of a planet is determined only by its initial composition and the rate at which molecules are lost from the top of the atmosphere. F
14. The atmosphere of Venus is mostly sulfuric acid. F
15. Venus has a surface atmospheric pressure about 9 times that of the Earth's atmosphere. F
16. The escape or retention of a molecule in the atmosphere of a planet is determined by how the average speed of the molecule, which depends on the temperature, compares with the escape velocity, which depends on planet's mass and radius. T

Multiple Choice

1. Venus rotates east to west (retrograde). This was discovered by radar.
   * A. correct
   B. wrong: Rotation must be from west to east to be called retrograde.
   C. wrong: It was discovered with optical telescopes.
   D. wrong: a Soviet probe landing on Venus discovered it.
   E. wrong: Both B and D corrections are needed.

2. The atmosphere of Venus is mostly
   A. oxygen
   B. nitrogen
   * C. carbon dioxide
   D. neon
   E. sulfuric acid

3. The clouds of Venus are composed of droplets of
   A. water
   B. nitrogen
   C. carbon dioxide
   D. salt
   * E. sulfuric acid

4. A cool, large planet can most easily keep its atmosphere.
   * A. correct
   B. wrong: The planet must be cool and small to keep its atmosphere.
   C. wrong: The planet must be hot and large to keep its atmosphere.
   D. wrong: The planet must be hot and small to keep its atmosphere.
   E. none of these

5. For a given temperature, the lighter the gas molecules, the ___ their average speeds.
   A. slower
   * B. higher
   C. bluer
   D. more primitive
   E. misleading: Temperature does not affect speed.

6. Venus is said to be hot because of a greenhouse effect. This means
   A. Venus is covered with glass
   B. Venus is green
   C. radiation can't get to the surface of Venus since it has clouds
   * D. the carbon-dioxide clouds keep the surface heat of Venus from radiating
   E. both A and B

7. Which of the following phrase(s) best describe the lower atmosphere of Venus?
   * A. high pressure
   B. low pressure
   C. Earth like
   D. both A and C
   E. all three A, B, and C

8. Venus is said to have a runaway greenhouse effect. This means __.
   A. most solar radiation is reflected by the atmosphere
   * B. infrared radiation is trapped by the CO_2 atmosphere
   C. the plants on Venus heat the surface
   D. the heavy atmosphere cannot escape.

9. The Earth and Venus have about the same amount of CO_2. Where is the Earth's CO_2?
   A. in the atmosphere
   * B. chemically in rocks
   C. in salt in the ocean
   D. wrong — the Earth has much less CO_2 than Venus

10. How can astronomers estimate the age of the surface of Venus?
    A. study the samples returned by space probes
    B. study atmosphere sample returned by Venera
    * C. count craters
    D. measure mountain heights
    E. misleading — astronomers have no idea of the age of the surface

11. Which of the following is a correct rule of thumb of comparative planetology?
    A. the older a planet, the younger its surface.
    B. the larger the planet, the older its surface
    C. the smaller the planet, the younger its surface
    * D. the larger the planet, the younger its surface
    E. all planets have the same surface age

Essay

1. Discuss conditions on the surface of Venus.
2. What is the difference between rotation and revolution?
3. What three principles govern the motions of gas molecules in atmospheres.
4. Discuss the atmosphere of Venus: composition, clouds, density, and pressure.
5. Give and discuss the three principles governing the motions of gas molecules in planetary atmospheres.
6. Discuss how planet surface features and planetary size are related.
7. Describe the possible cause of the retrograde rotation of Venus.

Word Practice (* denotes other words from the Chapter.)

1. The _____ _____ _____ _____ means that Venus rotates east to west.
2. The study of the origins and development of planets is termed ____.
3. The atmosphere that a planet develops as it outgasses and evolves is called its _____ _____.
4. The heating of a planet's atmosphere caused by CO_2 trapping infrared rays is called the _____.
5. The total energy striking a planet per unit area per second is the planet's _____ _____.
6. The initial gaseous atmosphere of a planet is the planet's __ __.
7. A planet that rotates from west to east is said to have __ rotation.
8. The clouds of Venus are mostly droplets of _____ _____.
9. _____ was the first spacecraft to successfully soft land on Venus.

10. The _____ is a series of depressed or raised circular rings of ridges or fractures. These _____ are found scattered over the surface of Venus.

Answers to Word Practice

1. retrograde rotation of Venus
2. planetology
3. secondary atmosphere
4. greenhouse effect
5. solar constant

6. primitive atmosphere
7. prograde
8. sulfuric acid
9. Venera 7
10. corona, coronas

Chapter 10
Mars

Answers to Problems in the Text

1. Main points: Day length ~ 24 h. Landscape: reddish soil with many rock fragments. Either still (19 mph) or strong winds (greater than 100 mph). If no clouds, sky reddish, occasional dust storms. Color of sky depends upon amount of dust. Temperature changes of 60°C, from sunrise to mid afternoon. May get a few degrees above freezing on a summer afternoon. Remember, Vikings landed at "dullest" or flattest place. There are impressive cliffs, canyons, craters, snowfields, and ice caps elsewhere. Might see one or two small moons in the sky.

2. Mars is more Earth like than the Moon. With frozen water and past free water, there is a chance of finding life, evidence of past life, or evidence of conditions that prevented life from arising. A colony on Mars could obtain its water by heating Martian soil, whereas the Moon apparently contains no water.

3. Craters on Mars show signs of erosion (by water for the oldest craters and by dust for the younger ones). In addition, on Mars we see the dark dust deposits downwind from the craters and in some crater interiors.
    a. Students should point out that on Mars erosion has caused "soft"-looking shallow craters with low or broken rims.
    b. The Martian environment has caused more topological changes—for example, erosion.

4.

	Mercury	*Mars*	*Earth*
Atmosphere	little or none	low pressure	1 atmosphere
Craters	surface well covered by craters	older craters are much eroded	most craters are eroded away
Plate tectonics	none	possible: break in one large canyon	active tectonics
Volcanism	volcanic lava flows form mare plains but no volcanic mountains	large, isolated, young volcanoes and lava flows covered by dust	active volcanic mountains; volcanoes in chains
Surface	old	mixed	young

5. These satellites can be used to answer questions such as:
Are the two moons of the same age and composition? Are they pieces of a single large primeval moon? Are they of different origins? Are they perhaps captured asteroids? Do they clarify the age and origin of our moon? Do their surfaces reflect the past history of the solar system?

6. a. The sample would most likely be seabed. Most seabed is sedimentary with organic sediment. About one out of six would land on the solid surface. They would probably get widely different soil types. However, the two Vikings found virtually identical soil at two widely separated sites, which implies that the dust is well mixed by the wind.

    b. The Earth is divisible into several distinct types off terrain—Arctic, plains, mountains, desert, tropic, and oceans—so 15–24 well-placed landings (three in each type of terrain) would give only a gross idea. If landings were random, 90–144 would be needed because most would be lost at sea. If we wanted to characterize people or other life forms, more would be needed.

    c. If landings were random, fewer might be needed—possibly 20–40, well placed, should give us a good characterization. Mars is smaller and it does not appear to be as different in various regions, yet there are volcanoes, canyons, sand dunes, rocky plains, dark and light soil, two kinds of ice cap, and so on, which we would like to understand.

Advanced Problems

7. Use weight = force = $G M m / r^2 = W$, then

$$W_{Phobos}/W_{Earth} = (M_{Phobos}/M_{Earth})(r_{Phobos}/r_{Earth})^2.$$

Use Table 8.1—since Phobos is not spherical, use an average value, say 12 km. The ratio then becomes

$$W_{Phobos}/W_{Earth} = 4.5 \times 10^{-4};$$

hence, $W_{Phobos} = 0.059$ lb. $= 0.9$ oz.

8. $t = \sqrt{2h/a}$; $a = 0.0042$ m/s

    a. Assume eye level is 1.70 m from ground (6 feet to top of head).

    $$t = \sqrt{\frac{2 \times 1.70}{0.0042}} \text{ s} = \sqrt{810} \text{ s} \approx 28 \text{ s}$$

    b. $t = \sqrt{\frac{2 \times 1.70}{10}} \text{ s} = \sqrt{34 \times 10^{-4}} \text{ s} = 0.058 \text{ s}$

9. $\dfrac{\alpha''}{206,265} = d/D$; $\alpha'' = 1''$; $D = 56 \times 10^6$ km $= 5.6 \times 10^{10}$ m;

$$d = (\alpha'' D)/(2.06 \times 10^5) = \frac{5.6}{2.06} \times 10^5 \text{ m} = 2.7 \times 10^5 \text{ m}$$

Objects larger than 270 km could be resolved. Lowell did not claim to see canals but rather what he thought was vegetation along the sides.

10. $V_{circ} = \sqrt{GM/R}$; $G = 6.67 \times 10^{-11}$ SI; $M = 6 \times 10^{15}$ kg;

    $R = 8$ km $= 8 \times 10^3$ m

    $V_{circ} = [2(6.67 \times 6/8) \times 10^{-11} \times 10^{15}/10^3)]^{1/2} = 7$ m/s

    If an object were not too massive, it could easily be put in circular orbit by hand.

    $V_{escape} = \sqrt{2} \, V_{circ} = 10$ m/s, so the object could also easily escape.

Sample Test Questions

True-False

1. The first successful Mars landing was Viking 1 in 1976. T
2. Mars appears as a uniformly reddish ball through a telescope. F
3. Mars shows seasonal changes. T
4. The term *canali* was first popularized by Lowell. F
5. The reddish color of Mars is caused by iron oxide. T
6. The sky of Mars is reddish-tan. T
7. Daytime air temperatures at the two Viking sites got above freezing (273 K). T
8. The air pressure at the surface of Mars is about 0.7% of that on Earth. T
9. The Martian polar caps consist of a permanent cap of CO_2 with an over layer of water ice that melts each year. F
10. The changing dark markings on Mars are not yet understood. F
11. The volcanoes of Mars are more numerous and smaller than those on the Earth. F
12. There is no evidence that there has ever been free water on Mars. F
13. The present lack of free water on Mars may have been caused by the volcanoes around Olympus Mons. T
14. The Viking experiments that were designed to directly detect organic molecules in the Martian soil did not detect any. F
15. Phobos is the inner satellite of Mars. T
16. Phobos is definitely an asteroid captured by mars. F
17. Mars' early atmosphere may have been frozen out when the inclination of the polar axis changed. T
18. Seasonal changes on Mars include both shrinking and swelling of the polar caps as well as changes in the Maria and desert regions. T
19. Deimos is the satellite closest to Mars. F
20. Mars appears as a uniformly reddish ball through a telescope. F
21. Mars atmospheric pressure was always about the same value it is now. F
22. The changing dark markings on Mars are not yet understood. F
23. The day on Mars is much shorter than the day on Earth. F
24. The Martian polar caps consist of a permafrost cap of carbon dioxide with an over layer of water ice that melts each year. F

Multiple Choice

1. The rotation period of Mars is about
   A. 2 hours, 10 minutes
   B. 59 days
   C. 6 hours
   D. 3 days
 * E. not near any of these

2. The dark areas of Mars are called
   A. Martian dark areas
 * B. maria
   C. canals
   D. deserts
   E. permafrost

3. The first spacecraft to reach the surface of Mars was
    A. Viking 1
*   B. Mars 2
    C. Mars 1
    D. Pioneer 10
    E. Mariner 10

4. Both of the Vikings landed on rocky plains.
*   A. correct
    B. wrong: Only Viking 1; Viking 2 landed on a smooth, featureless plain.
    C. wrong: Only Viking 2; Viking 1 landed on a smooth, featureless plain.
    D. wrong: Both Vikings landed on smooth plains.
    E. wrong: Only one Viking successfully landed.

5. The most common gas in the atmosphere of Mars is
*   A. CO_2
    B. N_2
    C. O_2
    D. H_2O
    E. none of these

6. The air pressure at the Viking sites was about __% of the Earth's normal pressure.
    A. 700
    B. 70
    C. 7
*   D. 0.7
    E. 0.07

7. The Martian air temperatures at the Viking landing sites ranged from a high of about 244 K to a low of 87 K.
    A. correct
    B. wrong: The high was 576 K.
*   C. wrong: The low was 187 K.
    D. wrong: Both B and C changes are needed to be correct.
    E. misleading: The Vikings were not equipped to measure air temperatures.

8. The Martian atmosphere is mostly CO_2. The next two compounds in order of amount are O_2 and argon.
    A. correct
    B. wrong: It is mostly H_2O.
*   C. wrong: The next two are nitrogen and argon.
    D. wrong: Both B and C changes need to be made.
    E. misleading: Only the major component, CO_2, is known.

9. That Martian volcanoes are larger than those on Earth is due to _____.
    A. the weaker surface gravity on Mars
*   B. the lack of plate tectonics on Mars
    C. the lowering of the lava-melting temperature by the weak Martian atmosphere
    D. the greater distance of Mars from the Sun
    E. misleading: Martian volcanoes are smaller, not larger.

10. The channels on Mars discovered by Mariner 9 show
    A. that intelligent life once existed on Mars
    B. that there were flaws in the Mariner 9 design
*   C. that there most likely once was free water on Mars
    D. That Schiaparelli was right
    E. misleading: There are no channels on Mars.

11. All of the Viking experiments could be interpreted to show that life exists, or at least once existed, on Mars.
    A. correct
*   B. wrong: Organic molecules were not found, and other experiments were ambiguous.
    C. wrong: All biological experiments were strongly negative.
    D. wrong: Only one experiment positively detected life.
    E. misleading: No Viking experiment checked this.

12. It is believed that beneath the surface of Mars lies a layer of frozen soil containing water ice that does not melt in the Martian summer. Such a layer is called a
    A. frozen layer
    B. maria
    C. channel
*   D. permafrost
    E. misleading: Most scientists do not believe this.

13. The Vikings and Mariners were able to show that Mars' moons Phobos and Deimos were once asteroids.
    A. correct
    B. wrong: They showed that they were once part of Mars.
    C. wrong: The moons are Phobos and Lowellos.
    D. wrong: Both B and C changes are needed.
*   E. misleading: The origin of the moons of Mars is not yet settled.

14. What was the most likely cause of the results of the Viking on-going-biological-process experiments?
*   A. Unexpected Martian soil chemistry
    B. Damage of the apparatus by ultraviolet light
    C. Microscopic life
    D. Contamination by terrestrial microbes
    E. None of these

15. Earth bound observers named which region(s) of Mars correctly?
*   A. Deserts
    B. Maria
    C. Canals
    D. All of them
    E. None of them

Problems Involving Optional Mathematical Equations from Other Chapters

* 16. (Optional Equation III) Calculate the escape velocity from Deimos starting from a mountain 8 km from the center if its mass is 6×10^{15} kg.
  A.   1 km/s
  * B.   10 km/s
  C.   30 km/s
  D.   7 km/s
  E.   15 km/s

* 17. (Optional Equation I) Mars at its closest is about 56 million km from Earth. Deimos is about 12 km in diameter and Phobos at largest is about 28 km long. Can either satellite be resolved (can their shape be seen) using an Earth-based telescope with a resolution of 1"?
  A.   Can resolve both
  B.   Can resolve Phobos but not Deimos
  C.   Can resolve Deimos but not Phobos
  * D.   Cannot resolve either

Essay

1. Describe the physical effect that caused the belief that Mars had canals.
2. With photographs of Mars (Viking orbiter) and the Moon, compare the surfaces and note three major differences. (Main points: erosion of craters; channels; dust patterns in lees of craters.)
3. Explain how Mars could have lost its free water.
4. Discuss the Martian surface features (craters, volcanoes). What do they tell us about the "geology" of Mars?
5. Discuss evidence for or against life on Mars.

Word Practice (* denotes an additional word from the chapter.)

1. There are _____ on Mars caused by meteoroid impacts.
2. The Viking spacecraft found no evidence for _____ ____.
3. ____ ____ containing carbon are essential building blocks of life as we know it.
4. A dark area on the surface of Mars is called _____.
5. The bright orange areas of Mars as seen through a telescope are called _____.
6. The shrinking of the northern Martian polar ice cap in summer and the growth of dark markings on the Martian surface are examples of _____ _____.
7. Mars was probably first seen through a telescope by _____.*
8. The _____ is a possible layer of ice-rich soil a few meters beneath the Martian surface.
9. Mars' outer satellite is called _____.*
10. The _____ of Mars are the largest known in the solar system. Olympus Mons is the largest.
11. The darkening of the Martian surface is caused by ___ storms.
12. The Martian atmosphere is mostly _____ _____.
13. The observatory at Flagstaff, Arizona, was founded by _____ to study Mars.
14. The first probe to reach Mars was the Russian probe _____ _____ , which crashed in 1971.*
15. The first successful landings of spacecraft on Mars were the __ __.
16. Both the surface and the sky of Mars appear _____.
17. The summer _____ _____ of Mars were measured between 187 K and 244 K by the Vikings.

18. The _____ of Mars is mostly CO_2 at low density.
19. The _____ _____ on Mars is about 0.7% of the Earth's.
20. The surface of Mars has _____ that look similar to dry riverbeds.*
21. The inner satellite of Mars is named _____.*
22. The _____ of Mars are an optical effect of poor observing conditions combined with the physiological tendency of the eye to connect dots into lines.
23. Mars's rotation _____ is $24^h 37^m$.
24. Rocks formed by melting within a planet are called ___ when they reach the surface.*
25. Martian _____ have been found on the Earth. They are believed to have been knocked off Mars by impacts.
26. The Martian volcanoes are formed by ascending currents of hot material known as _____ _____.
27. Apparently dry riverbeds or _____ suggest that Mars once had free water.

Answers to Word Practice

1. craters
2. life on Mars
3. organic molecules
4. maria
5. deserts
6. seasonal changes
7. Galileo
8. permafrost
9. Deimos
10. volcanoes
11. dust
12. carbon dioxide
13. Lowell
14. Mars 2

15. Viking missions
16. reddish
17. air temperatures
18. atmosphere
19. air pressure
20. channels
21. Phobos
22. canals
23. period
24. lava
25. meteorites
26. mantle plume
27. channels

Chapter 11
Jupiter, Saturn and Their Moons

Answers to Problems in the Text

1. a. Each of these planets has a different size, temperature, atmospheric pressure, rotation rate, and, most important, gravity, so they enable us to better understand how wind patterns depend upon these factors.

    b. Temperature, composition, atmospheric pressure, rotation period, planetary mass (gravity), and radius. The substances forming the "clouds" have different molecular weight and chemistry.

    c.

	Venus	Earth	Mars	Jupiter
Temperature	high	normal	low	low to moderate
Composition	CO_2	O_2, N_2	CO_2	H_2, He
Pressure	high	normal	low	high
Rotation period	slow	24^h	24^h	9^h
Planetary mass (Earth)	1	1	1/9	318
Surface features	some	some	high volcanoes	none known, if solid surface exists
Surface gravity/Earth's	0.9	1	0.4	2.6

    d. Mercury has no atmosphere; Uranus, Neptune, and Pluto are extremely cold and hard to study, so no data are available about cloud patterns and the like.

2. The gravitational force, F, at the surface of a body is given by
$$F = \frac{GM}{R^2}$$
where G is Newton's gravitational constant, M is the mass of the body and R is the radius of the body. To compare the Galilean satellites with the Moon, us
$$\frac{F_s}{F_M} = \frac{M_S}{M_M}\left(\frac{R_M}{R_S}\right)^2,$$
where "s" is the satellite and "M" is the Moon. Using Table 8-1, we find $\frac{F_{Io}}{F_M} = 1.1$ $\frac{F_{Europa}}{F_M} = 0.80$

$\frac{F_{Ganymede}}{F_M} = 0.88$ and $\frac{F_{Callisto}}{F_M} = 0.77$. These three bodies have about the same surface gravity. Tidal and solar heating are quite different for them than for the Moon.

3. Surface probably cratered; crunchy frozen ammonia frost and salt deposits underfoot; reddish and yellowish surface with possibly some stony soil in places. The sky would have a faint yellowish glow, its brightness depending on the position of Io in its orbit. Volcanic eruptions and sulfur flows.

4. Since the two planets have the same size and mass, we expect their composition to be similar. Also the surface gravity is about the same.

    a. Hydrogen content of the atmosphere is determined by the surface gravity as compared to the average speed of hydrogen molecules in the atmosphere. The planet further from the Sun will be cooler, so the average speed will be lower. As noted the gravity force is the same for the two, so we expect the planet further from the Sun to have more hydrogen in its atmosphere.

b. Volcanism releases CO_2 into the atmosphere. We would expect the more active planet to have more CO_2. We must realize that if one planet is extremely hot, it may lose its CO_2 faster than its more active volcanoes can release the CO_2.

5. The atmosphere of Titan is mostly nitrogen, with 10% methane and smog. The methane as well as ethane may also exist as both a solid and a liquid on the surface. This provides a good environment for complex organic compounds to form. Thus, Titan's surface is similar to the early terrestrial surface.

6. In both kinds of pass, the craft would be moving rapidly relative to the particles that make up the rings. In the plane, the probe would probably suffer many collisions (remember, 8 km/$\approx$ 1000 miles per hour). However, perpendicular passage would take only 0.1 second, so a collision is unlikely, but there would also be little time for collecting data. Of course, data have now been successfully collected as a probe passed through the ring structure.

Advanced Problems

7. Distance to Jupiter at closest approach: $4 \text{ AU} = 4 \times 1.5 \times 10^{11} \text{ m}$
   a. Use the small angle formula. For maximum angular separation satellite must be at maximum separation. Let us assume that real separation is $2 \times 10^6 \text{ km} = 2 \times 10^9$ for satellite-Jupiter distance. Then
   $$\alpha''/206,265 = d/D = 2 \times 10^9 \text{ m}/(6 \times 10^{11} \text{m});$$
   $$\alpha'' = \frac{2.06}{3} \times 10^3'' = 687'' = 0°2$$
   b. $0°2$ is about one-third the diameter of the full moon and well above the limit of resolution of the human eye, which therefore would easily see the satellites if they were bright enough. But Jupiter is so bright that its satellites are lost in the glare.

8. Take distance to Ganymede $= 6 \times 10^{11} \text{ m}$ (closest approach);
   $\alpha'' = 1/2''$, so $(1/2)/(2.06 \times 10^5) = d/(6 \times 10^1 \text{ m})$;
   $$d = \frac{3 \times 10^{11} \text{ m}}{2.06 \times 10^5} = 1.45 \times 10^6 \text{ m} = 1450 \text{ km}$$
   This is about $\frac{1}{3}$ to $\frac{1}{4}$ the size of Ganymede.

9. $W = \text{weight} = \dfrac{GMm}{r^2}$, so $\dfrac{W_{\text{Jupiter}}}{W_{\text{Earth}}} = \dfrac{\dfrac{GM_{\text{Jupiter}}m}{r^2_{\text{Jupiter}}}}{\dfrac{GM_{\text{Earth}}m}{r^2_{\text{Earth}}}}$.

   Use Table 8-1 to get numbers. $\dfrac{W_{\text{Jupiter}}}{W_{\text{Earth}}} = 2.5$

10. Use mean density = mass/volume = $3M/(4\pi^3) = 625 \text{ kg/m}^3$. This is less than water (1000 kg/m^3), so any rocky core of Saturn must be small.

11. $M_h = 5.7 \times 10^{26}$ kg

   a. $V_{circ} = \sqrt{(GM/R)}$; $G = 6.67 \times 10^{-11}$ SI Units

     Take $R = 2.5 \times 10^5$ km $= 2.5 \times 10^8$ m.

     $V_{circ} = \sqrt{(6.67 \times 5.7/2.5) \times (10^{-11} \times 10^{26} \times 10^{-8})}$

     $= \sqrt{1.52 \times 10^8}$ m/s

     $V_{circ} = 1.23 \times 10^4$ m/s $= 12.3$ km/s

   b. In principle, we just subtract the circular velocity at two nearby radii (1 km).

     $\Delta V \equiv V_{circ2} - V_{circ1} = \sqrt{GM/R_1} - \sqrt{GM/R_2}$

     $= \sqrt{GM}\left(1/\sqrt{R_1} - 1/\sqrt{R_2}\right)$

This type of calculation is worthwhile only if a calculator is available to carry answers to many significant figures so that the difference is meaningful. Otherwise, the solution is meaningless and we will have to use other mathematical methods. This point is important to make in a mathematically oriented course.

If the students have not had calculus, then to solve this problem we need only the expansion of $(1 + x)^n = 1 + nx$, if x is much less than 1. That is:

Let $R_1 = R_2 + dR$, so $1/R = (1/R_2)(1 - dR/R_2)^{-1}$

Use $(1 + x)^{-1} = 1 - x$ if x is small, so $1/R_1 = (1/R_2)(1 - dR/R_2)$; $\sqrt{1/R_1} = \sqrt{1/R_2}\sqrt{1 - dR/R_2}$

$(1 + x)^{1/2} = 1 + x/2$, if x is small, so $\sqrt{GM/R_1}\sqrt{GM/R_2}[1 - 1/2(dR/R_2)] = V_2[1 - 1/2(dR/R_2)]$;

hence,

$|dV| = \frac{1}{2}V_2\frac{dR}{R} = [(1/2) \times 12.3 \text{ km/s}]\frac{10^3 m}{2.5 \times 10^8 m} = 2.5 \times 10^{-5}$ km/s.

Relative velocity is 2.5 cm/s (if catch-up collision occurs). If the students have had calculus,

$V = (GM)^{1/2}R^{-1/2}$, $dV = -\frac{1}{2}(GM)^{1/2}R^{-3/2}dR = -\frac{V}{2R}dR$

12. $W = \text{weight} = GMm/r^2$, so

$W_{Titan}/W_{Earth} = \dfrac{\left(GM_{Titan}\dfrac{m}{r_{Titan}^2}\right)}{\dfrac{GM_{Earth}m}{r_{Earth}^2}} = \dfrac{M_{Titan}}{M_{Earth}}\left(\dfrac{r_{Earth}}{r_{Titan}}\right)^2.$

Use Table 8-1 to get numbers. $\dfrac{W_{Titan}}{W_{Earth}} = 0.13$

Sample Test Questions

True-False

1. The largest planet is Jupiter. T
2. All gas giant planets in the solar system have several natural satellites. T
3. Jupiter has many light and dark stripes parallel to its rotation. T
4. The dark bands on Jupiter are called belts. T
5. Jupiter's atmosphere is mostly hydrogen and nitrogen. F
6. The upper part of Jupiter's atmosphere is about 133 K. T
7. The lower atmosphere of Jupiter is much colder than the upper atmosphere. F

8. The Red Spot on Jupiter has existed at most for 100 years. F
9. Jupiter is radiating about two times the energy it receives from the Sun. T
10. Jupiter gets its heat from nuclear fusion. F
11. The synchrotron radiation from Jupiter is at a wavelength of about 1/10 meter. T
12. Saturn's moon Titan has an atmosphere. T
13. Jupiter's interior is about 60% hydrogen. T
14. The four largest satellites of Jupiter are called Galilean satellites. T
15. Ganymede is larger than Mercury. T
16. The Galilean satellites of Jupiter all have prograde orbits. T
17. There is a Red Spot in Saturn. F
18. Saturn has a day of between 10^h and 11^h. T
19. The large gap between the outer ring of Saturn and the bright inner ring is called Cassini's division. T
20. Each of Saturn's rings is one solid object encircling the planet. F
21. Saturn's rings are inside the Roche limit for Saturn. T
22. Not counting the rings, Saturn has at least 17 satellites. T

Multiple Choice

1. The largest planet in the solar system is
   A. Earth
 * B. Jupiter
   C. Saturn
   D. Uranus
   E. Pluto

2. Jupiter's atmosphere is mostly hydrogen and
 * A. helium
   B. neon
   C. water
   D. ammonia
   E. sulfuric acid

3. The upper atmosphere of Jupiter is about _____ K.
   A. 0
   B. 50
 * C. 133
   D. 273
   E. 670

4. Jupiter rotates with a day of about _____ hours.
   A. 1
 * B. 10
   C. 24
   D. 59
   E. 100

5. The lower atmosphere (60 km deep) of Jupiter probably has temperatures near those of Earth but with pressures 10 times Earth's.
   * A. correct
   B. wrong: cooler
   C. wrong: much warmer
   D. wrong: pressures 1000 times Earth's at that depth
   E. wrong: both C and D changes needed

6. Jupiter is warmer than can be expected from the Sun's heat. This extra heat is produced by thermonuclear reactions in the core.
   A. correct
   * B. wrong: The heat is produced by gravitational contraction.
   C. wrong: The heat is produced by radioactive decay.
   D. misleading: It has the temperature expected from solar heating.
   E. misleading: It is cooler than expected from solar heating.

7. Synchrotron radiation is caused by
   * A. electrons moving rapidly in a magnetic field
   B. hydrogen atoms moving rapidly in a magnetic field
   C. thermal heating
   D. Jupiter's moon Io
   E. poorly shielded CBs

8. Jupiter's decimeter radiation is
   A. thermal radiation
   B. from the surface of Jupiter
   * C. synchrotron radiation
   D. both A and C needed
   E. misleading: Jupiter radiates only at decameter wavelengths, not decimeter.

9. Jupiter's interior is mostly _____, which can conduct electrons.
   A. level
   B. granite
   C. carbon
   * D. metallic hydrogen
   E. metallic nitrogen

10. The second largest planet in the solar system is
    A. Earth
    B. Jupiter
    * C. Saturn
    D. Uranus
    E. Pluto

11. Saturn's atmosphere is mostly hydrogen and
    * A. helium
    B. neon
    C. water
    D. ammonia
    E. sulfuric acid

12. One of the largest outer satellites is Titan, which circles
    A. Jupiter
    B. Mars
  * C. Saturn
    D. Uranus
    E. none of these

13. The small moons that help confine particles in the F ring of Saturn are called _____ satellites.
    A. herding
    B. confining
  * C. shepherd
    D. sheep
    E. ring-moon

14. The broad division or gap between the outer ring of Saturn and the brighter inner ring is called _____.
    A. Encke's division
  * B. Cassini's division
    C. the gap
    D. the separator
    E. Galileo's gap

15. The particles in Saturn's rings come from
    A. a condensed gas as Saturn formed
    B. part of a satellite broken up by a collision
    C. a comet or asteroid broken apart by tidal forces
    D. either B or C
  * E. any of the three, A, B, and/or C

16. The fine structure in Saturn's rings is explained by ____ satellites.
    A. Galilean
    B. renegade
    C. voyager
  * D. shepherd
    E. artificial

17. A probable explanation of the source of Saturn's rings is that they _.
    A. are part of a satellite broken up by a collision
    B. are artificial debris
  * C. condensed as Saturn formed
    D. both a and c are possible explanations
    E. none of these

18. The inner moons of Jupiter and Saturn are _____.
    A. large
    B. medium sized
  * C. small
    D. solid ice
    E. green

19. Why do we not expect a liquid layer to exist on Ganymede like the one on Europa?
   A. Ganymede is too hot
 * B. Ganymede is far enough away that Jupiter's tides are too small
   C. Ganymede has no ices in its composition
   D. misleading — Ganymede has a liquid layer, Europa doesn't
   E. none of these

20. The satellite Iapetus is darker on the leading side than on the trailing side. This may be caused by
   _____.
   A. interplanetary dust swept up from Iapetus' orbit
 * B. collision with debris produced from Phoebe by meteorite impacts
   C. volcanoes on that side of Iapetus
   D. mining operations by inhabitants of Triton
   E. none of these

Problem Involving Optional Mathematical Equation from Another Chapter

21. (Optional Equation I) Cassini's division is 1500 km wide. When Saturn is closest to Earth, it is about 9 AU away from us. Which telescope listed below would show Cassini's division?
 * A. a telescope with a resolution of 0."1
   B. a telescope with a resolution of 1."0
   C. a telescope with a resolution of 10"
   D. both A and B
   E. all three, A, B, and C

Essay

1. Sketch the disk of Jupiter and any features visible through an Earth-based telescope. Label at least three major items.
2. Discuss the composition of the Jovian moons.
3. Discuss the volcanic features of Io.
4. Why do the giant planets have massive atmospheres?
5. Sketch the disk of Saturn and the surrounding region. Draw any features visible through an Earth-based telescope. Label at least three major items, including Cassini's division.
6. List the three possible sources of the particles of the rings of Saturn.

Word Practice (* denotes additional word not from the chapter)

1. _____ _____ is emitted when very fast electrons move through a magnetic field.
2. _____ rotation is east to west.
3. The _____ _____ of Jupiter is a long-lived storm.
4. The four large satellites of Jupiter are called the_____ satellites.
5. Jupiter's _____ thermal radiation is due to the planet's heat.
6. Jupiter's _____ is about 133 K.
7. The great Red Spot is often visible on the disk of _____.
8. Jupiter's satellite _____ is often surrounded by a sodium cloud.
9. Much of Jupiter's interior is _____ _____.
10. Within ____ limit a large natural satellite will be tidally torn apart.

11. The opposite of prograde is _____.
12. The giant planets are characterized by ____ ____ and large size.
13. Jupiter's _____ radiation is synchrotron radiation.*
14. Jupiter's infrared radiation is _____ radiation.
15. _____ _____ can help confine rings to a narrow zone.
16. Jupiter is such that it may be hard to say where the surface divides the planet from its _____.
17. Satellites that revolve about their parent body in the same sense as the planets revolve about the Sun are said to revolve _____.
18. Saturn's satellite _____ is a small black-surfaced object in retrograde orbit.
19. _____ satellites revolve counter to the planet's revolution.
20. _____ is a satellite of Saturn with one light and one dark side.
21. The dark lines across the disk of Jupiter are called _____.
22. Jupiter's outermost moons are _____ moons that were formally interplanetary bodies.
23. The bright cloud bands parallel to Jupiter's equator are called _____.
24. Jupiter's _____ is about 60% hydrogen.
25. The rocky matter making up the moons of Jupiter is a black _____ material.
26. The Galilean satellite covered with ice is _____.
27. _____ has rings easily visible through a telescope.
28. _____ division is a prominent gap in the rings of Saturn.
29. ___ ___ system is very thin and composed of many small particles.
30. _____ atmosphere is similar to Jupiter's.
31. ___ __ __ begins at the edge of the rings with five small satellites.
32. _____ occurs when a periodic force applied to a system has the same frequency as one of the natural frequencies of the system.
33. Saturn's satellite _____ seems to have a structure intermediate between Europa and Ganymede of Jupiter.*
34. ____, ____, and ____ are three small moons of Saturn just inside the orbit of Titan.*
35. The moon _____ of Saturn has an atmosphere.
36. _____ is a term used to describe a mixture of ice and carbonaceous dirt
37. To and Europa both show major _____ _____ effects. Io by volcanic action and Europa by a frozen surface which shows lines suggestive of an upwelling of water.

Answers to Word Practice

1. synchrotron radiation
2. retrograde
3. Red Spot
4. Galilean
5. infrared
6. temperature
7. Jupiter
8. Io
9. metallic hydrogen
10. Roche's
11. retrograde
12. low density
13. short-wave or decimeter
14. thermal
15. shepherd satellites

20. Iapetus
21. belts
22. captured
23. zones
24. interior
25. carbonaceous
26. Europa
27. Saturn
28. Cassini's
29. Saturn's ring
30. Saturn's
31. Saturn's satellite system
32. Resonance
33. Enceladus
34. Tethys. Dione, and Rhea

16. atmosphere
17. prograde
18. Phoebe
19. retrograde

35. Titan
36. Dirty ice
37. tidal heating

Chapter 12
The Outermost Planets and Their Moons

Answers to Problems in the Text

1. The atmospheres of Uranus and Neptune are too cold for the organic compounds found in the atmospheres of Jupiter and Saturn. The color of the outer two planets' atmospheres is dominated by a high-altitude methane-rich haze, which absorbs the redder light and reflects the blue light, the same roles played by water vapor in the Earth's atmosphere.

2. The rings of Jupiter, Saturn, and Neptune were probably formed by the fragmentation of moons that moved too close to the planet, or they may be due to material in orbit being unable to collapse into a moon. Both possibilities involve tidal effects.

3. The Earth is too warm to keep hydrogen and helium in its atmosphere. Optional Equation VI in Chapter 11 discusses the average velocity, and we previously discussed escape velocity in Optional Equation IV. The gas giants were cooler and hence kept this material; this made them more massive and hence able to keep even more material.

4. At mid-latitudes, a yearly cycle would include about four months of day and about two months of 24-hour day as the Earth's axis points, respectively, away from it at right angles to, toward, and again at right angles to the Sun. Seasons would be much more extreme than we now have.

5. Only the orbits of Pluto and Neptune. Of course, the orbits of some asteroids, comets, and Chiron cross planetary orbits.

6. Bode's rule: 4 + one of a series.
   0, 3, 6, 12, 24, 48, 96, 192, 384, 768 divided by 10
   >   >   >   >
   Mercury   Mars   Saturn   Pluto
   So, the rule predicts a tenth planet at 77.2 AU. Searches have yielded no large planet there. Snow because it reflects about six times more light than rock does.

Advanced Problems

7. $v = (3kT/m)^{1/2}$
   The H molecule has two atoms, so
   $m = 2 \times 1.67 \times 10^{-27}$ kg $= 3.34 \times 10^{-27}$ kg.
   Putting in the numbers for k and m, we get $v = 111 \times (T)^{1/2}$ m/s.
   a. $T = 1500\ K$, $T^{1/2} = 39$, $v = 4.33 \times 10^3$ m/s.
   Multiply by two for atomic hydrogen
   b. $T = 1500\ K$, so the answer must be the same as in part a.
   c. $T = 200\ K$, $T^{1/2} = 14$, $v = 1.55 \times 10^3$ m/s.
   d. Escape velocity is discussed in Chapter 4. $v(esc) = (2GM/r)^{1/2}$
   and the figure is 11 km/s for the Earth. We look at ratios for object (P) and Earth (E):
   $v(esc)(P)/(esc)(E) = (M_P/M_E)^{1/2} (r_E/r_P)^{1/2}$

Use the numbers in Table 8-1 and get 11 km/s for Earth, 2.3 km/s for the Moon, and 59 km/s for Jupiter. The Moon's escape velocity is clearly lower than the hydrogen speed, and the escape speed for Jupiter is clearly much higher. The figure for the Earth is about equal, but top speeds are often three times higher, and the 11 km/s is for the Earth's surface, not the upper atmosphere.

8. It is easiest to use ratios, since weight $= \dfrac{GM_1M_2}{r^2}$ where r and M_1 are the planet's size and mass and m_2 is the mass of the object. Then

$$\frac{\text{weight on Pluto}}{140 \text{ lb}} = \frac{\text{mass of Pluto}}{\text{mass of Earth}} \times \left(\frac{\text{Radius of Earth}}{\text{Radius of Pluto}}\right)^2 = 0.05,$$

where we have used Table 8-1.

Sample Test Questions

True-False

1. All gas giant planets in the solar system have several natural satellites. T
2. Uranus was discovered by accident. T
3. Uranus has an obliquity of 98°. T
4. Uranus' rotation is prograde. F
5. Saturn is the only planet with rings. F
6. Neptune was discovered by accident. F
7. Pluto is probably an escaped satellite of Neptune. T
8. There might easily be a planet as large as Neptune at 90 AU from the Sun if it lies in the plane of the solar system. F
9. The ring system of Uranus is as extensive as the one around Saturn. (F)
10. Neptune was discovered accidentally (during a star mapping project) but the existence of Uranus was predicted before it was discovered. (F)

Multiple Choice

1. Neither Neptune nor Uranus was known to the ancient astronomers. Uranus was discovered by accident, but Neptune was found by the effects it had on Uranus' orbit.
* A. correct
   B. wrong: The ancient Greeks knew of Uranus but not of Neptune.
   C. wrong: The second sentence is correct only if the words Uranus and Neptune are interchanged.
   D. wrong: Both B and C are true.
   E. wrong: The effects on Pluto's orbit were what led to the discovery of Neptune.

2. We expect the surface of Titan to be covered with liquid
   A. water
   B. helium
   C. sulfur dioxide
   D. hydrogen
* E. methane

3. Of all the outer planets, only Jupiter and Saturn have rings.
    A. correct
    B. wrong: Neptune also has rings.
    C. wrong: Uranus also has rings.
    *   D. wrong: Both Neptune and Uranus also have rings.
    E. wrong: Only Saturn and Neptune have rings.

4. Most of the moons of the outer planets are composed only of
    A. light-colored ices
    B. sooty black organic materials
    *   C. Both A and B are found alone or together.
    D. No ice is observed in the satellites of these planets.
    E. None of these

5. Which of the outer planets has the largest obliquity between its axis and its orbital plane?
    A. Neptune
    *   B. Uranus
    C. Earth
    D. Pluto
    E. Saturn

6. Neither Neptune nor Uranus was known to the ancient astronomers. Uranus was discovered by accident, but Neptune was found by studies of the changes it produced on Uranus' orbit. These statements are _____.
    *   A. correct
    B. incorrect; the ancient Greeks knew of Uranus but not of Neptune
    C. the second sentence is correct only if you interchange Uranus and Neptune
    D. both B and C
    E. incorrect; the small changes in Pluto's orbit led to the discovery of Neptune

7. A planet is said to have retrograde rotation whenever _____.
    *   A. it rotates east to west
    B. it has no rotation
    C. it has no obliquity
    D. it rotates west to east
    E. it rotates north to south

8. The current explanation of the arc-rings of Neptune is _____.
    A. the arc-rings were just formed
    B. meteors have broken up continuous rings
    C. perturbations introduced by Jupiter and Saturn
    *   D. gravitational effects of small moonlets
    E. astronomers have no suggestions as to the cause.

9. In general the giant planets in the solar system are better able to keep their atmospheres than the inner planets since _____.
    A. they are hotter
    *   C. they are colder
    B. they rotate slower
    D. they have lots of primordial gas
    E. None of these

10. Although Triton is only the seventh largest satellite in the solar system it is believed to have an atmosphere and seasonal changes while the much larger Moon of Earth has no atmosphere. This is possible since _____.
    A. Triton is far from Neptune
    B. Triton is close to the Sun
    * C. Triton is far from the Sun
    D. the Moon is close to Earth
    E. None of these

11. Compare two gases, one of whose molecular mass is four times the mass of the other. How will the typical velocities compare if their temperatures are the same?
    A. they will be the same
    B. the lighter will have a typical speed four times the heavier one
    C. the heavier will have a typical speed four times the lighter one
    * D. the lighter will have a typical speed two times the heavier one the heavier will have a typical speed two times the lighter one
    E. None of these

12. If the Kelvin temperature of a gas is increased by a factor of four, the typical velocity of the average particle of the gas will _____.
    A. Become ½ as great
    B. Become $1/\sqrt{2}$ as large as before
    C. Remain constant
    D. Becomes ($\sqrt{2}$ times as large as before
    * E. Double

13. Which will have the smallest average velocity (rms speed) at 300 K?
    A. Hydrogen with a molecular mass of 2 units
    B. Helium with a molecular mass of 4 units
    * C. Oxygen with a molecular mass of 32 units
    D. They all have the same average velocity (rms speed)
    E. Not enough information in principle to answer

Problems Involving Optional Mathematical Equation VI and Optional Mathematical Equations from Other Chapters

14. (Optional Equation V) Uranus has a mass about 15 times the Earth's and a radius about four times the Earth's. How many times stronger than the Earth's gravitational field is that of Uranus at its surface (approximately)? That is, surface gravity on Uranus = (approximately) _____ surface gravity on the Earth.
    A. 1/10
    B. 4
    C. 56
    * D. 1
    E. 9

15. (Optional Equation IV) The surface temperature of Pluto is about 50 K. At what wavelength is the most thermal radiation emitted (not reflected)?
    A. 3 cm
    B. 5.8 m
    C. .145 m
    D. 5.8×10^5 m
  * E. 5.8×10^{-5} m

16. (Optional Equation VI) If the Kelvin temperature of a gas is increased by a factor of four (4), the average velocity will increase by a factor of _____.
    A. ¼
    B. ½
  * C. 2
    D. 4
    E. 1.38

17. (Optional Equation VI) An oxygen molecule has twice the mass as monatomic oxygen. At the same temperature, how does the average velocity of monatomic oxygen compare with the average velocity of an oxygen molecule? Monatomic oxygen has _____ times the average velocity of molecular oxygen.
    A. $\dfrac{1}{\sqrt{2}}$
    B. ½
    C. 1 (the same)
  * D. $\sqrt{2}$
    E. 2

Essay

1. Explain the concept of shepherd satellites.
2. Describe how the rings of Uranus were discovered.
3. Discuss the typical composition of the satellites of the outer planets.
4. How is the average velocity of a gas related to the temperature of a gas?
5. Discuss the atmospheres of the gas giants.
6. Should Pluto still be considered a planet? Discuss why or why not.

Word Practice (* denotes additional word not from the chapter)

1. _____ can help confine rings to a narrow zone.
2. The planet _____ was discovered by its gravitational effects on the orbit of Uranus.
3. A rotation from East to West is termed _____ rotation.
4. The outermost planet of the solar system is_____.
5. In addition to rings about Uranus, the space probes showed that there were rings around _____.
6. Ring systems that contain thicker segments are called _____ systems.
7. _____ may be related to the peculiar orbit of Triton.*
8. The first planet discovered in recorded history is _____.
9. _____ occurs when the rotation rate and direction of a body axis changes irregularly.*

10. The _____ of a planet is the deviation of the axis of rotation from being perpendicular to the orbital plane.
11. Uranus' _____ were discovered only in 1977 when they passed in front of a star.
12. _____ satellites were mostly discovered by Voyager.
13. _____ is the innermost of the five largest satellites of Uranus. It has a highly fractured surface.
14. _____ is the largest satellite of Neptune. It may have a thin atmosphere.
15. _____ is the only known satellite of Pluto.
16. _____ is the term used to refer to a possible planet in orbit beyond Pluto.
17. The _____ is an atmospheric feature of Neptune discovered on Voyager 2 photos.

Answers to Word Practice

1. shepherd satellites
2. Neptune
3. retrograde
4. Pluto
5. Neptune
6. arc-ring
7. Pluto's origin
8. Uranus
9. chaotic rotation
10. obliquity
11. rings
12. Uranus'
13. Miranda
14. Triton
15. Charon
16. "Planet X"
17. Great Dark Spot

Chapter 13
Comets, Meteors, Asteroids, and Meteorites

Answers to Problems in the Text

1. Still being too cold to vaporize, it would not release a large gas cloud. Hence, it would be too small and faint to be seen. In addition, if it were seen, it would be hard to pick out from the same sized parts of Saturn's satellite system.

2. Yes. It applies to all bodies orbiting around the Sun or in fact all small bodies orbiting around a much more massive body. (Hence, the term "Keplerian motion.")
   If $a = 10^5$ AU; $p^2 = a^3 = 10^{15}$;
   $p = \sqrt{10} \times 10^7 = 3.2 \times 10^7$ years = 32 million years.

3.

Item	Useful Form	Non useful Form
Time	clock hour (e.g., 8:37 PM EST)	vague—at night (e.g., sometime last night)
Size	angular or relative to landmarks (e.g., 2° or as large as the width of	imprecise measurement (e.g., as large as a horse, as big as a 747, biggest
	the mountain visible from my house)	thing I ever saw)
Brightness	relative to stars (e.g., between Sirius and Venus in brightness)	absolute, un-testable, (e.g., brightest thing I ever saw)
Motion	relative to stars (e.g., passed between Mars and Jupiter in three minutes)	absolute (e.g., moved 100 mph or as fast as a plane)
Location	relative to sky objects (e.g., passed through Orion)	vague (e.g., overhead)

Make sure of location and time of fall. Notify nearest science museum, geology department, or astronomy department. Return and remain near fall. Protect it from being disturbed. Notify an astronomer through his or her textbook publisher if no local authority seems concerned or competent.

4. Meteors: glow as meteoroid hits atmosphere; fine debris of comets.
   Comets: gaseous pieces of asteroids kicked out into cometary orbits.
   Zodiacal light: microscopic meteoroid dust left in solar system (remnants of comets and asteroids? primordial?).
   Asteroids: small bodies mostly in orbit between Mars and Jupiter; some elsewhere; debris of solar system formation. Some objects listed as asteroids may be burned-out comets.
   Meteorites: probably pieces of asteroids (possibly comets) that survive as meteors and hit the ground.

5. An icy body some miles across. Icy surface or perhaps covered with a dusty layer of soil dislodged as ices sublime. It might not really have a surface as we think of it. Entire sky and region about the astronauts would glow from the vaporized material if in the inner solar system. Gravity would be

negligible. Short-period comets would have speeds closer to the Earth's velocity and would more likely lie in the plane of the solar system and hence be easier to match orbits with.

6. Neglect the fact that the Earth would accelerate particles as they got very close to it. All numbers are thus upper limits:
speed = 15 km/s.

a. time = distance/velocity;

distance = 15×10^6 km; time = 10^6 s = 11.6 days.

b. This is not much time to move many people. If the object were going to hit a body of water (which they do in five out of six cases), people could be evacuated to higher ground. The process of political decision might take several days, so even less time is left.

c. distance = 3.81×10^5 cm; time = distance/velocity = 2.56×10^4 s = 7.1 hours.

d. distance = 100 km; time = distance/velocity = 6.7 s.

Note: Many students may be helped by dimensional analysis, so you could set the problem up

as time = m $\times \dfrac{s}{m}$ = m/(m/s);

that is, time = $\dfrac{\text{distance}}{\text{velocity}}$.

7. Very small. Yes: Survivors might have reported a finger of God striking the area or destruction raining down from heaven because of the (local) gods. If the object fell into the sea, the surrounding coasts would have been flooded by tsunamis. This could have resulted in flood myths.

Advanced Problems

8. Since the comet is on a parabolic orbit, we may assume it is traveling at the speed needed to escape from the Sun when it is at closest approach. The Earth is in nearly circular orbit, so the Earth's speed is that of circular orbit. Thus, V comet =

$\sqrt{2}$ V circular as we saw in Chapter 4 (Optional Equation III). So the comet's speed is either ($\sqrt{2}$ −1) or ($\sqrt{2}$ + 1) times the Earth's speed. Earth velocity in orbit is

$V = \dfrac{2\pi R}{\text{period}} = \dfrac{2\pi \times 1.5 \times 10^{11} \text{m}}{3 \times 10^7 \text{s}}$ 3×10^4m/s

Therefore, 1.2×10^4 m/s or 7.2×10^4 m/s.

9. $\alpha" = 1"$, $d = 2$ km $= 2 \times 10^3$ m, so $\alpha"/(2.06 \times 10^5) = d/D \Rightarrow D = d \times 2.06 \times 10^5/\alpha"$ and
$D = 2 \times 10^3 \times 2.06 \times 10^5$ m $= 4.06 \times 10^5$ km
This distance is slightly more than the Moon's distance from the Earth; however, it would have to be closer to the Moon's orbit for us to be able to distinguish its shape.

10. Mass $= (4/3)\pi r^3 p = (4/3) \times 3.14 \times (10^2 \text{ m})^3 \times 8000 \text{ kg/m}^3 =$
3.35×10^{10} kg

Value $=$ mass $\times$ $\$.90$/kg $= \$3.02 \times 10^{10} = \$30$ billion

Thus, investors (or the government) could spend up to about \$30 billion to reach and mine this body if the price remained at this level. Future shortages of many essential substances may make the possible future return even greater.

11. $\text{Volume} = \dfrac{4}{3}\pi r^3 = \dfrac{1}{6}\pi(\text{diameter})^3 \Rightarrow \dfrac{\text{volume of Earth}}{\text{volume of asteroid}}$

$= \left(\dfrac{\text{dia} \oplus}{\text{diameter}}\right)^3 = \left(\dfrac{1.2 \times 10^7}{1.2 \times 10^5}\right)^3 = 10^6$

It would take about 1 million.

Sample Test Questions

True-False

1. The cosmic debris floating between the planets is known as the meteoritic complex. T
2. Comets are rocky-metallic worlds ranging from a few hundred meters or less up to 1000 km in diameter. F
3. Interplanetary rocks that collide with the Earth's atmosphere and survive to fall to the ground are termed meteors. F
4. The original small, pre-planetary bodies of the solar system are known as planetesimals. T
5. Comets are omens of things to come. F
6. Tycho Brahe was the first astronomer to determine that comets were more distant than the Moon. T
7. The Oort cloud is a swarm of millions of comets at 50 AU from the Sun. F
8. The Oort cloud is a swarm of millions of comets at 50,000 AU from the Sun. T
9. Nearby stars cause comets to leave the Oort cloud. T
10. Most meteors must be small bits of debris scattered from comets. T
11. The asteroid belt is the region between Mars and Saturn. F
12. Asteroids that cross the Earth's orbit are called Apollo asteroids. T
13. The smaller the meteorite, the rarer it is. F
14. There are four basic types of meteorites. F
15. The meteorite parent bodies formed 4.6 billion years ago. T
16. The zodiacal light is a faint glowing band of light diametrically opposite the Sun. T
16. The asteroids are mainly composed of metal poor stony compounds. F
17. Asteroids are probably planetesimals that never finished forming a planet. T
18. The asteroid belt is the region between Jupiter and Saturn. F
19. Comets begin to develop gaseous comas and tails when they are within 3 AU of the Sun. T
20. Comet tails are of three types: ionized gas, solid dust, and diffuse liquid. F
21. Passing stars can cause some comets to leave the Oort cloud. T
22. The zodiacal light is a faint glowing band of light diametrically opposite the Sun. F
23. The meteorite parent bodies formed 4.6 billion years ago. T

Multiple Choice

1. Icy worlds a few kilometers across are
   A. parent bodies
   B. meteoroids
   C. meteors
 * D. comets
   E. asteroids

2. A small nebulosity with one or more bright spots and an attached flowing streak extending several degrees across the sky is
   A. a meteor
   B. an asteroid
   C. a planet
 * D. a comet
   E. a galaxy

3. The dust tails of comets point
   A. toward the Sun
 * B. away from the Sun
   C. toward the Earth
   D. toward Jupiter
   E. toward the direction of travel

Consider the sketch of a comet:

4. The comet nucleus is denoted by
 * A. A
   B B
   C. C
   D. A and B together
   E. B and C together

5. The comet tail is denoted by
   A. A
   B B
 * C. C
   D. A and B together
   E. B and C together

6. The comet nucleus is denoted by
   A. A
   B B
   C. C
 * D. A and B together
   E. B and C together

7. Comets may have several tails, but they are of only two types.
 * A. correct
   B. wrong: only two tails at most
   C. wrong: only one tail
   D. wrong: at least five types
   E. wrong: both B and D

8. Most comets are believed to come from other nearby stars.
   A. correct
   B. wrong: ejected from the Sun
 * C. wrong: true members of the solar system
   D. wrong: from other galaxies
   E. wrong: astronomers have no idea

9. The comet model that suggests chunks of frozen gases several kilometers across, laced with bits of silicate dust, is called the _____ model.
   A. Oort
   B. frozen sherbet
 * C. dirty iceberg
   D. frozen lace
   E. silicate

10. Tails of comets are
    A. caused by ionization of the Earth's atmosphere as the comet enters it
    B. dust and gas captured by the comet
    C. the jet exhausts of the engines that make the comets move
 * D. dust and gas blown off the comet by the solar wind
    E. misleading: Comets do not have tails.

11. Most meteors are
 * A. small bits of debris scattered from comets
    B. small comets that never had long tails
    C. pieces of Jupiter
    D. pieces of Saturn's rings
    E. none of these

12. The asteroids that lie in two swarms 60° ahead of and behind Jupiter are the _____ asteroids
    A. Apollo
    B. Jupiter
    C. Lagrange
 * D. Trojan
    E. Greek

13. The asteroids are small bodies, most of whose orbits lie near the plane of the ecliptic between the orbits of Jupiter and Mars.
 * A. correct
    B. wrong: The asteroids are usually larger than the Moon.
    C. wrong: The orbits of the asteroids lie between Jupiter and Saturn.
    D. wrong: There is no preferred plane for asteroid orbits.
    E. None of these

14. The points 60° ahead of and behind a planet in its orbit are called the _____ points. At these points, the planet and the Sun permit other particles to exist in a stable orbit.
    A. Apollo
 * B. Lagrangian
    C. Trojan
    D. stable
    E. Oort

15. The _____ are a stony type of meteorite that has never been subjected to very much heat.
   * A. carbonaceous chondrites
   B. achondrites
   C. chondrites
   D. irons
   E. stony-irons

16. Most meteorites became solid objects 1.2 billion years ago as parts of parent bodies. These parent bodies broke up as late as a few million years ago.
   A. correct
   B. wrong: Parents broke up 1.2 billion years ago.
   * C. wrong: Most became solid objects 4.6 billion years ago.
   D. wrong: Both B and C changes are needed.
   E. misleading: There is no indication that meteorites ever were parts of larger bodies.

17. The chondrites come from the _____ of the parent body of meteorites.
   * A. outside
   B. core
   C. melted metals
   D. radioactive regions
   E. zodiac

Problems Involving Optional Equations from Other Chapters

18. (Optional Equation I) Ceres is about 1000 km in diameter and can be as close as 1.77 AU from the Earth. Which of the telescopes below could resolve Ceres?*
   A. a telescope with a resolution of 0.07"
   B. a telescope with a resolution of 0.7"
   C. a telescope with a resolution of 7"
   * D. both A and B
   E. all three, A, B, and C

19. (Optional Equation II) Ceres has an estimated mass of 1.2×10^{21} kg and a radius of 500 km. Thus, it has about 2×10^{-4} times the Earth's mass and about 0.079 times its radius. So the gravitational force of Ceres equals (approximately) _____ times the gravitational force on Earth.*
   A. 3×10^{-7}
   * B. 3.2×10^{-2}
   C. 0.32
   D. 3.2
   E. 965

20. (Optional Equation III) Vesta has an estimated mass of 2.4×10^{20} kg and a radius of 269 km. What is the approximate escape velocity from Vesta?*
   A. 0.035 km/s
   * B. 0.35 km/s
   C. 3.5 km/s
   D. 0.24 km/s
   E. 0.024 km/s

Essay

1. Distinguish among meteoroids, meteors, and meteorites, commenting on their origins.
2. Sketch a comet, labeling nucleus, head, and tail.
3. Discuss the cause of zodiacal light.
4. What can be learned from a study of meteorites?
5. Why are the small bodies in the solar system so useful in teaching us about the formation of the solar system?

Word Practice

1. Occasionally large meteors occur. Such a large meteor is called a(n) _____.
2. Whipple has proposed the _____ of comet nuclei—chunks of frozen gases laced with bits of silicate dust.
3. _____ are icy worlds of few kilometers across when they are far from the Sun.
4. _____ are small bits of debris in space.
5. _____, _____, and _____ of all sizes are all debris left over from the origin of the solar system 4.6 billion years ago.
6. A(n) _____ meteorite is made of mixed fragments of different types.
7. The believed cloud of comets at 50,000 AU from the Sun is called the _____.
8. The best samples of __ ___ ___ are the carbonaceous chondrites.
9. are the millimeter-scale spherical silicate inclusions in chondrites.
10. The particles blown off the Sun are referred to as the _____.
11. _____ are meteorites most nearly like terrestrial igneous rocks.
12. _____ are meteorites composed of the most primitive, least altered material.
13. A meteor _____ occurs when many meteors are seen in a short time interval, all coming from approximately the same place in the sky.
14. Meteorites with a large metal content are called _____ meteorites.
15. The _____ asteroids cross the Earth's orbit.
16. The _____ is sunlight reflected off the microscopic dust grains in the solar system.
17. A meteor is seen that seems to strike the ground. Later, _____ are found there.
18. Asteroids that cross the orbit of Mars but not the Earth are called _____.
19. The first comet predicted to return was _____ Comet.
20. _____ was the first asteroid discovered.*
21. The _____ asteroids lie in two swarms 60° ahead of and behind Jupiter.
22. _____ are what is left of meteoroids that reach the ground.
23. _____ appear as a glowing streak across part of the sky. They remain for the night, slowly moving with respect to the stars.
24. The nucleus and the coma of a comet make up the _____.
25. _____ _____ are composed of microscopic particles blown off comets and now freely orbiting the Sun.
26. _____ meteorites are mixtures of silicates and metals.
27. The ___ points of Jupiter are the points 60° ahead of and behind Jupiter in its orbit.
28. _____ ____ comets take only a few decades for a complete orbit.
29. Most of the asteroids lie in the _____ that is between Mars and Jupiter.
30. The _____ of a comet is the star like point in the comet head.
31. ____ were small pre-planetary bodies in the early solar system.
32. A glowing streak is seen across the sky and disappears in a few seconds. _____ produce such an effect.

33. Meteorites broke off of a larger body called the _____.
34. The _____ belt lies between Mars and Jupiter.
35. The part of the comet that appears to stream out from the head is called the _____.
36. When a material changes directly from a solid to a gas, it is said to have _____.
37. The concentration of asteroids beyond Neptune and near Pluto is called the ____ belt.
38. The largest of the asteroids near Pluto have been termed _____.
39. _____ asteroids present a physical danger to us. The question is not if one will hit us, but when.
40. Chondrites often contain BB-like glassy spherules called _____.

Answers to Word Practice

1. fireball
2. dirty iceberg model
3. comets
4. meteoroids
5. comets, meteorites, asteroids
6. brecciaed
7. Oort cloud
8. primitive planetary material
9. Chondrules
10. solar wind
11. achondrites
12. carbonaceous chondrites
13. shower
14. iron
15. Apollo
16. zodiacal light
17. meteorites
18. Mars-crossing asteroids
19. Halley's
20. Ceres
21. Trojan
22. meteorites
23. comets
24. head
25. dust trails
26. stony-iron
27. Lagrangian
28. short period
29. asteroid belt
30. nucleus
31. planetesimals
32. meteors
33. parent body
34. main asteroid
35. tail
36. sublimed
37. Kuiper
38. Plutinos
39. Earth-crossing asteroids
40. chondrule

Chapter 14
The Origin of the Solar System

Answers to Problems in the Text

1. This is expected, from the basic laws of physics, as a natural evolutionary behavior. Thus, for planets of terrestrial size and temperatures, there is no need to explain the lack of hydrogen as an initial condition or primeval process.

2. Rocks on the Earth have been subjected to erosion by water and cooking by plate tectonics. The meteorite rocks, with rare exceptions, are closer than Earth rocks to the form they had when the material condensed. Meteorites have somewhat different chemistries because they were formed in a different part of the solar nebula.

3. The planets in the hotter inner solar system could not hold hydrogen. That is, we would expect the inner planets to have a smaller percentage of H, N, and C than the outer planets and a correspondingly larger percentage of A1, Ti, Ca, Fe, Ni, and Si. See Table 14-2. Even the compounds formed can be explained. For example, Venus and Mercury were too hot for much water ever to form. Compared to the Earth, Mercury is richer in iron and Mars is poorer. The other planets have abundant H-rich ices.

4. The planets Mercury, Venus, Earth, and Mars contain much less "ices" than Jupiter, Saturn, Uranus, and Neptune, so we expect that the "inner boundary" for condensation of ices was between Mars and Jupiter. A visit to the asteroid belt may tell us where between these two planets the boundary was.

5. The whole idea of a condensing gas and dust cloud might have to be thrown out if the orbits were non circular and inclined. Studies show that a cloud of dust and gas should flatten to a disk shape, giving rise to planets with circular orbits in a plane.

6. See entries in Table 14-1. The disk shape of the solar system. Meteorites bear evidence of accumulation and collisions of rock material. Is the distribution of minerals in the right order from the Sun? Do asteroids, meteorites, and craters all imply the existence of planetesimals?

7. A solar system can start with a collapsing dust and gas cloud with elements already existing in the percentages observed in the solar system. Theories of the origin of the universe must explain where all matter comes from and why.

8. Most meteorites and Earth and Moon samples we have examined were formed from gases at that date. Radiometric dating shows that the formation interval from dust to planet was probably well under 100 million years. Much has happened to the material of the Earth since that date, but we still know that it became solid then.

9. You could say that the world began as a cloud of dust. The same thing that can make you fall down and hold you down (which we call gravity) brought the cloud together, making the galaxies, their stars, and all the planets.

Advanced Problems

10. At 100 K, the maximum radiation occurs at a wavelength W, given by $W = 0.00290/T = 2.9 \times 10^{-6}$ m, a much larger wavelength than red light—infrared (2900 nm). Use an infrared telescope to look at the 2.9×10^{-6} m range for bright (at this wavelength) objects of very small angular size.

11. 1 AU $= 1.5 \times 10^{11}$ m

    1 year $= 365 \times 24 \times 60 \times 60 = 3.16 \times 10^7$ s

    Note: It is handy to remind students that 1 year $\pi \times 10^7$ s.

    Circumference $= 2\pi r$

    velocity $= \dfrac{2\pi r}{\text{period}}$, or use $V = \sqrt{GM_\odot / R}$

    For Earth

    velocity $= \dfrac{2 \times 3.14 \times 1.5 \times 10^1}{3.16 \times 10^7} = 2.98 \times 10^4$ m/s

    Earth orbital velocity $= 29.8$ km/s,

    so 0.1% is 0.298 km/s or about 300 m/s.

    For Pluto, use $p^2 = r^3$ to get p with $r = 29.4$ AU. Then

    $r^3 = 5.5 \times 10^4 = p^2, p = 2.35 \times 10^2$ years

    period $= 235 \times 3.16 \times 10^7 = 7.42 \times 10^9$ s

    velocity $= \dfrac{6.28 \times 39.4 \times 1.5 \times 10^{11}}{7.42 \times 10^9} = 5 \times 10^3$ m/s

    Pluto orbital velocity $= 5$ km/s, so 0.190 is 0.05 km/s $= 50$ m/s.

    Alternative Method I: $v = 2\pi r/p$; $p^2 = r^3$.

    Then V in cm/s is $V = \dfrac{2\pi (r)_{AU} \times 1.5 \times 10^{11}}{(P)_{yr} \times 3.16 \times 10^7} = 2.98 \times 10^4 \dfrac{r_{AU}}{P_{yr}}$ m/s $= \dfrac{2.98 \times 10^4}{\sqrt{r_{AU}}}$ m/s.

    Alternative Method II:

    Use $V_{circ} = \sqrt{GM/R}$, where $M =$ mass of Sun.

12. To keep gases, the average velocity must be less than one-fourth the escape velocity.
    a. Let density P be 1000 kg/m^3, $T = 500$ K, and diameter $D = 38,000$ km. Then

       mass $= M = (4/3) \pi (D/2)^3 \times P = \pi P D^3/6$.

       Using the given numbers, we get $M = 2.87 \times 10^{25}$ kg.

       From Chapter 4, we have $v_{escape} = (2GM/R)^{1/2}$

       $v = \sqrt{\dfrac{2 \infty 6.67 \times 10^{-11} \times 2.87 \times 10^{25}}{1.9 \times 10^4}} = 14.2$ km/s.

       From Chapter 11, $v_{typical} = (3kT/m)^{1/2}$.

       Since we have hydrogen molecules,

       $v_{typical} = \sqrt{\dfrac{3 \times 1.38 \times 10^{-23} \times 500}{3.34 \times 10^{-27}}} = 2.5$ km/s

       $4 \times v_{typical} = 10$ km/s < 14.2 km/s

    b. Use Table 8-1—$M_{Earth} = 5.98 \times 10^{24}$ kg. The mass used is less than 8–30 times the Earth's mass but clearly bigger than the Earth's mass.
    c. We see that the gas giants are gas giants because they have large rocky cores. The Earth, on the other hand, is a rocky body because it is too small to retain the original hydrogen and possibly because it formed at a higher temperature.

Sample Test Questions

True-False

1. All of the solar nebula was ultimately either absorbed by the Sun or by the planets. F
2. The nebula that surrounded the contracting Sun is called the solar nebula. T
3. A theory of the origin of the solar system does not need to explain Kepler's laws. T
4. A theory of the origin of the solar system must explain Kepler's laws. F
5. A theory of the origin of the solar system must explain Newton's law of gravitation. F
6. Why Saturn's rings have divisions is one of the 13 things an origin theory must be able to explain. F
7. Wien's law is not something that we must explain in a proper origin theory for the solar system. T
8. Wien's law must be explained in a proper origin theory for the solar system. F
9. Why Saturn's rings have divisions is not one of the 13 things an origin theory must be able to explain. T
10. A theory of the origin of the solar system need not explain Newton's law of gravitation. T
11. A theory of the origin of the solar system need not explain Kepler's laws. T
12. A theory of the origin of the solar system must explain Kepler's laws. F
13. A theory of the origin of the solar system must explain why the planets differ in their composition. T
14. Why planets have satellites is not one of the questions to be asked of a solar system origin theory. F
15. Astronomers now believe that catastrophic theories best explain the origin of the solar system. F
16. Evolutionary theories tend to explain most things as due to relatively gradual processes. T
17. Astronomers now believe that evolutionary theories best explain the origin of the solar system. T
18. Rene Descartes proposed the first scientific evolutionary theory in 1644. T
19. The principle of conservation of angular momentum predicts that a spinning body will rotate faster if its mass moves closer to the axis of rotation. T
20. The principle of conservation of angular momentum predicts that a spinning body will rotate SLOWER if its mass moves closer to the axis of rotation. F
21. It would be harder to develop a solar system cosmology if the solar system consisted of planets orbiting the Sun in randomly inclined circular orbits, both prograde and retrograde. T
22. It would be easy to develop a solar system cosmology if the solar system consisted of planets orbiting the Sun in randomly inclined circular orbits, both prograde and retrograde. F
23. The smallest particles, such as dust grains, left after planetary formation were possibly carried away from the solar system by solar radiation and gas. T
24. The surface composition of the planets was not affected by differentiation. F
25. The final surface composition of the planets was affected by differentiation. T
26. The most abundant element in the solar system is hydrogen. T
27. The isotope distribution problem might be explained by the explosion of a nearby star at the time of the formation of the solar system, which added different mixes of isotopes to parts of the nebula. this combination of events could be explained if the explosion of the one star somehow triggered the collapse of the solar nebula. T
28. H. Alfven was among the first to realize the early Sun probably had a strong magnetic field. T
29. C. Impey was among the first to realize the early Sun probably had a strong magnetic field. F

Multiple Choice

1. Theories that explain things through sudden or uncommon events are _____ theories.
   - A. nebula
 * B. catastrophic
   - C. sudden
   - D. condensation
   - E. evolutionary

2. Any theory of the origin of the solar system must explain
   A. why planetary orbits are nearly circular
   B. why the planet-satellite systems resemble the solar system
   C. why Kepler's laws hold
*   D. both A and B
   E. none of these

3. Any theory of the origin of the solar system must explain
   A. why planetary orbits are nearly circular
   B. why the planets differ in composition
   C. why meteorites differ in chemical and geological properties from all known planetary and lunar rocks
   D. both A and B
*   E. all three, A, B, and C

4. The _____ explains both why the planets lie nearly in the same plane and why this is the plane of the Sun's rotation.
*   A. conservation of angular momentum
   B. theory of Helmholtz contraction
   C. condensation sequence
   D. conservation of parity
   E. retrograde rotation of Venus

5. An example of conservation of angular momentum is
   A. figure skaters slowing down their spin when they pull in their arms
*   B. figure skaters speeding up their spin when they pull in their arms
   C. a car going through a 90° turn at high speed
   D. what happens when you stand on a skateboard and throw a ball
   E. none of these

6. The collapse of the solar nebula when its atoms were far apart is technically called _____.
   A. Roman falling
   B. catastrophic contraction
*   C. free-fall contraction
   D. Helmholtz contraction
   E. none of these

7. The contraction of the solar nebula in which the shrinkage is slowed by outward pressure is
   A. pressure collapse
   B. catastrophic contraction
   C. free-fall contraction
*   D. Helmholtz contraction
   E. none of these

8. A cloud in space that is later incorporated into a planet is called _____.
   A. a cirrus cloud
   B. a grain
   C. a planetesimal
   D. a protoplanet
*   E. none of these

9. The order in which gases condensed out of the solar nebula is termed the _____.
   A. solidification order
 * B. condensation sequence
   C. condensation order
   D. Helmholtz order
   E. Alfvén sequence

10. One of the first elements to condense from the solar nebula was _____.
   A. silicon (Si)
   B. hydrogen (H)
   C. iron (Fe)
 * D. calcium (Ca)
   E. none of these

11. Of the nine elements considered in the condensation sequence in the solar nebula, one of the last to condense was __.
   A. aluminum (Al)
   B. iron (Fe)
 * C. carbon (C)
   D. silicon (Si)
   E. lead (Pb)

12. Intermediate bodies from which the planets were assembled are called _____.
   A. grains
   B. nebulae
 * C. planetesimals
   D. intermediate planets
   E. new planets

13. The most abundant element in the solar system is _____.
   A. potassium (K)
   B. sulfur (S)
   C. helium (He)
   D. oxygen (O)
 * E. carbon (C)

14. The second most abundant element in the solar system is _____.
   A. aluminum (Al)
   B. iron (Fe)
   C. silicon (Si)
 * D. helium (He)
   E. carbon (C)

15. The probable method of slowing the Sun's rotation and transforming the angular momentum to the planetary material was _____.
 * A. magnetic braking
   B. angular transfer
   C. viscous flow
   D. catastrophic collision
   E. none of these

16. The satellites of the planets were formed ____.
    A. around the planets
    B. separately and later captured
    C. much later than the planets themselves
    D. much earlier than the planets which later formed near the satellites
*   E. both A and B occurred

Problems Involving Optional Mathematical Equations from Other Chapters

17. (Optional Equation III) If a body is in circular motion about a point the distance of which is far greater than the body's size, the body's angular momentum is *mvr*, where *m* is the mass, *v* its velocity, and *r* the radius of its orbit. Jupiter has a mass of 1.9×10^{27} kg and an orbital radius of 5.2 AU (1 AU $= 1.5 \times 10^{11}$ m). What is the approximate angular momentum of Jupiter in SI units?
*   A. 6×10^{41}
    B. 6×10^{37}
    C. 4×10^{17}
    D. 2×10^{98}
    E. 13.5

18. (Optional Equation IV) Silicate materials condense out of the solar nebula at a temperature of about 1300 K. At that temperature, what would be the approximate wavelength at which the most thermal radiation would be emitted from the resulting mineral grains?
    A. 6.67×10^{-8} m
    B. 3.77×10^{-2} m
    C. 2.23×10^{-5} m
*   D. 2.23×10^{-6} m
    E. 2.06×10^{5} m

Essay

1. Distinguish between catastrophic theories and evolutionary theories.
2. List six observational items that must be explained by a theory of the origin of the solar system. (See Table 14-1.)
3. Give an example of conservation of angular momentum from your everyday experience.
4. List three items of evidence for the past existence of planetesimals.
5. Discuss the chemical compositions of the planets.

Word Practice (* denotes words not on the Concepts List.)

1. A(n) _____ is a cloud in space.
2. Microscopic solid particles in space are often called _____.
3. A(n) _____ theory explains things through sudden events.
4. _____ of angular momentum explains why figure skaters spin faster when they pull in their arms.
5. _____ was proposed by H. Alfvén to account for angular momentum transfer within the solar nebula.
6. The intermediate bodies from which the planets were assembled are called _____.
7. The _____ is the order in which particles condensed out of the solar nebula.

8. _____ are the bodies intermediate in size between grains and protoplanets.
9. The solar nebula began to collapse in _____ _____.
10. Catastrophic theories require _____ events.*
11. The _____ was the first body to form from the solar nebula.*
12. The third entry in the condensation sequence is _____.*
13. Atoms interacting in a gas cause _____.*
14. Meteorite _____ strongly supports the condensation theory.*
15. Magnetic braking explains the transfer of _____ within the solar nebula.*
16. When the solar nebula contraction is slowed by outward pressure, we call the contraction _____.
17. Minerals containing the element _____ formed the first stony material to condense from the solar nebula.*
18. The _____ surrounded the forming Sun.
19. The ____ grew into our Sun by absorbing most of the solar nebula.*
20. Theories that explain change by gradual processes are called _____ theories.
21. An orbit that diverges exponentially from a nearby orbit is called a(n) _____ orbit.

Answers to Word Practice

1. nebula
2. grains
3. catastrophic (WEB)
4. conservation
5. magnetic braking (WEB)
6. planetesimals
7. condensation sequence
8. planetesimals
9. free-fall contraction
10. sudden
11. protosun

12. silicon
13. pressure
14. composition
15. angular momentum
16. Helmholtz contraction
17. silicon
18. solar nebula
19. protosun
20. evolutionary (WEB)
21. chaotic

Chapter 15
The Sun: The Nature of the Nearest Star

Answers to Problems in the Text

1. Accepting the age of the Sun as 4.6 billion years, we know of no process that could have so long provided the energy for the Sun except nuclear fusion. From the known measurements of nuclear properties and the behavior of gases, plus our knowledge of the Sun's surface temperature, we can calculate approximate internal temperatures and pressure. These predict that nuclear reactions must be occurring in the Sun's hydrogen.

2. One-fourth the apparent solar rotation period: $27\dfrac{27\overset{d}{.}75}{4}\,75/4 = 6\overset{d}{.}83$. One apparent solar rotation period: $27\overset{d}{.}3$. It is unnecessary to correct for the Earth's motion if one uses the apparent rotation.

3. The number rises and falls every 11 years, but because the magnetic polarity is reversed every cycle, only after two cycles of rising and falling do all properties (polarity and numbers) repeat themselves.

4. Assume that the time required to make the observation is shorter than the interval of observation and that we are talking about the whole Sun, not just one spot.
   a. Changes in granulation spicules and super-granulation; prominences would have moved.

   b. Flares and solar rotation.

   c. Number of sunspots and location with respect to equator.

   d. Solar magnetic field and polarity of sunspots.

   e. Perhaps none, although some astronomers have speculated that known climatic changes on Earth with a 10-year time scale may reflect solar variations of that period.
   f. Nine billion years in the past the Sun would not yet have formed; nine billion years in the future the Sun will have consumed most of its available hydrogen. As later chapters show, its structure must change. We expect it to be a white dwarf by then. We would have missed the red giant stage, which occupies a much shorter period.

5. A radio disturbance is caused by electromagnetic radiation, which takes only $8\overset{m}{.}5$ to reach the Earth. An aurora is caused by particles trapped in the Earth's magnetic field. Particles released by solar flare take days to reach the Earth.

6. The Sun is 1.99×10^{30} kg; Jupiter 1.9×10^{27} kg; Saturn 5.69×10^{26} kg; the rest of the planets combined are negligible, so the planets = 2.5×10^{27} kg and $\dfrac{\text{mass of Sun}}{\text{mass of planets}} = \dfrac{1.99 \times 10^{30}}{2.5 \times 10^{27}} = 800$. We might liken the solar system to a bar of Ivory Soap: 99.9% Sun.

7. Hydrogen, helium.

8. See Chapter 14. The Earth is too small and warm to keep its free hydrogen and helium.

9. It will use up its available hydrogen.

10. Only at the center are the pressures and temperatures high enough for fusion to occur.

Advanced Problems

11. a. $\dfrac{\alpha\,''}{2.06\times10^5} = d/D$; $d = 1.28 \times 10^7$ m = diameter of Earth

    D $= 1.5 \times 10^{11}$ m $- 1.4 \times 10^9$ m $= 1.5 \times 10^{11}$ m = distance to Sun's surface

    $\alpha'' = \dfrac{1.28\times2.06}{1.5\times10^{11}} \times 10^5 \times 10^7 = 1.76 \times 10 = 17.''6.$

  b. The answer is obviously the same as for part a.

12. $V_{esc} = \sqrt{2}\, V_{circ}$; $V_{circ} = \sqrt{GM/R}$; $G = 6.67 \times 10^{-11}$; $M_\odot = 1.99 \times 10^{30}$ kg; $R_\odot = 6.96 \times 10^8$ m

    V_{esc} $= \sqrt{\dfrac{2\times6.67\times1.99}{6.96}\times10^{-11}\times\dfrac{10^{30}}{10^8}}$ $= \sqrt{3.82\times10^{11}}$ m/s $= 6.17 \times 10^5$ m/s $= 617$ km/s

13. Wien's law: $W = 0.0029/T$, so $T = 0.0029/W$, where $W = 5.1 \times 10^{-7}$ m, so $T = \dfrac{29\times10^{-4}}{5.1\times10^{-7}}$ K $= 5700$ K.

14. a. $v = (3kT/m)^{1/2}$ with $T = 2 \times 10^6$ K. We use the mass for a hydrogen atom or ion as the appropriate value for this problem. $v = \sqrt{\dfrac{3\times1.38\times10^{-23}\times2\times10^6}{1.67\times10^{-27}}} = 2.2 \times 10^6$ m/s

  b. From problem 12, $V_{escape} = 617$ km/s for the Sun. Thus, the typical velocity is less than the escape velocity; however, three times the typical velocity is greater than the escape velocity. We expect hydrogen ions and atoms to escape from the Sun.

Sample Test Questions

True-False

1. The Sun appears to rotate only because the Earth is revolving about the Sun. F
2. The study of the colors of light emitted by objects is called spectroscopy. T
3. The array of colors in a light beam, ordered according to wavelength, is called white light. F
4. A glow consisting of a mixture of all colors is called an emission line. F
5. A gas at very high pressure will produce bright emission lines. F
6. A hot gas may produce both a continuous spectrum and dark absorption lines at the same time. T
7. The bright red line emitted by hydrogen under the proper conditions is called the hydrogen alpha line. T
8. The element most abundant in the Sun is oxygen. F
9. Coal burning is an example of a chemical reaction. T
10. The Sun produces its energy by a nuclear reaction called the proton-proton chain. T
11. The Sun's central region is called the corona. F
12. Throughout most of the Sun's volume, energy moves primarily by conduction. F
13. The ability of a gas to obscure light passing through it is called the opacity of the gas. T
14. A device that artificially eclipses the Sun and allows study of the corona and the chromosphere is named an eclipograph. F
15. Sunspots are associated with magnetic fields. T
16. A gas with many ions is called a plasma. T

17. The solar cycle is 11 years long. F
18. Sunspots often appear in pairs. T
19. An out rush of gas from the Sun that reaches far beyond the Earth is called the solar wind. T
20. The solar radiation pressure pulls small particles toward the Sun. F
21. Throughout most of the Sun's volume, energy moves primarily by conduction. F
22. Bright regions consist of rising hot gases while the darker regions are cooler falling gases in the photosphere. T
23. The out rush of gas from the Sun that reaches far beyond the Earth is called the solar wind. T
24. The solar radiation pressure pulls small particles toward the Sun. F
25. The shortest wavelength of radiation that can be detected by the normal eye is about 400 nm. T
26. The shortest wavelength of visible radiation appears to be violet or blue to the human eye. T
27. The shortest wavelength of radiation that can be detected by the normal eye is about 700 nm. F
28. The array of colors in a light beam, ordered according to wavelength, is called white light. F
29. A glow consisting of a mixture of all colors is called an emission line. F
30. The element most abundant in the Sun is oxygen. F

Multiple Choice

1. The solar equatorial rotation rate relative to the Earth is ____ days.
    A. 1
    B. 15
    C. 25.4
*   D. 27.3
    E. 59

2. The dark lines on the solar spectrum are known as _____ lines.
*   A. Absorption
    B. Continuous
    C. Hot
    D. Missing
    E. None of these

3. A bright-line spectrum is
    A. Emitted by a luminous solid or liquid
*   B. Emitted by a luminous rarefied (low-pressure) gas
    C. Produced when light passes through a cool gas
    D. Nonexistent
    E. Real but is not produced by A, B, or C

4. The three laws governing continuous, absorption, and emission spectra are known as _____ laws.
    A. Kepler's
    B. Newton's
*   C. Kirchhoff's
    D. Van Allen's
    E. Oort's

5. The proton-proton chain is an example of a(n) _____ reaction.
* A. Nuclear
  B. Chemical
  C. Coronal
  D. Auroral
  E. Mechanical

6. Food burning in a hot pot is an example of a(n) _____ reaction.
  A. Nuclear
* B. Chemical
  C. Coronal
  D. Mechanical
  E. Auroral

7. The opacity of the Sun is caused by
  A. Positive helium ions
  B. Negative helium ions
* C. Negative hydrogen ions
  D. Positive hydrogen ions
  E. None of the above

8. Throughout most of the Sun's volume, energy is transferred by
  A. Conduction
  B. Convection
  C. Opacity
* D. Radiation
  E. Decay

9. In the region just below the photosphere of the Sun, energy is transferred by
  A. Conduction
* B. Convection
  C. Opacity
  D. Decay
  E. Radiation

10. When one end of a metal rod is stuck into a fire, the other end gets hot also. This is an example of energy transfer by
* A. Conduction
  B. Convection
  C. Opacity
  D. Decay
  E. Radiation

11. A gas with many ions is called
  A. Neutral
  B. Flarish
  C. Ionic
* D. A plasma
  E. Multion

In the figure shown below:

12. The core of the Sun is
*   A. A
    B. B
    C. C
    D. D
    E. E

13. The convective zone of the Sun is
    A. A
*   B. B
    C. C
    D. D
    E. E

14. The photosphere of the Sun is
    A. A
    B. B
    C. C
*   D. D
    E. E

15. The chromosphere of the Sun is
    A. A
    B. B
*   C. C
    D. D
    E. E

16. The corona of the Sun is
    A. A
    B. B
    C. C
    D. D
*   E. E

17. The sunspot cycle is approximately _____ years long.
   A. 1
   B. 5
   C. 11
 * D. 22
   E. 31

18. The solar constant is _____ in SI units (kw/m^2).
   A. 3×10^5
 * B. 1.368
   C. 1368
   D. 0.290
   E. 206,265

19. What we might term the visible surface of the Sun is the
 * A. Photosphere
   B. Chromosphere
   C. Corona
   D. Prominence
   E. Plage

20. The zone of the Sun's atmosphere, just above its opaque zone, is the
   A. Photosphere
 * B. Chromosphere
   C. Corona
   D. Prominence
   E. Plage

21. The outermost layer of the Sun's atmosphere is the
   A. Photosphere
   B. Chromosphere
 * C. Corona
   D. Prominence
   E. Plage

22. The charged atomic particles (mostly protons and electrons) emitted nearly continuously by the Sun are called the
   A. Photosphere
 * B. Solar wind
   C. Sunspots
   D. Solar emission
   E. None of these

23. In the photosphere, there are bright regions caused by rising hot gases and darker regions of cooler falling gases. This causes the mottling called
   A. Photosphere
 * B. Granulation
   C. Sunspots
   D. Corona
   E. Faculae

24. Apparently dark regions on the Sun's visible surface, which may be visible to the naked eye, are called
    A. Solar dark regions
    B. Granulation
    C. Solar wind
    D. Plages
 * E. Sunspots

25. Spikes of gas rising vertically through the chromosphere are
    A. Sunspots
    B. Flares
    C. Prominences
 * D. Spicules
    E. None of these

26. A sudden brightening of an area of the Sun's chromosphere, observed most commonly near sunspots, is termed a _____. This process throws material into the corona and emits vast amounts of ultraviolet rays and X-rays.
    A. Spicule
 * B. Flare
    C. Plage
    D. Granulation
    E. Photosence

27. Granulation is caused by
 * A. Rising and sinking gas columns in the photosphere
    B. Rising and sinking gas columns in the chromosphere
    C. Rising and sinking gas columns in the corona
    D. Sudden flares
    E. Magnetic fields causing local heating in the chromosphere

28. The Sun has a strong magnetic field except near the sunspots, where it is weak.
    A. Correct
    B. Wrong: weak everywhere
    C. Wrong: strong everywhere
 * D. Wrong: strong near sunspots, weak everywhere else
    E. Wrong: no magnetic field anywhere

29. A spectroheliograph
    A. Records the solar wind
 * B. Takes a picture of the Sun in a narrow spectral region
    C. Produces an artificial eclipse by occulting the photosphere with a black disk
    D. Measures time
    E. Does none of the above

30. Astronomers have recently been unable to detect as many __ from the Sun as expected.
    A. Photons
    B. Sunspots
    D. Granules
    C. Super-granules
 * E. Neutrinos

31. When we look toward the edge (the limb) of the Sun, we see less deeply into the photosphere. This produces what is (are) termed ____.
    A. Spicules
    B. Auroras
    C. Maunder minima
*   D. Limb darkening
    E. Limb brightening

Essay

1. What are Kirchhoff's laws?
2. What causes granulation?
3. Why is the sunspot cycle said to be 22 years instead of 11 years?
4. What is the Maunder minimum? What consequences might it suggest for mankind?
5. What are cosmic fuels? Contrast a global economy based on cosmic fuels with one based on fossil fuels concentrated in certain countries.

Word Practice (* denotes other words from the chapter.)

1. _____ laws relate emission and absorption spectra to gas density and temperature.
2. In most of the Sun's volume, energy moves primarily by ____.
3. Fire is an example of a(n) _____ reaction.
4. If energy is carried by actual matter flow, we have _____.
5. The Sun generates most of its energy by the _____ chain.
6. The atomic bomb is an example of a(n)_____ reaction.
7. Under high pressure, a hot gas emits a(n)_____ spectrum.*
8. The Sun's energy is generated in the_____ _____.
9. A cool gas between a light source and an observer will cause _____ lines.*
10. The rusting of iron is an example of a(n) _____ reaction.
11. _____ is the study of the colors of light emitted by glowing bodies.*
12. _____ law relates the temperature to the peak color of a body.*
13. The Sun's energy source is a(n) _____ reaction.
14. The discrete particle of light is the _____.
15. A(n) _____ allows a photograph of the Sun to be made in a single wavelength.*
16. A hot gas under low pressure produces _____ lines.*
17. _____ is the transfer of energy by adjacent molecules bumping each other.*
18. A(n) _____ is the array of colors from a source in order of wavelength.*
19. The _____ line is a strong red hydrogen line.*
20. The _____ is the visible surface of the Sun.
21. The solar _____ can be seen from the motion of sunspots.
22. Electromagnetic energy oscillations are seen as _____.*
23. A(n) _____ is a gas with many ions.
24. The rate at which solar radiation reaches the Earth is called the _____.
25. The solar_____ is an outrush of gas from the Sun.
26. The _____ is the Sun's lower atmosphere, just above the visible surface.
27. Solar radiation exerts a(n) _____ on small dust particles and expels them from the solar system.*
28. The _____ is the Sun's upper atmosphere.
29. The solar _____ is about 22 years.
30. Large blasts of material associated with sunspot sites are called _____.*
31. The _____ is a vivid glow caused by solar particles entering the Earth's magnetic field.

32. A cool region on the Sun's surface controlled by magnetic fields is called a(n) ____.
33. The opacity of the photosphere is mainly caused by negative _____ ions.*
34. The _____ is the period from 1645 to 1715 during which sunspot numbers were very low.*
35. Energy from basic planetary or astronomical sources is called _____ fuel.
36. The _____ consist of ions trapped in the Earth's magnetic field.
37. _____ are large clouds of gas shot out of sunspot regions.*
38. _____ are convection cells in the photosphere.*
39. A(n) _____ produces artificial eclipses of the Sun.
40. _____ are columns of gas between the photosphere and the chromosphere.*
41. The _____ of a gas is its ability to obscure light passing through the gas.
42. A gas composed of atoms or molecules with one or more electrons free from the atom or molecules is said to be a(n) _____ gas.
43. The _____ is a nearly (or completely) massless particle emitted when two protons fuse to produce 2H.
44. The study of the natural vibrations of the Sun is called solar _____.

Answers to Word Practice

1. Kirchhoff's
2. radiation
3. chemical
4. convection
5. proton-proton
6. nuclear
7. continuous
8. solar core
9. absorption
10. chemical
11. spectroscopy
12. Wien's
13. nuclear
14. photon
15. spectroheliograph
16. emission
17. conduction
18. spectrum
19. hydrogen alpha
20. photosphere
21. rotation
22. light (or color)
23. plasma
24. solar constant
25. wind
26. chromosphere
27. radiation pressure
28. corona
29. cycle
30. flares
31. aurora
32. sunspot
33. hydrogen
34. Maunder minimum
35. cosmic
36. Van Allen belts
37. prominences
38. granules
39. coronograph
40. spicules
41. opacity
42. ionized
43. neutrino
44. seismology

Chapter 16
Measuring the Basic Properties of Stars

Answers to Problems in the Text

1. Because most stars are much smaller in angular size (the Sun at one parsec would have an angular size of 0.009"), we could resolve only the closest large stars, such as Betelgeuse. But the Earth's atmosphere often degrades the useful resolution to 0.5" or 1". So a ground-based telescope is often useless for stellar diameters. On the Moon, there would be no atmosphere to blur the image (and no scattered light either). At higher magnifications, atmospheric movement and blur are magnified and the images actually look worse, as well as fainter.

2. 1 parsec = 3.26 light-years; 20 parsecs = 65.2 light-years. So, 65.2 years.

3. Hydrogen (80%) and helium (20%) and some heavy elements.

4. The bluish is hotter (Wien's law): Color is temperature. The bluish star has higher luminosity: Of two stars with the same surface area, the hotter star emits more per unit area.
   $E = \sigma T^4 A$ (Stefan-Boltzmann law)

5. Reddish, by the reasoning in problem 4: $E = \sigma T^4 A$. T is lower for reddish stars, so area A must be larger for the star to radiate the same energy per second (E).

6. It is nonlinear. Doubling the amount of light (brightness) does not double magnitude. In fact, a hundred fold increase only decreases magnitude by an additional five units. Also, as the quantity measured gets larger (that is, brightness increases), the magnitude gets smaller.

7. It has the same temperature (as judged from the spectrum). It is not moving radially with respect to the Sun (that is, it has no Doppler shift). It is probably the same size (again, the spectrum is the same). It must be far away from us; it is faint. 30 magnitude $\cong 10^{12}$ times fainter, so the star must be $\sqrt{10^{12}}$ = 10^6 times as far away as the Sun. Distance = 10^6 AU or about 5 parsecs. The star must be very similar in chemical composition to the Sun (again, judging from the spectrum).

8. Distance in parsecs = 1/(parallax in seconds of arc), so
   $$\text{distance} = \frac{1}{5 \times 10^{-2}} = \frac{100}{5} = 20 \text{ parsecs.}$$

9. The surface temperature of the Sun is such as to particularly excite calcium rather than hydrogen. The strength of lines is influenced mainly by gas conditions, not gas composition.

10. Rapid rotation or a turbulent atmosphere, causing both red and blue Doppler shifts.

Advanced Problems

11. This problem (or similar ones) is a key testy of the students understanding of the magnitude system. Difference in magnitude = 26.5 − 12.5 = 14. Each 5 = 100 factor; each 1 = 2.5 factor. That is

$$100 \times 100 \times 2.5 \times 2.5 \times 2.5 \times 2.5 \quad = \frac{100 \times 100 \times 100}{2.5} = \frac{10}{2.5} \times 10^5 = 4 \times 10^5 \text{ times as bright.}$$

Could also argue directly that 14 = 15-1, so $100 \times 100 \times 100 \times \frac{1}{2.5} = 4 \times 10^5$ times as bright.

An exposure of the Moon must be 4×10^5 times as long as an exposure of the Sun. Thus, a $\frac{1}{100}$-s exposure must be:

$$\text{Time} = \frac{1}{100} \times 4 \times 10^5 \text{ s} = 4 \times 10^3 \text{ s} \sim 1 \text{ hour.}$$

12. a. The red shift means it is moving away.
    b. Its speed is 1% of the speed of light = 300 km/s, so it is moving unusually fast.

13. In one year, the star moves an angle of 1" so the distance traveled per year is given by the small angle equation

$$\frac{1''}{2.1 \times 10^5} = \frac{d}{D}, \text{ where } D = 10 \text{ pc} = 3.08 \times 10^{16} \text{ m} \times 10; \text{ so } d = \frac{1 \times 3.08 \times 10^{17}}{2.1 \times 10^5} \text{ m} = 1.5 \times 10^{12} \text{ m} = 1.5 \times 10^9 \text{ km.}$$ Divide this by the number of seconds per year ($\sim \pi \times 10^7$) to set the velocity in km/s: velocity = 49 km/s.

14. The star is receding at 300 km/s and moving at right angles to the line of sight at 49 km/s. The

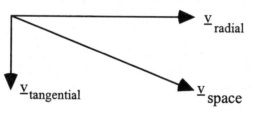

space velocity is the long side of the triangle whose other sides are the radial and tangential velocities, so

$$V \text{ space} = \sqrt{V_{\text{radial}}^2 + V_{\text{tangential}}^2} = 304 \text{ km/s.}$$

15. Use the Stefan-Boltzmann law (Optional Equation VIII): $L = \sigma A T^4$
    The problem is easier if we do a ratio. Let ∗ stand for the star and ⊙ for the Sun.

$$\frac{L_*}{L_\odot} = \frac{\sigma A_* T_*^4}{\sigma A_\odot T_\odot^4} = \frac{A_*}{A_\odot} \left(\frac{T_*}{T_\odot} \right)^4 \quad \text{We are given } L_* = L_\odot, \text{ so}$$

$$A_* = A_\odot \left(\frac{T_\odot}{T_*} \right)^4 = A_\odot \left(\frac{5700}{2850} \right)^4 = 16 A_\odot.$$

The area goes as radius squared, which means $R_* = 4 R_\odot$.

16. a. The average kinetic energy = $(3/2)kT$, so as T increases, the kinetic energy increases on the average.
    b. Since the kinetic energy increases with increasing temperature, the force of collision between atoms must increase also. Thus, a collision is more likely to cause ionization or excitation with higher temperature.

c.   To ionize, we need 2×10^{-18} joules. Find the temperature by
$E = (3/2)kT$. That is,

$$T = (2/3)\, E/k = \frac{\frac{2}{3} \times 2 \times 10^{-18} \text{ J}}{1.38 \times 10^{-23} \text{ J}/\text{K}} = 9.7 \times 10^{4} \text{ K}.$$

We could argue that each atom needs only half the ionization energy so that one needs only $T =$ 48,000 K.

d.   In any event, this is a ballpark figure near the 20,000–40,000 K temperature of O and B stars.

Sample Test Questions

True-False

1. Most of the brighter stars have English names. F
2. The disks of stars seen through the telescope are the images of the stellar diameters. F
3. The parsec is the distance light travels in one year. F
4. The light-year is a unit of time. F
5. The brightness of a star detected by an observer on Earth is termed apparent brightness. T
6. The magnitude system was devised by Hipparchus about 130 BC. T
7. The faintest star visible to the naked eye on a clear night has a magnitude of about 5. F
8. The device used to produce a photographic image of a spectrum is a spectrograph. T
9. A spectrometer produces a spectrum in the form of a chart or graph. T
10. Emission lines appear as dark vertical lines on a photographic spectrum and as notches or valleys on a scan. F
11. An M star is cooler than an A star. T
12. The stable arrangement of an atom is called its ground state. T
13. When electrons move from a higher to a lower energy level, they produce an absorption spectrum. F
14. The visible set of lines produced by hydrogen transitions ending on the $n = 2$ level is called the Balmer series. T
15. Temperature is a measure of the average speeds of atoms or molecules in a gas. T
16. If a light source is receding from us, we say it has a red shift. This means the light source will appear red. F
17. The Stefan-Boltzmann law tells us the wavelength at which most radiation from a star will be emitted. F
18. The distance limit for reliable parallaxes is about 20 parsecs. T
19. The luminosity of a star is the total amount of energy it radiates each second. T
20. Circumstellar material is detected from spectra by using the Zeeman effect. F
21. Star diameters are measured by first determining the luminosity and temperature and then using the Stefan-Boltzmann law. T
22. Stars with nearly identical spectra usually have nearly identical mass. T
23. Stars with rapidly rising and sinking gases in convection cells will show strong rotational line broadening. F
24. The Doppler shift enables us to detect the tangential velocity of a star. F
25. The tangential velocity of a star is its motion perpendicular to the line of sight. T
26. If a light source is receding from us we say it has a Red shift. This does not mean the light source will appear red. T
27. The tangential velocity of a star is its motion perpendicular to the line of sight. T
28. The Doppler shift enables us to detect the tangential velocity of a star. F

Multiple Choice

1. _____ causes even perfect lenses or mirrors to form images of stars as disks surrounded by rings.
   A. The finite speed of light
   B. Color
   C. The f-ratio
 * D. Diffraction
   E. Lasers

2. Which would be the normal units with in to express proper motion?
   A. Light-years per century
 * B. Seconds of arc per year
   C. Centimeters per second of time
   D. Kilometers per year
   E. Furlongs per fortnight

3. We can get the magnetic fields on a star's surface by studying its _____.
   A. Mass
 * B. Zeeman effect
   C. Opacity
   D. Doppler shifts
   E. Spectra

4. 1 parsec = _____ light-years.
   A. 2
 * B. 3.26
   C. 32.6
   D. 206,265
   E. 3×10^5

5. If two stars differ in magnitude by 5, the ratio of the amount of light received (brighter/fainter) is about _____ to 1.
   A. 1
   B. 2.5*
   C. 4
   D. 100
   E. 10,000

6. If star x appears to be 2.5 times as bright as star z, then the two stars differ in magnitude by
   A. 0
 * B. 1
   C. 0.5
   D. 10
   E. 2.5

7. If two stars are emitting the same amount of light, the closer star will appear to be
   A. Dimmer
   * B. Brighter
   C. The same brightness as the farther
   D. Red
   E. Blue

8. Consider three stars of apparent magnitudes 5, 2, and -1. Rank them in order of increasing apparent brightness.
   * A. 5, 2, -1
   B. -1, 2, 5
   C. 5, -1, 2
   D. -1, 5, 2
   E. 2, 5, -1

9. Consider three stars of apparent magnitudes 0, 7, and 3. Rank them in order of decreasing apparent brightness.
   A. 0, 7, 3
   B. 7, 3, 0
   * C. 0, 3, 7
   D. 7, 0, 3
   E. 3, 0, 7

10. The absolute magnitude is the magnitude a star would have if it were ___ parsecs away.
    A. 1
    B. 2.5
    C. 5
    * D. 10
    E. 100

11. The sun has an apparent magnitude of
    A. 26.5
    B. 5
    C. 0
    D. -12.5
    * E. -26.5

12. The sun has an absolute magnitude of about
    A. 26.5
    * B. 5
    C. 0
    D. -12.5
    E. -26.5

13. The letters classifying the spectral sequence of stars from red to blue (low temperature to high temperature) are
    A. BROYGBYGW
    B. NRAWDOP
    C. OBAFGKM
    * D. MKGFABO
    E. OBAFKMG

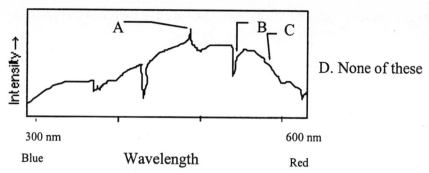

D. None of these

Refer to the spectrum graph shown above to answer questions 14–16.

14. The continuous spectrum is
    A. A
    B. B
* C. C
    D. Both A and B
    E. None of these

15. An emission line is
* A. A
    B. B
    C. C
    D. Both A and B
    E. None of these

16. An absorption line is
    A. A
* B. B
    C. C
    D. Both A and B
    E. None of these

17. An A5 star is
    A. Halfway from B0 to A0
    B. Halfway from A0 to B0
* C. Halfway from A0 to F0
    D. Red
    E. None of these

18. M stars are _____ in color.
    A. Blue
    B. Blue to white
    C. White to yellow
    D. Orange to red
* E. Red

19. Two rapidly moving atoms collide, exciting an electron in one atom to a higher energy level. Later this electron returns to its original energy level. This latter process produces a(n) _____ spectrum.
* A. Emission
   B. Absorption
   C. Decoration
   D. Off-line
   E. Defective

20. G stars have prominent spectral lines of
   A. Ionized metals
   B. Hydrogen Balmer
   C. Helium
* D. Both a and b
   E. All of these, a, b, and c

21. The Bohr model of the atom puts the _____ in shells around the nucleus.
   A. Protons
   B. Neutrons
* C. Electrons
   D. Patrons
   E. Positrons

22. An atom is said to be excited when
   A. One or more electrons are removed
* B. One or more electrons are in higher energy levels than normal
   C. One or more protons are in higher energy levels than normal
   D. One or more protons are removed
   E. It is in a gas

23. An atom is said to be ionized when
* A. One or more electrons are removed
   B. One or more electrons are in higher energy levels than normal
   C. One or more protons are in higher energy levels than normal
   D. One or more protons are removed
   E. It is in a gas

24. The change in observed wavelengths from a wave source that is approaching or receding from us is the _____ effect.
   A. Michelson
   B. Impey
   C. Einstein
   D. Hartmann
* E. Doppler

25. The distance limit for reliable parallaxes is _____ parsecs.
   A. 1
   B. 5
   C. 10
* D. 20
   E. 50

26. If a star is approaching us at 0.01 times the speed of light and it is emitting 500 nm of light, we will see a wavelength shift of*
    A. 5 nm to the red
    B. 0.5 nm to the red
    C. 0.05 nm to the red
    * D. 5 nm to the blue
    E. No shift

27. A star emitting light at a wavelength of 4.50×10^{-7} m is receding from us at 0.1 times the speed of light. We will see the light at a wavelength of _____ m.*
    A. 4.05×10^{-7}
    * B. 4.95×10^{-7}
    C. 1×10^{-4}
    D. 6.8×10^{-7}
    E. 4.50×10^{-7}

28. If the temperature of a perfect radiator is doubled, the energy emitted per unit area per unit time will be ___ times as large as originally.
    A. ½
    B. 8
    C. 4
    D. 2
    * E. 16

29. Which would emit more energy: star 1 of area 16a and temperature t or star 2 of area a and temperature 2t ?
    A. Star 1
    B. Star 2
    * C. Both would be the same
    D. Not enough information

30. A possible definition for the parsec is the distance to a star whose parallax is _____ seconds of arc (corrected for its relative position to the ecliptic).
    A. 0.1
    * B. 1.0
    C. 10
    D. 0.5
    E. None of these

31. The sun has a diameter of 1.4×10^{11} km and a surface area of 6.1×10^{19} m². If the temperature of the sun is 5700 k and the constant in the Stefan-Boltzmann law is 5.7×10^{-8} w/m² · K⁴, what is the approximate energy per unit time that the sun emits in watts?
    A. 4.0×10^{20}
    * B. 4.0×10^{33}
    C. 3×10^{10}
    D. 4.0×10^{45}
    E. 4.0×10^{15}

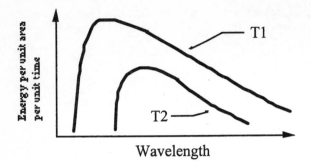

32. Refer to the diagram above. The perfect radiator with the greater temperature is ____.
*   A. T1
    B. T2
    C. Both are equal
    D. Not enough information
    E. None of these

33. The parallax of a star is the angle through which the star appears to move (against the background stars) in the course of a year (corrected for its relative position to the ecliptic).
    A. Correct
    B. Wrong: it is one-fourth the angle in a year.
*   C. Wrong: it is half the angle in a year.
    D. Wrong: the parallax of a star is its temperature divided by one-half its mass.
    E. Wrong: parallax has to do with color changes.

34. If a star has a parallax of 1 second of arc, its distance is ___ parsecs.
    A. 2
*   B. 1
    C. ½
    D. 10
    E. 13

35. If a star has a parallax of 0.1 second of arc, its distance is _____ parsecs.
    A. 2
    B. 1
    C. ½
*   D. 10
    E. 13

36. Which stars must have a large positive luminosity?
*   A. Intrinsically bright stars
    B. Intrinsically dim stars
    C. Red stars
    D. No stars
    E. Both B and C

37. Which stars must have large positive absolute magnitude?
   A. Intrinsically bright stars
 * B. Intrinsically dim stars
   C. Red stars
   D. No stars
   E. Both B and C

38. The magnitude based on all of the electromagnetic energy ideally reaching the earth is the ___.
   A. Visual magnitude
   B. Photographic magnitude
   C. Photovisual magnitude
 * D. Bolometric magnitude
   E. None of these

39. The bolometric magnitude is useful because it
 * A. Takes into account radiation at all wavelengths
   B. Corrects for year of observation
   C. Is the easiest to measure
   D. Is the same for all stars
   E. None of these

40. The rapid motion of atoms in a star's photosphere causes
   A. Rotation
   B. Photons
   C. Collisional broadening
 * D. Doppler broadening
   E. None of these

41. When we look at the center of the disk of the sun (or any star), we see deeper into the photosphere than when we look at the limb. This causes _____.
   A. Collisional broadening
 * B. Limb darkening
   C. Limb brightening
   D. Limb decoloration
   E. No effect

42. We can get the temperature for a star from
   A. Measuring its continuous spectral distribution
   B. Studying its line spectrum
   C. Looking at the total energy per unit area the star emits
   D. Both a and b
 * E. All three, a, b, and c

43. We can measure the radial velocity of a star from the
 * A. Doppler shifts of its spectral lines
   B. Doppler broadening of its spectral lines
   C. Presence or absence of particular lines
   D. Total energy per unit area emitted
   E. None of the above

44. We can get the chemical composition of a star by studying its
    A. Mass
    B. Zeeman effect
*   C. Spectrum
    D. Opacity
    E. Doppler shifts

45. If a source, emitting light of wavelength *l*, is approaching us at speed **v**, and if *c*, is the speed of light; the change in wavelength *dl* that we will observe is _____.
    A. *Dl* / **v** = < *c* / *l*
    B. *Dl* **v** = *c l*
*   C. *Dl* / *l* = **v** / *c*
    D. *Dl* / *l* = *c* / **v**
    E. *L* / *c* = *dl* **v**

Essay

1. Distinguish between apparent and absolute magnitude.
2. Compare some typical apparent magnitudes. (See Table 16-1.)
3. List the seven main spectral classes and the typical color associated with each. (See Table 16-2.)
4. What are the two important spectroscopy laws of this chapter?
5. List eight of the 12 important stellar properties we studied and the techniques for measurement.
6. Why is spectroscopy so important for astronomy?

Word Practice

1. The _____ system is a scale for measuring brightness of stars and other astronomical objects.*
2. A(n) _____ produces an emission line.*
3. The _____ of stars are arranged by temperature, as shown by the spectral lines.
4. The _____ magnitude of a star is its magnitude as we perceive it from the Earth.
5. The _____ is how bright the stars would appear if they were placed at some identical, standard distance.
6. A(n) _____ produces a spectrum in the form of a chart or graph.*
7. An atom is _____ if one or more electrons are in higher energy levels than usual.*
8. A(n) _____ is the distance light travels in one year.
9. The _____ magnitude of a star is the magnitude the star would have if it were 10 pc from us.*
10. The spectral classification scheme is a(n) _____ classification.
11. A(n) _____ produces a spectrum, which is a photographic image.*
12. The first letter of the Greek alphabet is _____.*
13. The _____ alpha line is a prominent red line in the hydrogen spectrum.*
14. The _____ is the general level of brightness between absorption or emission lines.
15. A(n) _____ is the distance at which 1 AU appears to be 1 second of arc in angular size.
16. A(n) _____ consists of a nucleus with a surrounding cloud of electrons.*
17. The _____ disk is produced by diffraction.*
18. A hot, low-pressure gas produces _____ lines.
19. The _____ of a star is how bright the star appears from Earth.
20. Electronic orbits in atoms are also known as _____ _____.*
21. _____ causes a star image to appear as a disk surrounded by faint rings.*
22. The Bohr model of the hydrogen atom has the electrons in _____.*

23. The _____ series is a set of visible lines of hydrogen ending on the $n = 2$ level.
24. _____ are objects that generate (or have generated) energy in their cores by nuclear reactions.
25. The _____ _____ magnitude of a star is measured using a system with the same color sensitivity as the human eye.
26. _____ is a measure of the average velocities of atoms or molecules in a gas.
27. Dark vertical lines on a photographic spectrum and notches or valleys on a scan are _____ lines.
28. _____ is the study of spectra.
29. A(n) _____ is the distribution of light into different wavelengths.
30. The _____ equation tells us the relative numbers of atoms in each state of excitation.*
31. The _____ of a star is a measure of the energy per unit time emitted from the star. It is calculated from the absolute magnitude.
32. The _____ luminosity is the calculated value of energy emission from the surface of the star at all wavelengths.
33. The _____ law gives the spectral distribution of radiation from an ideal black body given the area and the Kelvin temperature of that body.
34. The change in wavelength of light from a moving body is called the _____ effect.
35. Light from a source approaching us has a Doppler _____.
36. Light from a source receding from us has a Doppler _____.
37. The _____ velocity is velocity directly towards or away from us. It is often measured in km/s.
38. The _____ of a star is its angular motion across the sky relative to us. It is usually measured in $\dfrac{"}{year}$ or $\dfrac{"}{century}$.
39. _____ is the careful measurement of the positions of objects in t he sky.
40. The _____ velocity of a star is the true velocity of the star relative to the Sun. This included radial and tangential velocity.

Answers to Word Practice

1. magnitude
2. ionized atom
3. spectral classes
4. apparent
5. absolute brightness
6. spectrometer
7. excited
8. light-year
9. absolute
10. temperature
11. spectrograph
12. alpha
13. Balmer (or hydrogen)
14. continuum
15. parsec
16. atom
17. Airy
18. emission
19. apparent brightness
20. energy levels
21. diffraction
22. quantized orbits (or energy levels)
23. hydrogen (or Balmer)
24. stars
25. visual apparent
26. temperature
27. absorption
28. spectroscopy
29. spectrum
30. Saha
31. luminosity
32. bolometric luminosity
33. Stefan-Boltzmann
34. Doppler
35. blue shift
36. red shift
37. radial
38. proper motion
39. astrometry
40. space

Chapter 17
Behavior of Nearby Stars: The H-R Diagram

Answers to Problems in the Text

1. a. Main sequence stars, spectral classes, G-M, masses usually less than the Sun's mass.
    b. About 20% or less. (Use Table 7-1; assume unknown masses $< M_\odot$.)
    c. No. Most apparently bright stars are giants. Giant stars are rare.

2. No. They are larger in diameter. $E = \sigma T^4 A$. Thus, if they are of the same spectral class as the Sun, the Ts are equal. Thus, for a giant, denoted by $*$, and the Sun, indicated by $\odot$,

    $$E*/E_\odot = L*/L_\odot = A*/A_\odot = 100. \text{ (See Fig. 17-8.)}$$

    Thus, surface area is a factor of 100 larger, which means the diameter of the giant is a factor of 10 larger than the diameter of the Sun. This result checks with Fig. 17-5.

3. a. upper and lower left-hand corners
    b. upper right-and left-hand
    c. upper right-hand
    d. upper left-hand

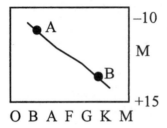

4. a. usually the one to the upper left
    b. the one toward the upper left
    c. same
    d. same

    Thus, star A in all cases.

5. The more massive will evolve faster, reaching main sequence first, becoming a giant star first, and also revolving to a white dwarf first. It is also more likely to become a supernova.

6. In 5–6 billion years, the Sun will rapidly grow (within a period of a few million years) to a red giant about 100 times its present size. From the Earth, the Sun would appear very roughly $100 \times 1/2 \sim 50°$ in diameter. Mercury and Venus (probably) would be absorbed by the Sun. The Sun would be cooler but more luminous (emitting more energy/second), so the Earth would heat and the oceans would evaporate. Life forms would perish from the heat. As one astronomer has put it, "Conditions would be quite miserable." Then, in just a few million more years, the Sun would shrink to a white dwarf. Perhaps it would be a variable star along the way. Everything on the Earth would freeze, assuming the planet had not been engulfed in the Sun's outer part during the red giant stage.
    The two coordinates of the H-R diagram fix 7. Temperature and luminosity. These fix the radius. Only the mass is not fixed by position on the H-R diagram, unless the star is known to be on the main sequence. For example, stars of different mass may be in the giant region.

7. Temperature and luminosity are fixed by the two coordinates of the H-R diagram. These fix the radius. Only the mass is not fixed by position on the H-R diagram, unless the star is known to be on the main sequence. For example, stars of different mass may be in the giant region.

8. Rate of concentration slows. Objects much less than 0.08 of the Sun's mass never become stars because they do not get hot enough inside to start nuclear reactions. Thus, Jupiter is not a star.

9. Main-sequence life for a Sun like star is 9 billion years. Our estimates are that the solar system is 4.6 billion years old and took about 100 million years to form. This is consistent with data. The Sun has been roughly the same for the last 4 billion years. The solar system could hardly be 4.6 billion years if the Sun were only 1 billion years old.

10. Radiation from the Sun's center exerts a pressure that supports the star. This pressure lasts as long as nuclear reactions create energy. It takes a long time to burn up the hydrogen in normal stars.

11. There is now more helium and less hydrogen and also some additional heavier elements. The only difference is in the core, where reactions have taken place. There is no mixing with most of the Sun's volume.

12. Blanket statement not correct. Teachers should distinguish "chronological age" (years) from "evolutionary age" (stage). A massive star evolves faster than a low-mass star. Many of the chronologically very old $1/10\ M_\odot$ stars have yet to reach the main sequence. The Sun is chronologically older than a $10\ M_\odot$ red giant star.

Advanced Problems

13. $W = 0.0029/T$; $W_M = 0.0029/2900\ K = 10^{-6}\ m = 1000\ nm$, greater than visible wavelength: This is infrared light.
$W_K = 0.0029/29,000\ K = 10^{-7}\ m = 100\ nm$, shorter than visible light: This is ultraviolet light.
Each star must show color characteristic of the end of the spectrum at which it lies, so an M star is very red and a K star is very blue. Both peaks lie outside the visible range.

14. a. Energy radiated is proportional to T^4 by Stefan-Boltzmann law: $(20,000/2000)^4 = 10^4$.
    b. Use line $10\ R_\odot$, and read off the luminosity difference on the left-hand scale. From 2500 K to 20,000 K, it looks like about 10,000 or 20,000 in luminosity. This checks approximately.

15. a. Density $= \dfrac{\text{mass}}{\text{volume}}$. For this star, mass $= 0.8\ M_\odot$;

    volume $= \dfrac{4}{3}\pi R^3 = \dfrac{4}{3}\pi(0.015 R_\odot)^3$;

    density $= 2.4 \times 10^5 \times$ density of Sun. Using Table 8-1, we find density of Sun $= 1.4 \times 10^3\ kg/m^3$, so density $= 3.4 \times 10^8\ kg/m^3$. This is between 10^4 and 10^5 times the density of normal matter.
    b. Assume the question means the Earth. We need to calculate the volume of a matchbox and multiply by acceleration due to gravity and by density. Weight $=$ density $\times$ volume $\times\ 9.8\ m/s^2$. This gives weight in Newtons.

Sample Test Questions

True-False

1. The principal differences in the stellar spectra of main-sequence stars arise in general from variations in a single condition in the stellar atmosphere. T
2. The letters in the H-R diagram stand for Herman-Russell. F
3. Unusually small white stars are called white dwarfs. T
4. On the H-R diagram, a line of constant star radius slants down from left to right. T

5. The stars with an apparent magnitude brighter than first magnitude are called representative stars. F
6. The 40 known stars within 4 parsecs of the Sun are known as representative stars. T
7. There are more red giants and supergiants on the list of prominent stars than are found on the list of representative stars. T
8. Stars stay on the main sequence as long as the internal chemistry and energy production change rapidly. F
9. On the main sequence, a star with less mass than the Sun's will be brighter than the Sun. F
10. The relationship between mass and magnitude, called the mass-luminosity relation, holds for all stars. F
11. The equilibrium structure of an ordinary star is determined uniquely by its mass and past history. F
12. The Russell-Vogt theorem explains the cause of stellar evolution. T
13. Stars evolve through most of their life cycle with essentially constant composition but changing mass. F
14. As the Sun evolves, it will first become cooler and brighter. T
15. The more massive a star, the more rapidly it evolves. T
16. The H-R diagram can serve as a tool for dating groups of stars that formed together. T
17. Usually small white stars are called white dwarfs. T
18. The letters in the H-R diagram stand for Herman-Russell. F
19. The relationship between mass and magnitude, called the mass-luminosity relation, holds for all stars. F
20. Any point on the H-R diagram corresponds to a certain temperature, hence, it must correspond to a given energy emission per unit area. T
21. The stars with an apparent magnitude brighter than first magnitude are called representative stars. F
22. Hayashi was one of the astrophysicists who pioneered in calculating evolutionary tracts.
23. The Hayashi phase is a short low-luminosity phase. F
24. Newly formed stars are cooler than main-sequence stars. T
25. Newly forming stars must be above and to the right of the main sequence. T
26. More massive stars evolve more slowly to the main sequence than less massive stars. F
27. The cocoon nebula hides the star from view during its earliest formation. T
28. The high luminosity phase is easily visible through the cocoon nebula. F
29. Maser is an acronym for "molecule amplification by stimulated emission of radiation." F
30. T Tauri stars are so named because they are only observed in the region of Taurus and the neighboring constellation Orion. F

Multiple Choice

1. Small, hot, faint stars, often called degenerate, are termed
   A. Supergiants
   B. Giants
   C. Main sequence
 * D. White dwarfs
   E. None of these

2. The most common star masses are _____ $M_\odot$.
   A. 0.001–0.01
   B. 0.01–0.1
 * C. 0.1–1.0
   D. 1.0–10
   E. 10–100

Refer to Diagram 1 for questions 3–6.

Diagram 1

3. The spectral class of star A is
    A. G5
    B. A3
    C. M0
*   D. B7
    E. M6

4. The spectral class of star C is
    A. G5
*   B. M0
    C. M6
    D. A3
    E. B7

5. The star that has an absolute magnitude of +10 is
*   A. A
    B. B
    C. C
    D. D
    E. E

6. The star that is a supergiant is
    A. A
    B. B
    C. C
*   D. D
    E. E

Refer to diagram 2 for questions 7 and 8.

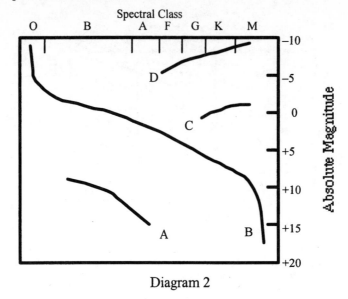

Diagram 2

7. Main-sequence stars are denoted by line
   A. A
 * B. B
   C. C
   D. D
   E. E

8. Supergiant stars are denoted by line
   A. A
   B. B
   C. C
 * D. D
   E. E

9. Consider the following data on five stars. The hottest star is

Star	Apparent Magnitude	Spectrum
A	15	G2 main sequence
B	20	M3 supergiant
C	10	M3 main sequence
* D	15	B9 main sequence
E	15	M5 main sequence

10. Most of the apparently bright stars in the sky are bright because they are close to our Sun (within 4 parsecs).
    A. Correct
 * B. Wrong: Most are intrinsically bright and lie far from the Sun.
    C. Wrong: Close means closer than 1 parsec.
    D. Wrong: This is true only for the green ones.
    E. Wrong: Both C and D changes are needed.

Refer to Diagram 3 for questions 11-16.

Diagram 3

11. The A0 white dwarf star is
*   A. A
    B. B
    C. C
    D. D
    E. E

12. The absolute magnitude of the A0 white dwarf star is
    A. +4
    B. +6
*   C. +11
    D. -1
    E. -7

13. The spectral class of the star with absolute magnitude -7 is
    A. A0
*   B. G8
    C. K2
    D. B3
    E. Z2

14. The supergiant is
    A. A
    B. B
*   C. C
    D. D
    E. E

15. Of the stars on Diagram 3 labeled A–E, the brightest of the hotter stars is
    A. A
 * B. B
    C. C
    D. D
    E. E

16. In Diagram 3, of the stars in the main sequence, the most massive is
    A. A
 * B. B
    C. C
    D. D
    E. E

Diagram 4

17. Refer to Diagram 4 (ABOVE). Which line shows the approach to the main sequence?
    A. Line I
    B. Line II
 * C. Line III
    D. Line IV
    E. None of these

18. The Russell-Vogt theorem tells us that the equilibrium structure of an ordinary star is determined uniquely by its
    A. Mass
    B. Age
    C. Chemical composition
 * D. Both A and C
    E. All three, A, B, and C

Spectral Class

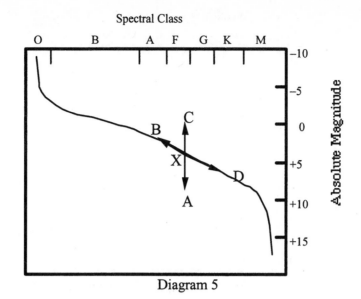

Diagram 5

19. Refer to Diagram 5 (ABOVE). Suppose a star is located at X on the main sequence. Which direction will it move as it evolves off the main sequence?
    A. Direction A
    B. Direction B
  * C. Direction C
    D. Direction D
    E. None of these

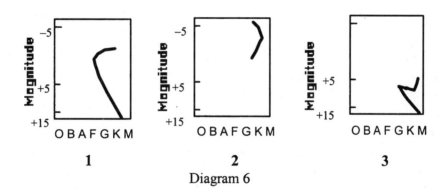

Diagram 6

20. Refer to Diagram 6 (ABOVE), a Hertzsprung-Russell diagram for a hypothetical cluster from birth to old age. Place the diagrams in the correct sequence of increasing time.
    A. 1, 2, 3
    B. 2, 3, 1
    C. 1, 3, 2
  * D. 2, 1, 3
    E. None of these

21. In simple models, just before reaching the main sequence, a star has a(n) _____ magnitude (or luminosity).
  * A. Approximately constant
    B. Decreasing
    C. Increasing

Diagram 7

22. Refer to Diagram 7 (ABOVE) Which part of the path is the evolution from the red giant stage toward the white dwarf stage?
    A. 6 to 5
    B. 1 to 2
    C. 5 to 4
*   D. 3 to 5
    E. 5 to 3

23. The main sequence for a star can best be described as the first state in which the energy produced by _____ balances the energy lost by radiation from the surface.
    A. Gravitational contraction
*   B. Fusion of hydrogen into helium
    C. Fission of helium into hydrogen
    D. Fission of helium into carbon
    E. None of the above

Essay

1. List the spectral classes in order of increasing temperature. Explain why the stars were first listed in alphabetical order but are now listed by classes in a very different order. (Answer to first part: MKGFABO.) As astronomers studied stars, they found that the original order was wrong and that some classes did not really exist.
2. Distinguish between prominent and representative stars.
3. If there is a giant star, a supergiant star, and a main sequence star all of the same spectral class, say K0, what can you say about their relative sizes? Why? (Size: largest, supergiant; next, giant; smallest, main sequence. Temperature: same. Definition of spectral classes and Stefan-Boltzmann law.)
4. What is the Russell-Vogt theorem?
5. Draw an H-R diagram, label the axes, and indicate main sequence, giant, supergiant, and white dwarf regions. (See Diagram 3 in Sample Multiple Choice Questions: A, white dwarf; B, main-sequence; C, giant; D, supergiant.)
6. Explain why the H-R diagram has been useful in interpreting and discussing star data and theory, both historically and in the present. Give examples of how it is used in such discussions.

(Main points: It can be plotted with observational data such as *M* versus spectrum [as Hertzsprung and Russell did] or with theoretical data [such as temperature and luminosity]. It can be used for describing clusters of stars, showing dwarfs and giants.)

Word Practice

1. Stars undergo change as they age. This is called stellar _____.
2. Most stars on the H-R diagram are _____ _____.
3. Stars in the upper half of the H-R diagram are intrinsically _____.*
4. The _____ theorem states that "the equilibrium structure of an ordinary star is determined uniquely by its mass and chemical composition.
5. Stars with an apparent magnitude less than 1 (these are bright stars) are called _ stars*
6. One of the astronomers who first plotted absolute magnitude against spectral class was _____.*
7. A plot of absolute magnitude against spectral class is the _____ diagram.
8. _____ are small hot stars.
9. Stars to the right on the H-R diagram are _____.*
10. The path a star traces out on the H-R diagram as it evolves is the star's _____.*
11. Stars on the lower half of the H-R diagram are intrinsically _____.*
12. A statement of the _____ relation is that "on the main sequence each different mass corresponds to a different luminosity."
13. Stars that suddenly and unpredictably brighten are called _____.*
14. Large red stars are _____ stars.
15. The stars within 4 pc of the Sun are called _____ stars.*
16. The largest of the red stars are the _____ stars.
17. Stars to the left on the H-R diagram are _____.*
18. A tabulation (or display) of the relative amounts of light received from a star as a function of the wavelength of the light is the star's _____.*
19. If a star is hotter or cooler than the Sun, we must add the _____ _____ to their absolute visual magnitude to correct for their color.*

Answers to Word Practice

1. evolution
2. main sequence
3. bright
4. Russell-Vogt
5. prominent
6. Hertzsprung or Russell or Hertzsprung-Russell or H-R
7. spectrum-luminosity
8. white dwarfs
9. cool
10. evolutionary track
11. dim
12. mass-luminosity
13. novae
14. giant
15. representative
16. supergiant
17. hot
18. spectrum
19. bolometric correction

Chapter 18
Stellar Evolution I: Birth and Middle Age

Answers to Problems in the Text

1. The last half.

2. a. Hinder, because there would be no areas of greater density.
    b. Any substantial enough random collection of material will begin to collapse under gravitational attraction. Supernovae and novae shear from galactic rotation; passage of stars through the gas might cause dense regions.
    c. Yes.

3. Fragmentation is an almost inevitable consequence of the cloud collapse process. Because each large cloud that has many star masses breaks up into sub-clouds that form stars, many stars form together.

4. The two time scales are consistent. Star formation theories give us stars forming inside cocoon nebulae, which would also provide the material for planetary formation. And, indeed, silicate dust has been observed to be near young stars. For planetary theory, we have the data from the solar system and satellite system, plus samples from the Moon and meteorites. Much of the data we have collected is geochemical and dynamical. For star formation, we have only what we can observe by telescope in a time that is short compared to the lifetimes of stars.

5. Even these short evolutionary time scales are long compared with the length of time in which we have been observing the stars. Of the few changes that have occurred, most are too small for us to be sure what consequences they imply.

6. The very high-mass end would have evolved off the main sequence because those stars evolve rapidly. The low-mass stars would not yet have reached the main sequence.

7. We would not see much with the naked eye, but infrared telescopes would see an object that was brightening and shrinking in size. The star would reach its high-luminosity phase in about 1000 years and then spend several million years fading toward the main sequence. During this time, its cocoon nebula would probably hide the star, so it would be visible only in infrared. But after the first thousand years, it would be hard to detect even by infrared observation.

8. Many clouds are too low in density and size to collapse. Even some dense clouds have enough turbulence to keep gravity from causing them to collapse.

9. At that point the internal temperature is high enough for hydrogen to fuse into helium, releasing energy. This energy provides a pressure that prevents the collapse. A star with very large amounts of hydrogen in its core will have a long period of stability.

Advanced Problems

10. $W = 10\ \mu m = 10^{-5}$ m; $T = 0.00290/W = 290$ K; $v/c = \dfrac{\text{change in wavelength}}{\text{wavelength}} = 10^{-3} \rightarrow v = 10^{-3}\ c = 300$ km/s

We have a G-type star surrounded by an opaque dust cloud. The dust cloud has been heated to 290 K and probably contains silicates (other solids might be present as well). The blue shift indicates that the part of the dust cloud between us and the star is approaching us at a speed of 10^{-3} times the speed of light = 300 km/s. Two interpretations:

a. Between us and the G-type star is a warm dust cloud of $T = 290$ K approaching us. This is unlikely since the cloud is too warm to be truly interstellar; it must be heated by being near a star.

b. A newly born G-type star is in the process of blowing away its cocoon nebula. Thus, it is very much like the hypothesized early solar system.

Explanation b is the most probable because the interstellar cloud would not have a heat source.

Sample Test Questions

True-False

1. We have only theory, not proofs, that stars are being born today. F
2. We know of massive stars that must be only a few million years old. T
3. On the average, in space there are only 1–5 atoms/cm^3. T
4. In star-forming regions, there may be as many as 10,000 atoms and molecules/cm^3. T
5. The relationship needed between mass and density for a gas cloud to collapse is given by the Jeans theory. T
6. A collapsing gas cloud first subdivides into regions containing enough mass for thousands of stars. T
7. The average density of the universe is believed to be 10^{-27} or 10^{-28} kg/m^3. T
8. Hayashi was one of the astrophysicists who pioneered in calculating evolutionary tracks. T
9. The Hayashi phase is a short, low-luminosity phase. F
10. Newly forming stars must be above and to the right of the main sequence. T
11. The cocoon nebula hides the star from view during its earliest formation. T
12. The cocoon nebula is eventually completely absorbed by the star it surrounds. T
13. Objects too big to be planets but too small to become stars are called brown dwarfs. T
14. Stars of sun like mass produce their energy by the set of nuclear reactions called the carbon cycle. F
15. Dark clouds 1000 to 100,000 AU, common near young star clusters, are called T Tauri globules. F
16. If there were no in homogeneities in the interstellar gas then stars would never form. T
17. In star forming regions the density of gas is lower than normal for interstellar space. F
18. There are more red giants and supergiants on the list of prominent stars than are found on the list of representative stars. T
19. Newly formed stars are cooler than main-sequence stars. T
20. More massive stars evolve more slowly to the main sequence than less massive stars. F
21. The high luminosity phase is easily visible through the cocoon nebula.
22. Maser is an acronym for "molecule amplification by stimulated emission of radiation." F
23. The distinctive feature of Herbig-Haro objects is that there are no visible stars in them. T
24. T Tauri stars are so named because they are only observed in the region of Taurus and the neighboring constellation Orion. F

Multiple Choice

1. Some (or one) of the proofs that stars are forming today are (is)
    A. Short-lived massive stars
    B. The youth of the solar system
    C. Existing dust clouds
    * D. Both A and B
    E. All three, A, B, and C

2. A well-tested body of ideas that has a mathematical formulation and, usually, has been confirmed by observation is called a(n) ___.
    A. Hypothesis
    B. Speculation
    C. Idea
    * D. Theory
    E. Guess

3. A cocoon nebula surrounds
    A. α-Centauri
    * B. R Monocerotis
    C. Sirius
    D. Both B and C
    E. None of these

4. The line on the graph at right that best represents the prediction of the virial theorem (Jeans theorem) is
    * A. A
    B. B
    C. C
    D. D
    E. None of these

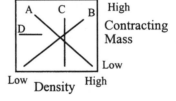

5. The energy radiated during the initial phases of stellar formation comes from
    A. Resistance loss
    * B. Helmholtz contraction
    C. Hayashi transport
    D. Nuclear fusion
    E. Nuclear fission

6. The short, high-luminosity phase of stellar formation occurs when the star is below and to the left of the main sequence.
    A. Correct
    B. Wrong: below and to the right
    C. Wrong: above and to the left
    * D. Wrong: above and to the right
    E. Wrong: occurs on the main sequence

7. A star of solar mass spends about a thousand years in the high-luminosity stage and reaches the main sequence after _____ years.
   A. 100
   B. 1 million
   C. 10 million
 * D. 100 million
   E. 10 billion

8. The high-luminosity phase is easily visible to an outside observer.
   A. Correct
 * B. Wrong: hidden by the cocoon nebula
   C. Wrong: hidden by the master cloud
   D. Wrong: hidden by the Bok globule
   E. None of these

9. _____ are small, highly variable nebulae often found in galactic clusters.
   A. T Tauri stars
 * B. Herbig-Haro objects
   C. Bok globules
   D. Hayashi blobs
   E. None of these

10. Young, rapidly rotating variable stars surrounded by an expanding gas and dust cloud are _____.
 * A. T Tauri stars
   B. Herbig-Haro objects
   C. Bok globules
   D. Hayashi blobs
   E. None of these

11. Near young star clusters, it is common to find dark clouds, usually 1000–100,000 AU across with densities at least a million times that of interstellar space. These clouds are called _____.
   A. T Tauri stars
   B. Herbig-Haro objects
 * C. Bok globules
   D. Hayashi blobs
   E. Stars

12. Objects often found in young star clusters include _____.
   A. T Tauri stars
   B. Bok globules
   C. Red giants
 * D. Both A and B
   E. All three, A, B, and C

13. The process of nuclear fusion in which protons directly collide to form deuterium is called the
   A. Carbon cycle
 * B. Proton-proton cycle
   C. Deuterium process
   D. Collision process
   E. Direct process

14. Stars of the Sun's mass or less primarily operate on the _____ while they are on the main sequence.
    A. Carbon cycle
    * B. Proton-proton cycle
    C. Triple-alpha process
    D. Protein cycle
    E. None of these

15. The nuclear process that involves collisions between hydrogen and carbon to finally (after a few steps) produce helium is the _____.
    A. Direct process
    * B. Carbon cycle
    C. Proton-proton cycle
    D. Triple-alpha process
    E. None of these

16. Stars more massive than 1.5 $M_\odot$ primarily generate their energy while on the main sequence by the

    _____.
    A. Direct process
    * B. Carbon cycle
    C. Proton-proton cycle
    D. Triple-alpha process
    E. None of these

17. The proton-proton cycle dominates when central temperatures are
    A. Less than 15 K
    B. Less than 15,000 K
    * C. Less than 15 million K
    D. Greater than 15 million K
    E. Greater than 100 million K

18. The carbon cycle dominates when the central temperatures are
    A. Less than 15 K
    B. Less than 15,000 K
    C. Less than 15 million K
    * D. Greater than 15 million K
    E. Greater than 100 million K

Problem Involving Optional Mathematical Equation from Another Chapter

19. (Optional Equation VIII) A T Tauri star consists of an A star of $T = 9000$ K and luminosity of 4×10^{28} joules/s and is surrounded by a spherical cocoon nebula at 3000 K. Use the Stefan-Boltzmann law to calculate the size of the nebula. The nebula's radius is _____ AU.*
    A. 5.7
    B. 57
    * C. 570
    D. 5700
    E. 390
    (Assume that energy radiated by star = energy radiated by nebula. Use $E = \sigma T^4 A$ with T temperature and A area of nebula, $E = 4 \times 10^{28}$ joules/s [one joule/s = 1 watt].)

Essay

1. Describe three kinds of observational data that are interpreted as indicating present-day star formation.
2. Draw an H-R diagram and show the approaching path to the main sequence (simplest model) for a 1 M_o and a 10 M_o, assuming you could see through the cocoon nebula. How would the cocoon nebula modify this?
3. List at least three of the four features of young, forming stars that tie in with the evidence we have about the nebula that surrounded our own Sun.
4. Describe Herbig-Haro objects.
5. Describe T Tauri stars.
6. Comment on the old concept of "fixed stars" as permanent, immovable objects on the distant "celestial sphere."

Word Practice (* denotes other selected words from the chapter.)

1. The nebula surrounding a forming star is the _____ nebula.*
2. Newly formed stars are very bright for short periods, known as the ____ ____.*
3. Our solar system is relatively _____, so all stars did not form at the same time.*
4. Dense enough interstellar nebula may collapse under the pressure of _____ ____.
5. A cloud of gas and dust in space is called a(n) _____.*
6. Fragmentation appears to be an almost _ consequence of the cloud collapse process.*
7. The plural of nebula is _____.*
8. _____ globules are small (1000–100,000 AU), dark clouds with a density about a million times that of normal interstellar space.*
9. ____ ____ exist that are younger than the species *Homo* Sapiens.*
10. The high-luminosity phase is often referred to as the ___ ____.*
11. We know that stars are forming _____.*
12. ___ ___ ___ are believed to represent a transitional stage between newly formed stars with opaque nebulae and stars that have blown off their cocoons.
13. The theory of _____ _____ seems to have a good basis because all stages of star formation are reasonably well understood.
14. A(n) __ __, such as an open star cluster, shows that star formation occurred recently.*
15. ___ __ are small, highly variable nebulae often found in clusters.*
16. _____ occurs on shrinking protoclusters to form individual stars.
17. _____ fields can provide magnetic support for molecular clouds.
18. The _____ _____ is part of the Orion star-forming region.*
19. _____ stars are very faint in the visible range but are bright in the 1–2 micrometer range.*
20. The _____ region is a young star-forming region.*
21. _____ is an example of a black dwarf.*
22. The _____ _____ nebula is a dark, round cloud that obscures part of the Milky Way in the Southern Hemisphere.*
23. In a(n) _____ jet, gas flows out in two narrow streams in opposite directions.
24. The _____ theory enables us to calculate how collapsing clouds should fragment.*
25. The intense emission from OH and H_2O molecules in molecular clouds is caused by _____ emission.*
26. A _____ is a cloud of gas and dust that is cool enough and dense enough to contract gravitationally.

27. A star which has started form to form but has not yet reached the main-sequence is called a _____ sequence star.
28. Objects more massive than planets but with a masses less than 80 times Jupiter's mass are called _____ dwarfs.
29. A star on the _____ _____ generates sufficient energy from nuclear fusion to halt the collapse process.
30. A star is said to be _____ main sequence when it just begins to generate energy by nuclear fusion.
31. Main sequence stars of the Sun's mass and less generate their energy by the _____ chain reaction.
32. Main sequence stars with 1.5 times the solar mass or more generate their energy by the _____ cycle.

Answers to Word Practice

1. cocoon
2. high-luminosity phase
3. young
4. gravitational contraction
5. nebula
6. inevitable
7. nebulae
8. Bok
9. short-lived stars
10. Hayashi phase
11. today
12. T Tauri stars
13. star formation
14. short-lived cluster
15. Herbig-Haro objects
16. subfragmentation
17. magnetic
18. Orion nebula
19. infrared
20. Orion
21. Jupiter
22. Coal Sack
23. bipolar
24. Jeans
25. maser
26. protostar
27. pre-main
28. brown
29. main-sequence
30. zero-age
31. proton-proton
32. carbon

Chapter 19
Stellar Evolution II: Death and Transfiguration

Answers to Problems in the Text

1. The center contracts and produces more total energy. (Thus, contraction may be viewed as the significant process.) This increased energy flow pushes the outer layers of the star farther out, where they become cooler. The available helium is soon consumed, so the energy flow outward declines and contraction begins again. Teachers should emphasize contraction in the evolutionary sequence.

2. Because they are so bright that we can see them far away, we see an exaggerated sample. The more numerous red main-sequence stars are so faint that we do not see them at such a great distance.

3. Blue-shifted absorption lines around M giants and supergiants and Wolf-Rayet; O and B stars; P Cygni stars; novae; supernovae with visibly expanding nebulae. The expansion of the Crab nebula has been measured photographically.

4. a. Stars of mass less than 1.4 $M_\odot$. Slightly more massive stars may shed enough mass. Thus, the limit might be 6 $M_\odot$ initially.
    b. Medium mass stars 12–30 $M_\odot$ initially.
    c. High-mass stars 30–100 $M_\odot$ initially.
    d. White dwarf.

5. It burns its fuel much more rapidly and with a process that requires this higher rate. A main sequence B3 has an absolute magnitude of possibly -4 compared with the Sun's +5, so it loses 4000 times as much energy/s but has only 10 times the fuel.

6. When the star collapses, it rotates faster. Even after the outer layers are blown off, the remaining matter keeps shrinking and reaches a higher spin rate.

7. Theorists in the 1930s predicted objects such as neutron stars and black holes long before they could be observed. Without means to test the predictions, these predictions lay forgotten in the journals until observational techniques were available. Accidental discovery of neutron stars led to the realization that the theory could now be tested. This strongly spurred observations in the 1970s. Black holes are not yet completely understood. More observational evidence is needed.

Advanced Problems

8. a. $V_{circ} = \sqrt{GM/R}$; $G = 6.67 \times 10^{-11}$,
        $M = M_\odot = 1.99 \times 10^{30}$ kg; $R = R_\oplus = 6.38 \times 10^6$ m
        $V_{circ} = 4.56 \times 10^6$ m/s $= 4560$ km/s $= 1.5\%$ speed of light
    b. $V_{circ} = \sqrt{2}\, V_{circ} = 6450$ km/s $= 2.1\%$ speed of light
    c. Both values are $\sqrt{M_\odot/M_H}$ times values for Earth.
        $\sqrt{M_\odot/M_H} = 577$
    d. White dwarf.

9. $E = \sigma T^4 A$; for star $*$, $L_* = \sigma T_*^4 A_*$.

    Evolution to the right on the H-R diagram means T is decreasing.
    If $L_* =$ constant and T_* decreases, A_* must increase.: $A_* =$ area, so size is increasing.

10. $L_* = \sigma T_*^4 A_*$

    $L_{WD} = \sigma T_{WD}^4 A_{WD} \leftarrow$ white dwarf (WD)

    $L_{MS} = \sigma T_{MS}^4 A_{MS} \leftarrow$ main sequence (MS) of same spectral class

    $T_{MS} = T_{WD}$, so $\dfrac{L_{WD}}{L_{MS}} = \dfrac{A_{WD}}{A_{MS}}$. If $A_{WD} < A_{MS}$, then

    $L_{WD} < L_{MS}$, so white dwarf is below main sequence.

11. We are concerned with material that moves at right angles to the line of sight so we can take distance
    = 500 parsecs = constant. First find how big the cloud must be to resolve it.

    $\dfrac{\alpha"}{206,265} = d/D$; $D = 500$ parsecs $= 500 \times 3 \times 10^{16}$ m, $\alpha = \dfrac{1}{2}$ "

    $d = \dfrac{\alpha D}{2.06 \times 10^5} = \dfrac{5 \times 3}{2 \times 2.06} \times \dfrac{10^{18}}{10^5} = 3.47 \times 10^{13}$ m. The time this takes is

    $\dfrac{d}{\text{speed}} = \dfrac{3.47 \times 10^{13} m}{10^6 m/s} = 3.47 \times 10^7$ s $= 1.1$ years (Remember, 1 year $= \pi \times 10^7$ s.)

12. Use Wien's law, $L = 0.00290/T$ with L in meters and T in Kelvin degrees. For $T = 10^9$ K, we get

    $L = \dfrac{0.0029}{10^9} = 2.9 \times 10^{-3} \times 10^{-9} = 2.9 \times 10^{-12}$ m $= 0.0029$ nm

    This is X-ray.
    Such observation would not be possible on the ground since the atmosphere is opaque. See Chapter 5.

13. For the ideal gas, Kinetic Energy (KE) = $(3/2)kT$, where $k = 1.38 \times 10^{-23}$ in SI units. So KE $= 3.5 \times 10^{-13}$ and: $J = (3/2) \times 1.38 \times 10^{-23} T$, which gives: $T = 1.7 \times 10^{10}$ K $= 17$ billion K.
    If the faster atoms move at about 4 times average, then since KE =: $(1/2)mv^2$, the highest KE is about
    $16 = 4^2$, so T is about 1 billion K. We should also consider the possibility that both particles are
    moving, so the relative velocity would be used. This reduces the temperature by a factor of 2.

14. There would be no change in the Earth's orbit or the orbital velocity. At 1 AU the Newtonian
    universal law of gravity is unchanged, and still $F = GM$ m/r^2. Since the mass is unchanged, so is the
    force on the Earth and the circular velocity is still

    $\sqrt{\dfrac{GM}{R}}$.

Sample Test Questions

True-False

1. When a star first moves off the main sequence, its photosphere expands. T
2. When a star first moves off the main sequence, it's surface gets cooler. T
3. Stars that become supergiants have a mass greater than 6 $M_\odot$. T
4. A star begins burning helium as soon as it leaves the main sequence. F

5. The helium flash is the turning of the entire star into helium. T
6. FG Sagittae is an example of a giant star. F
7. Most variable stars represent pre-giant stages. F
8. The instability strip is a nearly horizontal region of the H-R diagram. F
9. Low-mass ($<0.4\,M_\odot$) stars never become variable stars. T
10. The Hertzsprung gap is a vertical band nearly empty of stars. T
11. A star of the Sun's mass may become a black hole. F
12. White dwarfs are about the size of our planet. T
13. White dwarfs are kept from collapsing by the Pauli exclusion principle. T
14. White dwarfs always have a mass greater than $1.4\,M_\odot$. F
15. A neutron star can be as small as a few kilometers in diameter. T
16. Pulsars may have solid surfaces. T
17. The event horizon surrounds black holes. T
18. Small black holes ($<10^{12}$ kg) may radiate energy. T
19. Cygnus X-1 is believed to contain a black hole. T
20. A main sequence B3 star has about ten times the mass of the Sun and therefore has about ten times as much potential nuclear fuel. This means it will spend more time on the main sequence than the Sun. F
21. When stars with mass greater than about 4 solar masses leave the main sequence they evolve into supergiants. F

Multiple Choice

1. The helium of a star begins to burn when the star is
*   A. At the extreme right top of the giant region
      B. At the extreme left top of the giant region
      C. Leaving the main sequence
      D. Approaching the main sequence
      E. It never burns.

2. For a star to become a supergiant, its mass must be greater than about _____ $M_\odot$.
      A. 0.1
      B. 0.6
      C. 1
*   D. 6
      E. 16

3. Most stars become variable stars _____ the red giant stage.
      A. Before
*   B. After
      C. Instead of
      D. During
      E. Between

4. Which is the correct order of evolutionary stages for a medium-mass star?
      A. Main sequence, black dwarf
      B. Main sequence, variable star, giant, white dwarf
*   C. Main sequence, giant, variable star, white dwarf
      D. Main sequence, giant, white dwarf, variable star
      E. None of these

5. Hot stars resembling O stars except for their expanding gaseous shells (shown by ionized carbon, nitrogen, and helium) are called
   A. M-giants
   B. Supergiants
 * C. Wolf-Rayet stars
   D. Main sequence
   E. Novae

6. The variability of Cepheids is caused by
   A. Ionized hydrogen
   B. Doubly ionized hydrogen
   C. Ionized helium
 * D. Doubly ionized helium
   E. None of these

7. An example of a fast-evolving supergiant is
   A. M5
   B. The Crab nebula
   C. Mira
 * D. FG Sagittae
   E. Cygnus X-1

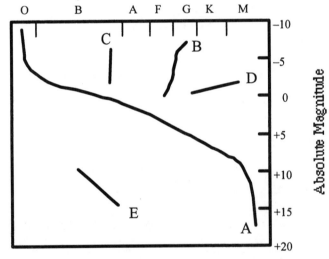

8. The line on the diagram that indicates the instability strip is
   A. A
 * B. B
   C. C
   D. D
   E. E

9. If one of the lines on the diagram is the instability strip, the Hertzsprung gap is
   A. A
   B. B
 * C. C
   D. D
   E. E

10. The Chandrasekhar limit is
    A. The upper limit of size for all stars
    B. The upper limit of mass for all stars
* C. The upper limit of mass for white dwarfs
    D. The lower limit of mass for white dwarfs
    E. The maximum mass a star can have without becoming variable sometime in its life

11. The Chandrasekhar limit is about _____ $M_\odot$.
    A. 0.8
* B. 1.4
    C. 2.3
    D. 6
    E. 59

12. Supernovae can be as bright as magnitude _____.
    A. 20
    B. 3
    C. 0
    D. -3
* E. -20

13. Supernovae explosions result from _____.
* A. Neutrino emission
    B. Proton absorption
    C. Electron absorption
    D. Gas loss
    E. Star collisions

14. The period of the Crab nebula pulsar is about
    A. 0.33 years
    B. 0.33 months
* C. 33 milliseconds
    D. 3.3 seconds
    E. 33 seconds

15. The supernova remnant for stars with masses between 12 and 30 $M_\odot$ is most likely a(n) _____.
    A. G2 star
    B. white dwarf
    C. black hole
* D. neutron star
    E. exohole

16. A good analogy of how a neutron star is a pulsar is a _____.
    A. Blinking neon sign
* B. Lighthouse
    C. Greenhouse
    D. Metronome
    E. Traffic light

17. A _____ is so dense that its gravitational field keeps light from escaping.
    A. White dwarf
    B. Supergiant
    C. Neutron star
  * D. Black hole
    E. Shell star

18. The periods of variation in light output of certain classes of _____ are known to be related to their absolute magnitudes.
    A. Binary stars
  * B. Variable stars
    C. White dwarfs
    D. Red stars
    E. None of these

19. The surface surrounding a black hole where the escape velocity is the speed of light is the _____.
    A. Photon sphere
    B. Singularity
    C. Last surface
    D. Einstein-Rosen bridge
  * E. Event horizon

20. Refer to the diagram above. Of the plots in the diagram, ____ shows the period-luminosity behavior for Cepheids.
    A. A
  * B. B
    C. C
    D. D
    E. E

Essay

1. Describe why and how Cepheid variables oscillate.
2. List and describe three types of stars that blow off mass.
3. Describe why neutron stars pulse.

4. Describe some of the paradoxical properties of black holes.
5. How were the early analysis of white dwarfs and the prediction of neutron stars historically related to the development of the atomic bomb?
    (Main point: The studies of high-density jamming together of atoms as a part of nuclear physics led to developments in both astrophysics and weapons technology.)
6. Discuss how evolved stars may lose mass.

Word Practice (* denotes other selected words form the chapter.)

1. A(n) _____ _____ is a planet-sized, super-dense star.
2. The ____ ____ is a vertical band on the H-R diagram that is nearly empty of stars.*
3. The ___ ____ ____ keeps the electrons in a white dwarf from collapsing further.*
4. The stars of 1–5 $M_\odot$ form __ __ after they leave the main sequence.*
5. The ___ ___ gives a value for the upper mass limit of white dwarfs.
6. The ____ effect describes the motion of main sequence stars toward the giant region.*
7. A(n) ____ is a pulsating radio source believed to be a rapidly rotating neutron star.
8. The variations in Cepheid stars are caused by a(n) _ layer of doubly ionized helium.*
9. _____ holes are surrounded by an event horizon.
10. Light loses energy as it travels away from a gravitating body. This causes the gravitational _____.
11. The balance between pressure and gravity is termed ___ equilibrium.*
12. __ ___ have regular variations in light with periods related to the intrinsic brightness.
13. Doubly ____ ____ provides a dam that drives the Cepheid variables.*
14. _____ stars are similar to O stars except for their expanding gaseous shells.*
15. A star that varies irregularly is called a(n) _____ _____.*
16. When matter is squeezed so densely that only the electrons provide the support, we have _____.
17. When the gravitational pressure in a star is able to overcome the electric repulsion and collapse the atoms, a(n) ____ ____ is formed.
18. A star with more than 6 $M_\odot$ will evolve into a(n) ___ as it leaves the main sequence.
19. The _____ _____ is a near-vertical region of the H-R diagram in which Cepheid and RR Lyrae variables are found.*
20. A rapidly rotating neutron star may appear as a(n) _____.
21. A(n) _____ _____ is a star that varies in brightness.
22. _____ _____ is the fastest-evolving supergiant known.*
23. A(n) ___ ____ results when a star becomes so small that even light cannot escape.
24. The ___ ___ around a black hole is defined as that surface from which no radiation can escape.
25. The _____ is the most energetic of all stellar explosions.
26. The sudden increase in the density of a supergiant's core is called _____ collapse.
27. The sudden release of neutrinos during core collapse is called the _____ _____.*
28. X-ray _____ are produced when a layer of helium around a neutron star becomes thick enough to fuse.*
29. One of the principles of special _____ is that the speed of light is the same to all observers.
30. The _____ theory of relativity tells us that gravity distorts space.
31. The _____ radius gives us the size of a simple black hole.
32. Betelgeuse, a cool bright red star is an example of a ____ _____.
33. The _____ _____ process generates energy by fusing helium into carbon.
34. Since it occurs very rapidly. the helium burning in giant stars is called a _____ _____ .
35. The glowing bubble of expanding gas surrounding a mass-shedding star is called a _____ nebula.
36. The first step in the death of a massive star takes only seconds as _____ _____ occurs producing heavy elements.

37. The expanding nebula surrounding the location of a supernova is called a supernova _____.
38. The disk of matter slowly spiraling into a black hole is called the _____ disk.

Answers to Word Practice

1. white dwarf
2. Hertzsprung gap
3. Pauli exclusion principle
4. giant stars
5. Chandrasekhar limit
6. funneling
7. pulsar
8. opaque
9. black
10. redshift
11. hydrostatic
12. Cepheid variables
13. ionized helium
14. Wolf-Rayet
15. irregular variable
16. degenerate matter
17. neutron star
18. supergiant
19. instability strip

20. pulsar
21. variable star
22. FG Sagittae
23. black hole
24. event horizon
25. supernova
26. core
27. neutrino burst
28. bursters
29. relativity
30. general
31. Schwarzschild
32. red giant
33. triple-alpha
34. helium flash
35. planetary nebula
36. explosive nucleosynthesis
37. supernova
38. accretion

Chapter 20
Interstellar Atoms, Dust, and Nebulae

Answers to Problems in the Text

1. The thicker atmosphere and dust are able to scatter the blue light better than the red. The blue has been bent away from the line of sight. Looking away from the Sun, we see that scattered light.

2. Because the dust on Mars is red, it reflects red light better than blue.

3. Two ways: (1) Strong radiation pressures and stellar winds stir up nearby interstellar material. (2) They lose mass and even explode as supernovae.

4. More and more carbon compounds of greater and greater complexity are being found—even some that could make biologically significant compounds. So carbon chemistry seems the same elsewhere in the universe.

5. (See Table 20-1.) Masses range from $0.1\ M_\odot$ to $100,000\ M_\odot$. Since stars form in clusters, we expect those nebulae associated with star formation to have masses hundreds to thousands of times that of the Sun. Dark and emission nebulae behave this way.

6. Emission nebulae must, by definition, be near a hot star to be excited enough to have emission lines. Solar-type stars are not hot enough to cause emission nebulae over a significant volume of space.

7. Planetary nebulae are expanding. They are bubble-like shells thrown off by stars, perhaps in a cyclic sequence, whereas emission nebulae are chaotic gas clouds within which hot, young, violent stars are forming.

Advanced Problems

8. N = total number of atoms = $(4/3)\pi r^3 n$, where n = number per unit volume and r = size. Take r = 10 atoms/cm^3, $N = 10^{57}$ atoms; then:

$$r^3 = \frac{3N}{4\pi n} = \frac{3 \times 10^{57}}{4 \times 3.14 \times 10/\text{cm}^3} = 2.38 \times 10^{55}\ \text{cm}^3, \text{ so } r = 2.88 \times 10^{18}\ \text{cm} = 0.96\ \text{parsecs}$$

   a. Much larger than the solar system, by a factor of 10,000 in linear size.
   b. Small compared to the dark and emission nebulae in Table 20-1, all of which (except 1) have a larger density.

9. a. $0.005 = v/c = v/(3 \times 10^8\ \text{m/s})$
   $v = 1.5 \times 10^6\ \text{m/s} = 1500\ \text{km/s}$
   b. $D = 1.5 \times 10^3$ parsecs $= 4.5 \times 10^{19}$ m in one year $\alpha = 0''2$
   $\alpha/2.06 \times 10^5 = d/D$

$$d = \frac{\alpha D}{2.06 \times 10^5} = \frac{9 \times 10^{18}}{2.06 \times 10^5} = 4.36 \times 10^{13}\ \text{m}$$

   So, in one year, it expands 4.36×10^{13} m; hence, in one second

$$v = \frac{4.36 \times 10^{13}\text{m}}{\pi \times 10^7\,\text{s}} = 1.39 \times 10^6 \text{m/s} = 1390\ \text{km/s}$$

c.   Agree to within 11 parts in 150 = 0.073. Agree to within 7.3%.

10. Use escape velocity $= (2GM/R)^{1/2}$, where $M = 100$ solar masses and R is the distance from the center. We also have

$(1/2)\, mv^2 = (3/2)kT$, where $m = 1.67 \times 10^{-27}$ kg. Then $v = \sqrt{\dfrac{3kT}{m}} = 1.58 \times 10^5$ m/s,

while the escape velocity = 210 m/s. Thus, the cloud clearly continues to expand.

Sample Test Questions

True-False

1.   The interaction of any wavelength of radiation with matter depends only upon the wavelength and is independent of the size of the particles making up the matter. F
2.   An atom is excited if one or more electrons are knocked completely out of the atom. F
3.   When molecules absorb light, they affect a range of wavelengths (bands) rather than discrete, individual wavelengths. T
4.   The sky of the Earth is blue because more blue than red light is scattered by air molecules. T
5.   The most common gas in interstellar space is sodium. F
6.   Metastable states are states of atoms with unusual electron distribution that last for several minutes. T
7.   Metastable states give rise to forbidden lines. T
8.   The gases in space are too rare for molecules to form. F
9.   The 21-cm radiation can be emitted by atomic hydrogen. T
10. Interstellar obscuration is caused by hydrogen gas. F
11. The interstellar grains (dust) are from 0.0001 to 0.011 mm in size. T
12. The interstellar dust is spherical in shape. F
13. The redder the light, the more energy each photon carries. F
14. In HII regions, the hydrogen gas is neutral. F
15. The Orion nebula is an emission nebula. T
16. At 1000–2000 nm, the brightest object in the sky is Eta Carinae. T
17. The Gum nebula has an angular diameter of 6°. F
18. Planetary nebulae are more irregular in shape than the larger emission nebula. F
19. An interstellar cloud is believed to contain only gas. It is observed that there are absorption bands in light from a star passing through the cloud. Thus, the cloud probably contains molecules. T
20. When dust absorbs light its affects a range of wavelengths (bands) rather than discrete individual wavelengths. T
21. Metastable states are electronic states of atoms with unusual distributions that last for times long when compared to most similar electronic states. T
22. Only five interstellar molecules have been discovered. F
23. Molecules are believed to form in cocoon nebulae around young stars. T
24. The interstellar grains (dust) are from one-hundredth to twice the wavelength of visible light in size. T
25. The electromagnetic fields of a polarized wave vibrate in all directions. F
26. The light scattered through dust clouds is polarized, this is an indication that the dust particles are spherical. F
27. The shorter the wavelength of the radiation the more energy each photon contains. T
28. Cooler sources radiate more blue light than hot sources. F

Multiple Choice

1. The interaction between radiation and matter depends upon
    A. The wavelength of radiation
    B. Types of particles
    C. Sizes of particles
    D. Both A and C
*   E. All three, A, B, and C

The following diagram is for questions 2–4.

Gas Cloud

2. Where in the diagram will you see absorption lines added to the star's spectrum by the gas cloud?
    A. A
    B. B
*   C. C
    D. D
    E. E

3. Where in the diagram will you see bright emission lines from the gas cloud?
    A. A
*   B. B
    C. C
    D. D
    E. E

4. Where in the diagram will you see the source reddened by the gas cloud? (*Note:* Gas clouds do not cause reddening.)
    A. A
    B. B
    C. C
*   D. D
    E. E

5. The bluer the light, the _____ each photon contains.
*   A. More energy
    B. Less energy
    C. More wavelength
    D. None of these
    E. More speed

The following diagram is for questions 6 & 7.

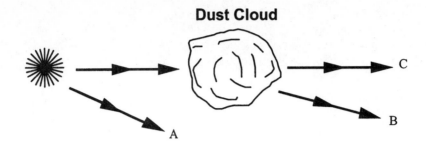

Dust Cloud

6. Where in the diagram will you see only redder light from the star?
   A. A
   B. B
   * C. C
   D. D
   E. E

7. Where in the diagram will you see the cloud glowing bluish?
   A. A
   * B. B
   C. C
   D. D
   E. E

8. Calcium and _____ provide the major absorption lines in HI regions.
   A. Helium
   B. Gold
   C. Uranium
   D. Oxygen
   * E. Sodium

9. In addition to interstellar gas and dust, five interstellar molecules have been found.
   A. Correct
   B. Wrong: no gas known
   C. Wrong: no dust known
   * D. Wrong: over 30 known
   E. Wrong: both C and D

10. The 21-cm radiation from HI regions happens when
    A. Two molecules collide
    B. Two atoms collide
    * C. The spin of the electron in a hydrogen atom flips with respect to the spin of the nucleus
    D. An O or B star is near
    E. Both B and D occur

11. One of the interstellar molecules found is an amino acid.
    - A. Correct
    - B. Wrong: Two are.
    - C. Wrong: Three are.
    - D. Wrong: But the spectrum of bacteria has been found.
    - * E. Wrong: No amino acids have been found, only two molecules that could make an amino acid.

12. The interstellar grains (or dust) are
    - * A. Small, smoke-like particles
    - B. All the same size
    - C. Spherical
    - D. Both A and C
    - E. All three, A, B, and C

13. Planck's law relates _____.
    - A. The change in wavelength to radial velocity
    - B. The break in radiation to temperature
    - * C. The wavelength of light to energy per photon
    - D. The luminosity to temperature and source size
    - E. None of these

14. HI regions contain mainly ionized hydrogen, while HII regions contain mainly neutral hydrogen.
    - A. Correct
    - B. Wrong: Replace hydrogen with helium.
    - * C. Wrong: Interchange HI and HII.
    - D. Wrong: Both B and C changes are needed.
    - E. Wrong: HI regions contain mainly helium dust, and HII regions contain mainly helium gas.

15. To exist, HII regions need _____ .
    - A. An M star
    - B. A source of radiation longer than 91.2 nm
    - * C. A source of radiation shorter than 91.2 nm
    - D. Sodium atoms
    - E. Both A and B

16. Clouds that look brighter than the background by virtue of emitted or scattered light are called _____ nebulae.
    - A. Planetary
    - B. Dark
    - * C. Bright
    - D. Crab
    - E. Emission

17. Clouds rich in dust silhouetted against a bright background region are called _____ nebulae.
    - A. Planetary
    - * B. Dark
    - C. Bright
    - D. Reflection
    - E. Emission

18. Several bright stars seem to have been ejected at high speed from the Orion nebula. They are called runaway stars.
    * A. Correct
    B. Wrong: called ejected stars
    C. Wrong: seem to be approaching the nebula, not leaving
    D. Wrong: called injected stars
    E. Wrong: both C and D are needed

Problems Involving Optional Mathematical Equations from Other Chapters

19. (Optional Equation I) The Crab nebula was seen about 925 years ago (1 year $\cong \pi \times 10^7$ s). It is about 2200 parsecs from us and appears at 4.7 minutes of arc. The linear size of the nebula (when the light we now see left the nebula) was _____ parsecs.
    A. 0.1
    B. 0.3
    * C. 3
    D. 30
    E. 100

20. (Optional Equation VII) In the last 925 years (approximately) since the Crab nebula was first seen, the nebula has appeared to expand at an average rate of 1550 km/s. Neglecting the turbulence of the expansion, what should the average Doppler shift be in the light from the outer parts of the nebula in the side toward us?
    * A. 0.5% blue
    B. 0.5% red
    C. 5% blue
    D. 5% red
    E. No shift

Essay

1. Describe the two main principles that govern what happens when light from a star passes through clouds of interstellar atoms, molecules, and dust grains.
2. Explain why the sunset is red and the sky is blue.
3. List the five main properties of the interstellar grains.
4. Name and describe three of the four types of interstellar regions.
5. Describe some of the interesting properties of the Orion nebula.
6. Describe some of the interesting properties of the Eta Carinae nebula.

Word Practice (* denotes other selected words from the chapter.)

1. _____ are bright nebulae close enough to a hot star that ionization or excitation has occurred.*
2. The ____ ____ is an effect of dust that makes objects look redder.
3. _____ nebulae are bright nebulae that are near enough to a star to reflect measurable light.*
4. _____ scattering causes the sky to appear blue.*
5. Entries in the New General Catalog are identified by ____ ____.*
6. _____ of an interstellar gas occurs when electrons are knocked to a higher energy level.
7. _____ are interstellar clouds that look brighter than the background.*

8. _____ nebulae are tight, expanding spherical shells of gaseous material.*
9. The Vela pulsar lies at the center of _____ which appears to have an angular diameter of 60°.*
10. High-speed stars racing out from the center of the Orion nebula are called _____.*
11. _____ nebulae are clouds rich in dust silhouetted against bright background clouds or against a star-rich region.*
12. Regions where hydrogen is neutral are called _____ regions.
13. A cloud in space is called a(n) _____.
14. Cold regions (~ 10 K) of dark clouds of dust and gas are ___ ___.
15. _____ such as sodium produce prominent absorption lines.
16. _____ occurs when electrons are knocked out of atoms.
17. _____ causes the red appearance of the Sun at sunset.
18. Interstellar _____ cause reddening and general dimming of starlight.*
19. _____ tells us that hotter sources emit more blue light than cooler sources.*
20. Interstellar grains cause a general dimming of starlight called _____.
21. The _____ is a strange emission nebula near the Coal Sack region.
22. _____ arise from unusual states of interstellar atoms.
23. _____ were assigned in 1781 to non-stellar objects, including the particularly vivid nebulae.*
24. The ____ ____ is a star-forming region about 460 pc from us.
25. _____ states are possible for interstellar atoms because the density of material is so low.*
26. _____ regions contain ionized hydrogen.
27. Neutral hydrogen emits radiation at about _____ wavelength.
28. _____ identify nebulae in the Index Catalog.*
29. _____ law relates photon energy to light wavelength*.
30. A _____ is a very hot cloud of gas created by a supernova.*
31. Cold regions of dark clouds are comprised of _____ molecules.
32. Regions of space where the molecules have been superheated by supernovae comprise the ____ _____ _____.

Answers to Word Practice

1. emission nebulae
2. interstellar reddening
3. reflection
4. Rayleigh
5. NGC numbers
6. excitation
7. bright nebulae
8. planetary
9. Gum nebulae
10. runaway stars
11. dark
12. HI
13. nebula
14. molecular clouds
15. interstellar atoms
16. ionization

17. Rayleigh scattering
18. grains
19. Wien's law
20. interstellar obscuration
21. Eta Carinae nebula
22. forbidden lines
23. Messier numbers
24. Orion nebula
25. metastable
26. HII
27. 21-cm
28. IC numbers
29. Planck's
30. superbubble
31. interstellar
32. hot interstellar medium

Chapter 21
Companions to Stars

Answers to Problems in the Text

1. Space program, binary stars. In 1827, Xi Ursa Majoris, a binary in Ursa Majoris, was found to fit a Keplerian ellipse.

2. Often highly elliptical orbits in binaries. In multiples, the relative inclination of orbits may vary; that is, for most multiple star systems (open), there is no common *plane of the system*. The masses of companions in known star systems are "of course" much greater than planetary masses.

3. Close binaries have a different mass distribution than open binaries. The text mentions one coplanar triple star system, possibly related to a planetary system.

4. All known novae have occurred in either known or suspected binary systems. Apparently, mass transfer moves the smaller star into the nova state. Supernovae are not related to binaries.

5. The 3 $M_\odot$ will evolve faster and transfer some mass to the 1 $M_\odot$ star. This may make the 1 $M_\odot$ star unstable. The 1 $M_\odot$ star, now having extra mass, will evolve faster than before. When the 1 $M_\odot$ star (now possibly more massive) becomes a giant, matter is transferred to the 3 $M_\odot$, which may become a nova.

6. The matter density would be higher in a region of star-cluster birth. Thus, that nearby stars would form—or protostars fission—is much likelier in clusters.

Advanced Problems

7. Very nearly that of the Earth. One approach is to use Kepler's third law as modified by Newton: $(M_1 + M_2)P^2 = r^3$,
   where M = mass in $M_\odot$, P = period in years, and r = distance in AU. For Earth, $(1 + \text{small})1^2 = 1^3$. For $M_2 = 0.05$,

   $(1 + 0.05)P^2 = 1^3 \rightarrow P^2 = \dfrac{1}{1.05}$; $P = 0.985$ years

   Students may either neglect the 0.05 and get $P = 1$ year or use $V_{circ} = \sqrt{GM/R}$ and period $= 2\pi/V$ and again get $P = 1$ year.

8. $V_{circ} = \sqrt{GM/R}$; $G = 6.67 \times 10^{-11}$, $M = 2 \times 10^{30}$ kg
   $R = 7.8 \times 10^{11}$ m
   $V_{circ} = 1.31 \times 10^4$ m/s $= 13.1$ km/s
   a. This agrees with the velocity for Jupiter (as it must).
   b. $\sqrt{2} \times 13.1$ km/s $= 18.5$ km/s

9. Since $5M \gg 0.5M$, $V_{circ} = \sqrt{\dfrac{GM}{R}}$; $G = 6.67 \times 10^{-11}$, $M = 5\,M_\odot = 10^{31}$ kg, so using $R = \dfrac{GM}{V^2}$

$(4.7 \times 10^4 \text{ m/s})^2 = \dfrac{GM}{R}$ which gives $R = \dfrac{6.67 \times 10^{-8} \times 10^{31}}{(4.7)^2 \times 10^8}$ m $= 3.02 \times 10^{11}$ m $= 2$ AU.

If we use Kepler's law as we did in question 7, get $(5 + .05)P^2 = R^3$; $P = \dfrac{2R}{V}$ (V in AU/year).

$5.5 \dfrac{4\pi^2 R^2}{V^2} = R$; $R = \dfrac{5.5 \times 4\pi^2}{V^2}$, so $V = 4.7 \times 10^4$ m/s $\times \dfrac{\text{AU}}{1.5 \times 10^{11} \text{m}} \times \dfrac{\pi \times 10^7 \text{s}}{\text{year}}$

So $V = 9.85$ AU/year; $R = \dfrac{5.5 \times 4 \times \pi^2}{(9.85)^2} = 2.25$ AU

Expect the first method to have an error of $(0.5)/5 \sim 10\%$, which is about the difference given by the two approaches.

10. Since the problem does not give a radius, we can give only relative data.
    a. $v = (GM/R)^{1/2}$. Let the orbital radius be R (in AU) and $M = 10$ solar masses, so $v = (10/R)^{1/2} \times V$, where V is the Earth's orbital velocity.
    b. $F = GMm/R^2$. Since M changes from 10 to 4 solar masses, $F_{afterward}/F_{before} = .4$.
    c. Neglect any direct forces from the explosion. Then from part a, the new orbital speed for circular orbit is $(4/10)^{1/2} = .64$ of the old, so it is going too fast for circular motion and hence it probably escapes.

Sample Test Questions

True-False

1. All optical doubles are true binaries. F
2. The first discovery of gravitational orbital motion beyond the solar system was Xi Ursa Majoris. T
3. The brighter star in a binary is denoted by the letter B for brighter. F
4. If orbital motion of a pair of stars is revealed by periodic Doppler shifts, we have a Doppler binary. F
5. A plot of brightness versus time is called a light curve. T
6. Binary systems revealed by the superposition of spectral lines from stars of two different temperatures are astrometric binaries. F
7. All estimates and counts give more than 50% of all stars as single stars. F
8. Close binaries are those binary systems that are close to us. F
9. Close binaries may be related to planetary systems. T
10. The material in each lobe of the Lagrangian surface is bound to the star in the other lobe. F
11. In contact binaries, both lobes of the Lagrangian surface are filled. T
12. One-half of all novae are believed to be binary systems. F
13. W Ursa Majoris stars are contact binaries. T
14. The only way binary or multiple-star systems can form is by common condensation. F
15. Many seemingly single stars probably have companions that are not massive enough for us to detect. T
16. We are more likely to observe a visual binary system in which the stars are widely separated. T
17. We are more likely to observe a visual binary system in which the stars are not widely separated. F
18. All estimates and counts give over 50 percent of all stars as single stars. F
19. Single stars are believed to be more common than binary star systems. F
20. No more than about one-half of all novae are believed to have occurred in binary systems. F

21. Nova explosions may be caused by catastrophic instabilities in a red giant star occurring when the red giant, which has exhausted all its own nuclear fuel, suddenly receives a new layer of burnable hydrogen from its binary companion, the white dwarf. F

22. One of the problems with the fission theory is that it does not explain how contact binaries are formed. F

23. The only way binary or multiple star systems can form is by subfragmentation. F

24. Theories of binary star formation in which a fast spinning protostar splits in two are called common condensation theories. F

25. Astronomers classify physical binaries according to methods of detecting them. T

26. Not all optical doubles are true binaries. T

27. The brighter star of a binary pair is not always the primary. T

28. If orbital motion of a pair of stars is revealed by periodic Doppler shifts we have a Doppler binary. F

29. In a spectroscopic binary it is always possible to resolve the individual stars. F

30. The center of mass of a star system is called its barycenter. T

31. Astrometric binaries can give us estimates on stellar sizes. F

Multiple Choice

1. A gravitationally associated pair of stars, both of which can be separately observed, is called a(n) _____ binary.
   A. optical
   B. spectrum
   C. eclipsing
   D. astrometric
 * E. visual

2. If what appears to be a single star undergoes wavy motions, we know it as a(n) _____ binary.
   A. visual
   B. spectroscopic
   C. optical
 * D. astrometric
   E. spectrum

3. Spectroscopic binaries show Doppler shifts. This means we measure their
   A. temperatures
   B. colors
 * C. radial velocities
   D. tangential velocities
   E separation

4. If the spectrum of a star shows spectral lines both of a hot and of a cool star, we have a(n) _____ binary.
   A. spectroscopic
 * B. spectrum
   C. visual
   D. eclipsing
   E. heliometric

5. A reasonable estimate of the percentage of stars that are multiple is _____%.
   A. 3
   B. 5
   C. 10
   D. 20
* E. 60

6. Most multiple stars differ from planetary orbits in that
   A. orbits are often highly elliptical
   B. orbits have all values of inclination
   C. they obey Kepler's laws
* D. both A and B
   E. all three, A, B, and C

7. In a contact binary, _____ Lagrangian lobe.
   A. one star fills its
   B. neither star fills its
* C. both stars fill their
   D. only one star has a
   E. there is no

8. There is evidence that all supernovae are members of binary systems.
   A. correct
   B. wrong: only about 50% D.
* C. novae, not supernovae
   D. both B and C changes needed
   E. None of these

9. Only the evolution of the more massive star in a close binary system is affected by the presence of the other star.
   A. correct
   B. wrong: Only the less massive is affected.
   C. wrong: The only effect is in triple systems.
* D. wrong: Both are evolutionary affected.
   E. wrong: Neither is evolutionary affected.

10. Which of the following is a contact binary?
* A. W Ursa Majoris
   B. Cygnus X-1
   C. Alpha Centauri
   D. Barnard's star
   E. None of these

11. In Algol, the originally more massive star has transferred matter to the originally less massive. Thus, the more massive star is now on the main sequence and the less massive is a white dwarf.
   A. correct
   B. wrong: The less massive has transferred matter to the more massive.
   C. wrong: The more massive is a white dwarf.
* D. wrong: The less massive is a giant star.
   E. wrong: Both C and D changes are needed.

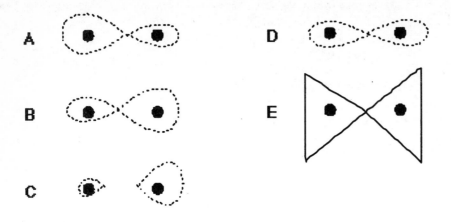

12. Which of the above figures best represents the Lagrangian surface for a binary system of equal mass?
    A. A
    B. B
    C. C
 * D. D
    E. E

13. Which of the above figures best represents the Lagrangian surface for a binary system with the stars of unequal mass?
    A. A
    B. B
    C. C
 * D. both A and B
    E. both A and C

14. Which of the following is a binary system that is also a strong X-ray source?
    A. Ursa Majoris X-3
 * B. SS-433
    C. Algol
    D. W Ursa Majoris
    E. Polaris

15. Formation of binary stars by chance encounter is the principle behind the _____ theories of binary star formation.
 * A. capture
    B. fission
    C. condensation
    D. encounter
    E. van de Kamp

Problems using Kepler's third law as modified by Newton

16. A star of 1 solar mass has another star rotating about it with a sidereal period of 10 years at 5 AU distance. The mass of second star is _____ solar masses.
    A.
    * B. ¼
    C. ½
    D.
    E. 2

17. A star of 2 solar masses has another star rotating about it with a sidereal period of 10 years at 6 AU distance. The second star has a mass of _____ solar masses.
    A. 0.06
    B. 0.9
    C. 9.6
    D. 0.76
    * E. 0.16

18. The separation (in AU's) of a star of 3 solar masses rotating about one of 7 solar masses with a period of 10 years is _____.
    A. 3
    B. 7
    C. 4
    * D. 10
    E. 35

19. A binary system consists of two equal stars of 2 solar masses each. If they are 4 AU apart, what is the sidereal period of the system?
    A. 2 years
    * B. 4 years
    C. 8 years
    D. 10 years
    E. 12 years

Essay

1. Give four of the six types of physical binary star systems classified according to the method of detecting them. For each, give the detection method. Discuss whether these types are physically different in origin, and so on.
2. Discuss the estimates of the incidence of multiplicity.
3. Give the main stages in the evolutionary path of a close binary that at first had neither star filling its Lagrangian lobe but ended up with both lobes filled. Assume the masses were initially very unequal.
4. Briefly describe and name the three groups of theories of binary star origin.

Word Practice (* denotes other words from the chapter.)

1. _____ are the results of binary star evolution.*
2. The ___ ___ ___ is a measure of the probability of a star's belonging to a multiple system.*

3. If observational effects tend to make observational data non-representative of the whole population, we have _____ _____.
4. In _____ binary systems, our line of sight is such that the stars pass in front of each other.
5. In _____ binary systems, the two stars are touching and share a common envelope.
6. The _____ theory proposes that binaries form by one star splitting into two.*
7. A plot of luminosity versus time for a binary system is called a(n) _____ curve.
8. A pair of co-orbiting stars is called a(n) _____ star.
9. According to _____ theories of binary formation, the stars of a binary system formed from separate sub fragments of a single cloud.*
10. In _____ _____, both stars fill their Lagrangian lobes.
11. _____ double stars are not co-orbiting.*
12. Eclipses in binary systems are detected by plotting the _____.*
13. _____ are binaries in which both stars fill their Lagrangian lobes.
14. _____ binaries are revealed by motions measured with respect to background stars.
15. _____ binaries show both Doppler shift and eclipses.*
16. A(n) _____ _____ of binary stars would have the two stars forming separately and later becoming gravitationally bound.*
17. In _____ binaries, we can resolve both stars.
18. As binary stars age, matter can be transferred across the Lagrangian surfaces, leading to different _____ than for single stars.*
19. _____ binaries are detected by observing spectral lines characteristic of stars at two different temperatures.*
20. In _____ binaries, the stars pass in front of each other and have measurable Doppler shifts.*
21. The _____ surface separates the regions where matter is bound to the individual stars of a binary from the region where the matter is in common.*
22. A(n) _____ consists of two stars gravitationally bound.
23. The Lagrangian surface of a binary system has two _____.*
24. _____ star systems contain three or more stars.
25. Xi Ursa Majoris was the first binary system shown to obey _____'s laws.*
26. _____ is an unusual eclipsing binary in that the less massive companion is the more evolved giant.*
27. In _____ binaries, orbital motion is detected by periodic Doppler shifts in spectral lines.
28. The _____ surface separates regions about binary stars into regions with possible orbits that belong only one star from the region belonging to both stars.
29. The large number of _____ pulsars found in globular clusters suggests that binary neutron stars can exchange matter.
30. The optical identification of a few _____ bursters suggests they are extremely bright and scattered throughout the universe at great distances.
31. _____ bursters are mostly found near the galactic center and are believed to be due to neutron stars in binary systems.
32. Recent discoveries of _____ planets support the theoretical arguments that other planetary system exist.

Answers to Word Practice

1. novae
2. incidence of multiplicity
3. selection effects
4. eclipsing
5. contact
6. fission

17. visual
18. evolution
19. spectrum
20. eclipsing spectroscopic
21. Lagrangian
22. physical binary

7. light
8. binary
9. subfragmentation
10. contact binaries
11. optical
12. light curve
13. contact binaries
14. astrometric
15. eclipsing spectroscopic
16. capture theory

23. lobes
24. multiple
25. Kepler
26. Algol
27. spectroscopic
28. Roche
29. millisecond
30. gamma-ray
31. X-ray
32. extrasolar

Chapter 22
Star Clusters and Associations

Answers to Problems in the Text

1. O and B stars are young stars. Open clusters are young enough that the O and B stars have not "burned out." Since they are massive, they are hot and so burn their hydrogen rapidly, at a great rate, making them the brightest main sequence stars. Globular clusters are old enough that the O and B stars have run out of fuel and become faint stars, such as supernova remnants. The next most massive stars have evolved to giants.

2. Globular clusters (so many stars).
   Globular clusters.
   Globular clusters.

3.

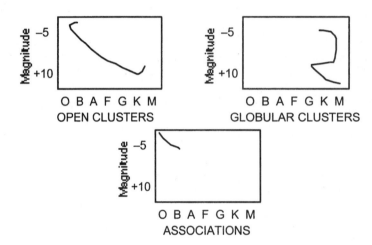

4. We might see 10,000 stars as close as, if not closer than, the Centaur's system. The sky would be a lively spectacular at night. If we were at 1 AU from a G star, it would still be easy to tell night from day. However, many globular clusters are X-ray sources, so internal conditions might be bad for us.

Advanced Problems

5. Volume with diameter 4 parsecs $V = \frac{4}{3}\pi r^3 = \frac{4}{3}\pi \left(\frac{4}{2}\right)^3 = 33.5$ parsecs^3.

   In 33.5 parsecs^3, there are 350 stars $\rightarrow$ 10.4 stars/parsecs^3, so there is a volume of 1/10.4 parsecs^3 per star. Set this equal to a volume and find the size of the volume. Make the volume a cube; a side of the cube is separation of

   $$\left(\frac{1}{10.4}\right)^{1/3} = (9.62 \times 10^{-2})^{1/3} \quad 0.5 \text{ parsecs.}$$

   In solar neighborhood, about 1 parsec separation. About a factor of 2 in separation or $2^3 = 8$ in density.

6. Again, $V = \dfrac{\pi d^3}{6} = 114$ parsecs^3 or $\dfrac{2 \times 10^5}{114} = 176$ stars/parsec^3.

   Separation $= \left(\dfrac{1}{176}\right)^{1/3}$ parsec $= 0.178$ parsec.

   Near the Sun, 1 parsec separation.

   About a factor of 5.6 in separation or $(5.6)^3 = 176$ in density.

7. $\alpha''/206{,}265 = d/D$; $D = 10^3$ parsecs; $\alpha'' = 1''$.
   a. $d = (\alpha'' D)/(2.06 \times 10^5) = 4.9 \times 10^{-3}$ parsecs   1000 AU
   b. $D = 10 \times D$ of part a, so $d = 4.9 \times 10^{-2}$ parsecs $= 10{,}000$ AU

8. a. $V_{circ} = \sqrt{GM/R}$; $G = 6.67 \times 10^{-11}$, $M = 6 \times 10^{35}$ kg, so $R = 1.5 \times 10^{17}$ m

   $V_{circ} = [(6.67 \times 6/1.5) \times (10^{-11} \times 10^{35}/10^{17})]^{1/2} = (26.7 \times 10^7)^{1/2} = 1.6 \times 10^4$ m/s $= 16$ km/s
   b. Look for a Doppler shift in light from the stars at the edges of the cluster. But if the axis of revolution around the cluster points toward the Earth, it may be hopeless! If the orbital plane is properly oriented, shift is $\dfrac{v}{c} = \dfrac{16}{3 \times 10^5} = 5.4 \times 10^5$, so the change in wavelength is about 0.005% of the original wavelength, which might be possible to detect.

9. The small angle equation, $\dfrac{\alpha''}{2.1 \times 10^5} = \dfrac{d}{D}$ requires α'' to be in seconds of arc. The cluster measures about $1.4° = 4.8 \times 10^3{''}$. Then

   $d = \dfrac{4.8 \times 10^3}{2.1 \times 10^5} \times D = \dfrac{4.8 \times 10^3}{2.1 \times 10^5} \times 127$ parsecs $= 3.0$ parsecs,

   which compares favorably with the figure of 2 parsecs quoted in Fig. 22-3.

Sample Test Questions

True-False

1. Moderately close-knit, irregularly shaped groupings of stars are called globular clusters. F
2. Associations are called O associations or B associations, depending on whether the brightest stars are O or B. F
3. The Pleiades are an example of an open cluster. T
4. Cluster distances are determined by measuring parallaxes. F
5. Cepheid variables can be used as distance indicators. T
6. The open clusters lie in a disk in our galaxy. T
7. The globular clusters form a spherical cloud in our galaxy. T
8. About half of the identified open clusters are less than 100 million years old. T
9. Most open clusters are older than globular clusters. F
10. Most associations are more than 1 billion years old. F
11. Globular clusters are more than 12 billion years old. T
12. A sphere is the final stable state for a contracting, rotating, self-gravitating system with substantial initial rotation. F
13. Globular clusters should last less than 20 million years before breaking up. F
14. A disk is the final stable state for a contracting, rotating, self-gravitating system with substantial initial rotation. T

15. About half of the identified open clusters are more than 100 millions years old. F
16. Globular clusters are generally confined to the galactic plane. F
17. Globular clusters are probably less than 9 billion years old. F
18. Globular clusters should last less than 5 billion years before breaking up. F
19. Moderately close-knit, irregularly shaped groupings of stars are called open clusters. T
20. Most open clusters are old. F
21. Most open clusters are young. T
22. O associations have T Tauri stars as their prominent members. F
23. Open clusters are less massive than globular clusters. T
24. Open clusters are more massive than globular clusters. F
25. The open clusters in our galaxy, lie in the galactic disk. T
26. The point at which the stars of a cluster leave the main sequence is a measure of the cluster's age. T

Multiple Choice

1. Moderately close-knit, irregularly shaped groupings of stars 4 to 20 parsecs in diameter are called
   A. groupings
 * B. open clusters
   C. globular clusters
   D. associations
   E. clumps

2. Loose-structured, irregularly shaped groupings of stars very rich in O and B or T Tauri stars are called
   A. groupings
   B. open clusters
   C. globular clusters
 * D. associations
   E. clumps

3. Massive, tightly packed spherical, symmetrical groupings of stars are called
   A. groupings
   B. open clusters
 * C. globular clusters
   D. associations
   E. clumps

4. Some (or one) of the methods of measuring cluster distances are (is) by
   A. parallaxes
   B. star luminosities
   C. cluster diameters
 * D. both B and C
   E. all three, A, B, and C

5. Interstellar dust throws off estimates of cluster distances since it dims the stars. This effect can be corrected by measuring the amount of
   A. Doppler shift
   B. interstellar bluing
   * C. interstellar reddening
   D. both A and B
   E. both A and C

6. The most useful method of determining the distances of distant clusters is to use
   A. parallaxes
   * B. Cepheid variables
   C. star luminosities
   D. cluster diameters
   E. Doppler shifts

7. Which clusters lie in a spherical distribution about the center of our galaxy?
   A. associations
   * B. globular
   C. open
   D. peanut
   E. both A and C

8. Which clusters lie nearly in a disk (the plane of the galaxy)?
   A. associations
   B. globular
   C. open
   D. peanut
   * E. both A and C

9. A reasonable range for the ages of open clusters is _____ years.
   A. 1–30 million
   * B. 1–100 million
   C. 12–13 billion
   D. 1–10,000
   E. 10–40 billion

10. A reasonable range for the ages of associations is _____ years.
   * A. 1–30 million
   B. 1–100 million
   C. 12–13 billion
   D. 1–10,000
   E. 10–40 billion

11. A reasonable range for the ages of globular clusters is _____ years.
   A. 1–30 million
   B. 1–100 million
   * C. 12–13 billion
   D. 1–10,000
   E. 10–40 billion

12. Globular clusters are spherical rather than flattened because the initial angular momentum was
    A. high
    B. moderate
*   C. low
    D. Clockwise
    E. counterclockwise

The following diagrams are for questions 13–15.

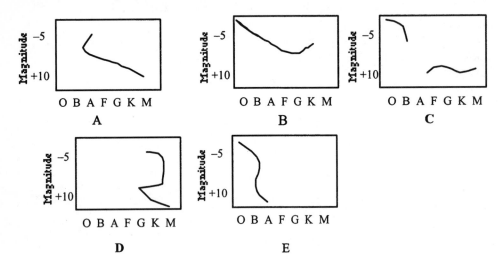

13. Which of the 5 diagrams above
    best represents the H-R diagram
    for an association?
    A. A
*   B. B
    C. C
    D. D
    E. E

14. Which of the 5 diagrams above
    best represents the H-R diagram
    for an open cluster?
*   A. A
    B. B
    C. C
    D. D
    E. E

15. Which diagram above best represents the H-R diagram for a globular cluster?
    A. A
    B. B
    C. C
*   D. D
    E. E

16. Globular clusters are sometimes X-ray sources. One (or more) possible explanations is (are)
    A. many neutron stars and black holes colliding
    B. high-mass black holes disrupting stars
    * C. neutron stars and black holes.capturing binary members and then transferring mass
    D. both A and B
    E. all three, A, B, and C

Essay

1. Name and describe the three types of clusters.
2. What are the three methods of determining cluster distances? Which is the best? (*Note:* Parallax is not a method used for determining cluster distances.)
3. Describe the distribution of the three types of clusters in our galaxy.
4. Discuss the origin of clusters.

Word Practice (* denotes other words for the chapter.)

1. The nearest cluster is the _____ _____ cluster.*
2. Interstellar _____ makes determination of cluster distances more difficult, but the associated reddening can be used to make a correction for this effect.*
3. The _____ of open clusters occurs because of fast-moving stars and tidal forces.*
4. _____ are often larger than open clusters and are rich in young stars.
5. The best method to determine cluster distances is to use __ __ stars.
6. _____ clusters are moderately close-knit, irregularly shaped groupings of stars.
7. Star ___ can be used to determine cluster distances by fitting the cluster to an H-R diagram.*
8. The ___ of globular clusters show that they formed with very little angular momentum.*
9. The _____ of globular clusters are all about 12.5 billion years.
10. Cluster _____ can be used to estimate cluster distances by applying the small angle equation.*
11. _____ clusters are massive, spherically symmetric star systems.
12. Some globular clusters are sources of _____ of irregular variation.*
13. _____ _____ have prominent T Tauri variables.*
14. _____ _____ have prominent O and B stars.*
15. _____, the most basic method of star distance measurement, are almost useless for clusters because most clusters are too far away.*
16. The _____ are an example of a naked eye, open cluster.*
17. The __ __ of a cluster can be used to estimate the age of the cluster.
18. _____ are basic groupings of stars of probable common origin.
19. The _____ of clusters of various masses depends on the density and temperature of the original diffuse medium.*
20. _____ is a globular cluster located about 13,000 parsecs from us.*
21. The process of _____ fitting involves using computer models to calculate the shape of the H-R Diagram plot for a cluster.
22. Open clusters are mostly _____. (age)
23. Globular clusters are mostly _____. (age)

Answers to Word Practice

1. Ursa Major
2. obscuration
3. disruption
4. associations
5. Cepheid variable
6. open
7. luminosities
8. dynamics
9. ages
10. diameters
11. globular
12. X-rays
13. T associations
14. O associations
15. parallaxes
16. Pleiades
17. H-R diagram
18. clusters
19. origin
20. M3
21. isochrone
22. young
23. old

Chapter 23
The Milky Way Galaxy

Answers to Problems in the Text

1. Take recorded history as 3000–4000 years. Use approximately 70 years for the time we have known about our galaxy. Using 3500 years for recorded history gives $\dfrac{3500 - 70}{3500} \times 100 = 98\%$.

2. The Milky Way appears as a relatively thin region lying on a great circle across the sky, although we are slightly out of the plane and can see part of one side of the nuclear bulge. That is, it cuts the celestial sphere in roughly two equal parts. If we were well above the plane of the Milky Way, the division of the sky would be uneven, with more sky above the Milky Way visible on the side on which we lie. Also, if we were above, we would be able to see the spiral arms and the disk more clearly.

3. The swarm of open clusters occupies a disk, whereas the globular clusters are distributed in a sphere. The open clusters are Population I, which is younger, whereas the Population II, older, stars are distributed in a more spherical volume. This implies that early star formation occurred before the collapse to a disk.

4. Calculate the center and size of the sphere that the globular clusters define. The size is the size of the galaxy. We can also use radar astronomy to measure the distances of HI clouds.

5. Assume that globular clusters are spherical in distribution. Calculate the distance and direction of this sphere's center. This is also consistent with the direction obtained from 21-cm hydrogen (HI) radiation.

6. First, we see spiral structure in certain other galaxies. Second, if we map open clusters, associations, nebulae, and so on, they fall into bands that can be interpreted as parts of spiral arms. Finally, the 21-cm radiation traces out details of the rest of the arm structure. The following objects reveal strong spiral structure: a, c, d, and f.

7. No. The stars' proper motions will cause them to appear to distort. Most constellations are composed of more than one cluster, so the changes will be extreme. Also, the stars will have gone halfway around the galaxy. Thus, we expect quite a bit of mixing and different neighbors.

8. From the point of view of the rest of the universe, it is the spiral-arm stars that are revolving about the galactic center. Although individual Population II stars are revolving about the galactic center, they have mixed orbits of all inclinations. The net sum of all this motion is no rotation with respect to external galaxies. High-velocity stars are halo stars. So it is the spiral arms that have systematic high velocity relative to the external galaxies.

9. Only old stars (Population II) are in the galactic halo. All original O and B stars have evolved off the main sequence. No new stars are forming there.

10. A 3-kiloparsec arm that is an expanding hydrogen cloud moving outward at 53 km/s; strong infrared and radio radiation from the center; our galaxy is similar to other galaxies that have bright, violent nuclei.

Advanced Problems

11. Distance to galactic center = 9 kiloparsecs = 9×10^3 parsec = D;

    $\alpha'' = 1''$, $d = (\alpha''D)/206{,}265 = \dfrac{9 \times 10^3}{2.06 \times 10^5}$ parsec = 4.4×10^{-2} parsec = 0.044 parsec

    a. No, dust blocks off visible light.
    b. Yes, if it is a radio source since radio waves pass through galactic dust. However, there would be no Doppler shift from which to get distances.

12. Convert 230 km/s to parsecs/year.

    $V = 230 \text{ km/s} \times \dfrac{\text{parsec}}{3 \times 10^{18} \text{cm}} \times \dfrac{10^5 \text{cm}}{\text{km}} \times \dfrac{\pi \times 10^7 \text{s}}{\text{year}} = \dfrac{2.3 \times \pi \times 10^{14}}{3 \times 10^{18}}$ parsec/year = 2.4×10^{-4}

    parsecs/year

    $\text{period} = \dfrac{\text{circumference}}{V} = \dfrac{2\pi \infty 9 \infty 10^3 \text{ pc}}{2.4 \infty 10^{-4} \text{ pc/year}} = 2.3 \times 10^8$ years = 230 million years

13. $V_{\text{circ}} = \sqrt{GM/R} \rightarrow M = RV^2/G$; $G = 6.67 \times 10^{-11}$, $R = 9 \times 10^3 \times 3 \times 10^{16}$ m = 2.7×10^{20} m

    $V^2 = (2.3 \times 10^5 \text{m/s})^2 = 5.3 \times 10^{10}$ m^2/s^2, so $M = \dfrac{2.7 \times 5.3 \times 10^{30}}{6.67 \times 10^{-11}} = 2 \times 10^{41}$ kg

    Two reasons why this is incorrect: (1) Value of r is only approximately known. (2) We made the approximation that all the mass of the galaxy is at the center.

14. Probable student response: Diameter 30,000 parsecs = 30,000 parsecs $\times$ 3.26 light-years/parsec= 100,000 light-years.

    In 70 years, it could go 70 light-years. $\% = \dfrac{70}{10^5} \times 100 = 0.07\%$

    This result is incorrect since rapidly moving clocks slow down; however, students do not have the background from this course to correctly calculate the result (at light speed, no time elapses). The results given in this and the next problem tell us how much time would pass on Earth for those who stayed behind.

15. Student response: The Orion nebula is 1600 years away at the speed of light. At 20 years per generation,

    number of generations $= \dfrac{1600}{20} = 80$. This result is incorrect: See comment after problem 14.

16. This problem is only an approximation since large relativistic effects would occur.
    a. $v = (GM/R)^{1/2}$, $M = 10^5$ solar masses, $R = 10$ AU; $v = 100 \times$ velocity of Earth in orbit
       Velocity of Earth in orbit = circumference/time = $2 \times \pi \times 1.5 \times 10^{11}$ m/($\pi \times 10^7$ s) = 3×10^4 m/s
       so $v = 3 \times 10^6$ m/s.
    b. $(1/2)mv^2 = (3/2)kT$, so $T = mv^2/(3k)$
       Assume hydrogen, so $m = 1.67 \times 10^{-27}$ kg and, $k = 1.38 \times 10^{-23}$ in SI. This gives T = 3.6×10^8 K.
    c. $L = \dfrac{0.00290}{T} = 8 \times 10^{-12}$ m = 8 pm (picometer)
    d. This is too short a wavelength to observe on the Earth's surface since the atmosphere is opaque. We need a space-based gamma ray detector.

Sample Test Questions

True-False

1. The first astronomer to confirm that the Milky Way was made of stars was Galileo. T
2. Herschel, in the late 1700s and early 1800s, counted many stars in the Milky Way. T
3. The first astronomer to put the Sun out toward one edge of the disk of the galaxy was H. Shapley. T
4. The overall diameter of the galaxy is 9000 parsecs. F
5. The disk shape of the spiral arms shows that this part of the galaxy has no net angular momentum. F
6. The spiral-arm structure of our galaxy is indicated by the distribution of O and B stars. T
7. Radio waves do not pass as easily through dust as visible light does. F
8. HII regions are most useful for mapping the distant parts of the galaxy's structure. F
9. The galaxy has spiral arms because matter is being jetted out at the center of the galaxy. F
10. The spiral arms can be explained by the density-wave theory. T
11. There are about 2×10^{11} stars in the galaxy. T
12. The mass of the galaxy is about 2×10^{30} kg. F
13. Population I stars are older than Population II stars. F
14. Population II stars have less-heavy elements than Population I stars. T
15. Population I Cepheids are the same as Population II Cepheids. F
16. The 3-kiloparsec arm is between us and the galactic center. T
17. Population I stars contain 1-4 per cent of their total mass in the form of elements heavier than hydrogen and helium and are younger than Population II stars. T

Multiple Choice

1. It is believed that the globular clusters are distributed spherically with a central concentration in the vicinity of the galactic center.
   * A. correct
     B. wrong: This describes the stars on spiral arms.
     C. wrong: This describes associations.
     D. wrong: They are disk-shaped with spiral arms, not spherical.
     E. wrong: They are centered about the Sun.

2. The Sun is about _____ kiloparsecs from the galactic center.
     A. 2.5–3.5
     B. 4.5–6.5
   * C. 6.5–8.5
     D. 8.5–10.5
     E. 10.5–12.5

3. The overall diameter of the galaxy is estimated at ____ kiloparsecs.
     A. 6–8
     B. 8–10
     C. 20
     D. 25
   * E. 30

4. The Sun's galactic motion is toward the center of the galaxy.
   A. correct
   B. wrong: The Sun is moving away from the galactic center.
   C. wrong: The Sun's motion is an elongated ellipse.
   * D. wrong: The Sun moves in a circular orbit.
   E. wrong: None of the above is correct.

5. The time it takes the Sun to travel around the galaxy is about _____ years.
   A. 240
   B. 2.4×10^5
   * C. 2.4×10^8
   D. 2.4×10^{11}
   E. 2.4×10^{24}

6. Spiral-arm stars that are farther from the galactic center than the Sun move more slowly than the Sun, while stars closer to the center move faster. This is called _____.
   A. splitting
   B. rigid body motion
   C. passing motion
   * D. differential rotation
   E. spiraling

7. Optically, we can see the parts of _____ arms of our galaxy.
   A. 1
   B. 2
   * C. 3
   D. 4
   E. 5

8. The reference direction for the galactic system is the _____.
   A. vernal equinox
   B. star Vega
   C. north point
   * D. galactic center
   E. celestial pole

9. Galactic latitude is measured
   * A. perpendicular to the plane of the Milky Way
   B. in the plane of the Milky Way
   C. perpendicular to the celestial equator
   D. by stars' proper motion
   E. none of the above

10. The general structure of the spiral arms of our galaxy can be mapped using _____.
    A. visible light
    * B. the 21-cm radiation of neutral hydrogen
    C. the 10-megahertz frequency of WWV
    D. both A and B
    E. all three, A, B, and C

11. We are able to see optically most of the spiral arms in our galaxy. These spiral arms are believed to be density waves.
    A. correct
*   B. wrong: Optically, we can see only nearby stars in spiral arms.
    C. wrong: The spiral arms are permanent in the sense that a star in the middle of a spiral arm remains in the middle of that arm.
    D. wrong: Both B and C are needed.
    E. misleading: The galaxy has no spiral arms; it is a globular galaxy.

Use the diagram to answer questions 12 and 13.

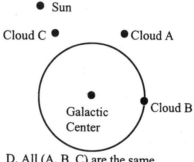

12. Which cloud will have the largest space velocity?
    A. A
*   B. B
    C. C
    D. D
    E. E

13. Which cloud will have the largest Doppler shift?
    A. A
*   B. B
    C. C
    D. D
    E. E

14. To understand why the spiral arms are not wound tighter than they are, it seems necessary to assume
    A. that the spiral arms are very young
    B. misleading: We are wrong about how tightly the spiral arms are wound.
*   C. that the spiral arms are density waves
    D. both A and C
    E. none of the above

15. The mass of the galaxy is about _____ kilograms.
    A. 3×10^{10}
    B. 3×10^{23}
    C. 2×10^{33}
*   D. 2×10^{42}
    E. 7×10^{69}

16. There are about _____ stars in the Milky Way galaxy.
    A. 3×10^{10}
    * B. 2×10^{12}
    C. 2×10^{44}
    D. 92×10^{42}
    E. 9×10^{57}

17. Which of the following are composed of Population I stars?
    A. globular clusters
    * B. spiral arms
    C. the corona
    D. both B and C
    E. all three, A, B, and C

18. Which of the following is not evidence for two types (or populations) of stars?
    A. stellar chemistry
    B. ages
    C. motions and orbits
    D. different types of Cepheid stars
    * E. All those listed are evidence for two populations

19. Which are the older stars in the galaxy?
    A. Population I
    * B. Population II
    C. Population A
    D. Population B
    E. Blue Stars

20. Which stars have virtually no elements heavier than hydrogen and helium?
    A. Population I
    * B. Population II
    C. Population A
    D. Population B
    E. Blue Stars

21. The galactic nucleus had a large energy release about _____ years ago, as shown by the 3-kiloparsec arm.
    A. 10 million
    B. 50 million
    * C. 100 million
    D. 1 billion
    E. 12 billion

22. Which of the following is not proposed as a condition that could have released large amounts of energy in the galactic center?
    A. unstable stars of very large mass undergoing nova
    B. stellar collisions
    * C. many K and M stars going through their life cycle
    D. dust falling on high-density, high-gravity objects
    E. All of the above are possible mechanisms.

23. The general vicinity of the center of our galaxy contains a strong gamma ray source so the nucleus of our galaxy is believed to contain a black hole.
    A. correct
    B. wrong — the nucleus does not show any evidence of a black hole
    * C. wrong — it is a compact radio source, the gamma ray source is not in the nucleus
    D. wrong — both B and C statements are correct.
    E. None of these

24. The point in the sky toward which the Sun appears to be moving is the _____.
    * A. solar apex
    B. local standard of rest
    C. peculiar velocity
    D. motion point
    E. Polaris

Problem Involving Optional Mathematical Equation from Another Chapter

25. (Optional Equation VII) A high-velocity star is approaching the Sun at 120 km/s. At what wavelength (approximately) would a 479.6 nm line be observed?*
    A. 477.6 nm
    * B. 479.4 nm
    C. 479.6 nm
    D. 479.8 nm
    E. 481.6 nm

Essay

1. Describe some of the problems astronomers had to overcome to discover the structure of our galaxy.
2. Describe how radio astronomy is able to map the spiral-arm structure.
3. Explain how the density-wave theory works.
4. Describe the modified coffee cup model (stochastic model) of the spiral arms.
5. Discuss three of the types of evidence for two stellar populations.
6. What are the three pieces of evidence for high-energy events in the galactic nucleus, and what are three possible mechanisms to cause these events?
7. Summarize the evolution of the galaxy.

Word Practice (* denotes other selected words form the chapter.)

1. The spiral arms are contained in the _____ of the galaxy.*
2. The galactic ____ is a spherical swarm of stars and globular clusters.
3. The _____ of our galaxy is its center.
4. ____ stars belong to the galactic halo and are usually Population II.*
5. ____ ____ is the coordinate from the galactic system that is measured in the plane of the Milky Way.*
6. The __ __ of our galaxy is best investigated with radio telescopes.*
7. ____ ____ ____ ____ is an imaginary point in the middle of our local swarm moving in a circular orbit around the galactic center.*
8. Two periodic motions may combine to produce the _____ that is the spiral arms.*
9. The ____ ____ stars are the younger stars in our galaxy.

10. _____ is the abbreviation for local standard of rest.*
11. Star formation is most rapid in the spiral _____ of our galaxy.
12. Galactic _____ is measured perpendicular to the Milky Way.*
13. The __ __ __ __ is about 12 billion years, so the spiral arms must be patterns.
14. The galaxy has a(n) _____ of about 30,000 parsecs.*
15. The _____ velocity of a star is its velocity relative to the LSR.*
16. The spiral arm ___ of the galaxy rotate about the nucleus in approximately circular orbits with a velocity that depends upon their distance from the galactic center.*
17. The _____ theory explains how the spiral arms can last so long.
18. The __ ____ is the point in the sky toward which the Sun appears to move.*
19. Both Cepheid II and _____ _____ _____ are Population II stars.*
20. One thousand parsecs equal one _____.
21. The period _____ of the Sun about the galactic center is 230 million years.*
22. _____ regions can emit 21-cm radiation.*
23. _____ rotation of the galaxy means that the period of rotation of a disk star depends upon its distance from the galactic center.*
24. The _____ of the galaxy is about 10^{11} $M_\odot$.
25. The _____ of the Population II stars more closely reflects the percentages of elements in the early galaxy than that of Population I stars.
26. The two types of _____ have different period-luminosity curves.*
27. _____ are used to map the spiral arm structure of our galaxy.
28. The ____ ____ runs along the center of the Milky Way.*
29. The ____ ____ stars comprise the older population of the galaxy.
30. _____ telescopes are the most useful for studying the spiral arm structure of our galaxy.*
31. The ____ of globular cluster stars differs from that of the disk stars.*
32. Our own galaxy is called the _____ _____ galaxy.
33. The old, red stars concentrated towards the center f the galaxy comprise the galactic ____ .
34. The _____ star-formation theory uses the chain-reaction nature of stellar formation to explain the spiral arms.

Answers to Word Practice

1. disk
2. halo
3. nucleus
4. high-velocity
5. galactic longitude
6. spiral (or galactic) structure
7. local standard of rest
8. pattern
9. Population I
10. LSR
11. arms
12. latitude
13. age of the galaxy
14. dimension (or diameter)
15. peculiar
16. stars
17. density-wave

18. solar apex
19. RR Lyrae stars
20. kiloparsec
21. revolution
22. HI
23. differential
24. mass
25. composition
26. Cepheids
27. 21-cm radio waves
28. galactic equator
29. Population II
30. radio
31. chemistry (or composition)
32. Milky Way
33. bulge
34. stochastic (coffee cup)

Chapter 24
The Local Galaxies

Answers to Problems in the Text

1. Spiral. Spiral and giant elliptical. Elliptical. (The largest and brightest galaxies, although rare, are probably giant ellipticals.)

2. Ordinary elliptical.

3. 670 kiloparsecs = 670 × 3.26 kilo-light years = 2.18×10^6 light years = about 2 million years

4. The one with the K spectrum would probably be an elliptical (predominant red giants); the one with B and A could not be an elliptical and would presumably be a spiral galaxy (Population I).

5. Galaxy size = 30 kiloparsecs; distance from Milky Way to Andromeda galaxy = 670 kiloparsecs, so separation is 670/30   24 disk diameters.

6. No. The local group has a common center of mass (barycenter). If there is a net rotation about this center, it would define an axis of rotation, but this would be hard to detect and has not been found. Distant galaxies recede from each other and appear to be directly receding from us also so that no axis of symmetry or rotation is known. Commonly, astronomers use the Milky Way galaxy.

7. They are too faint to be observed at those distances.

8. No. This only shows that star formation is going on at a rapid rate in these galaxies. The galaxies themselves may be very old.

9. Hot blue stars are young, the only other stars as bright as red supergiants, which are old stars. Young red stars are very faint. Star-forming regions would be expected to have young stars, the brightest of which are blue O and B.
    a. O and B stars evolve quickly. When star formation is slow, there is no longer a large source of Os and Bs, so they are not seen.
    b. Population I.

Advanced Problems

10. a. $\dfrac{\alpha''}{206,265} = \dfrac{d}{D} = \dfrac{40}{670}$, so $\alpha'' = \dfrac{40 \times 2.06 \times 10^5}{670} = 1.2 \times 10^4$ seconds of arc = 3°.

    This is six times the angular size of the Moon! But most of it is too faint to be seen. Consider the sky's appearance, if it were not so faint.

    b. $\alpha'' = \dfrac{d}{D} \times 2.06 \times 10^5 = \dfrac{3 \times 10^{-3}}{670} \times 2.06 \times 10^5 = 0.9''$. This is at the limit of resolution.

11. $\dfrac{\text{change in wavelength}}{\text{wavelength}} = \dfrac{v}{c} = \dfrac{0.165}{500}$. So, $v = 3.3 \times 10^{-4} c = 99$ km/s.

12. $V_{circ} = \sqrt{GM/R} \rightarrow M_{\odot}\dfrac{RV^2}{G}$,. This gives $M = \dfrac{4 \times 10^3 \times 3 \times 10^{16} \times [9.9 \times (10^4)]^2}{6.67 \times 10^{-11}}$

$= 1.8 \times 10^{40}$ kg or $10^{10}\, M_{\odot}$ .This is enough mass for 10 billion Suns or about 1/10 of our galaxy's mass.

Sample Test Questions

True-False

1. A galaxy's age depends upon its location on the "tuning fork" diagram. F
2. The Doppler shift can be used to determine the rotation of some other galaxies. T
3. The Magellanic clouds are satellite galaxies of the Milky Way. T
4. The Magellanic clouds are regular galaxies. F
5. The Tarantula nebula (30 Doradus) is believed to be the partially formed nucleus of the Large Magellanic cloud. T
6. The Magellanic clouds contain only Population I stars. F
7. Galaxies resembling our galaxy but without the spiral arms and dust are called elliptical galaxies. T
8. Galaxies tend to cluster in different-size groups. T
9. All elliptical galaxies are relatively small galaxies. F
10. The classification system for galaxies is often referred to as the "tuning fork" diagram. T
11. Approximately 70% of all galaxies are believed to be spirals. F
12. Our determinations of the distances to galaxies are not affected by errors in our estimates of distances to closer objects. F
13. Since they have few young (O) and (B) stars, elliptical galaxies are clearly older than spiral galaxies. F
14. The mass of a galaxy may be determined from the Doppler shift. F
15. The rotation of a galaxy may be determined from the Doppler shifts. T
16. The spiral-arm stars formed when the first stars were formed in the galaxy. F
17. Blue globular clusters contain only old Population II stars. F

Multiple Choice

1. The mass of a galaxy can sometimes be obtained from _____.
    A. Kepler's laws and the rotation speed of the galaxy
    B. the motion of binary galaxies
    C. Wien's law
  * D. both A and B
    E. none of these

2. Which of the following nearby galaxies is a spiral galaxy?
    A. Large Magellanic cloud
    B. Maffei I
    C. Draco system
  * D. both C and D
    E. Andromeda galaxy

3. Which of the following nearby galaxies is an elliptical galaxy?
   A. Large Magellanic cloud
   * B. Draco system
   C. Andromeda galaxy
   D. Maffei I
   E. both C and D

4. Which of the following nearby galaxies is an irregular galaxy?
   * A. Large Magellanic cloud
   B. Draco system
   C. Andromeda galaxy
   D. Maffei I
   E. both C and D

5. The Magellanic clouds are _____ galaxies.
   A. regular
   * B. irregular
   C. spiral
   D. elliptical
   E. intergalactic globular cluster

6. The chief importance of the Magellanic clouds to modern astronomy is that they
   A. are irregular galaxies
   B. have many O and B stars
   C. show that galaxies can have satellite galaxies
   * D. provide us with a collection of objects all at effectively the same distance
   E. none of the above

7. Which galaxies are dominated by Population II stars and have little gas or dust?
   A. spiral
   B. irregular
   C. intergalactic globular
   D. elliptical
   * E. both C and D

8. In the Andromeda galaxy, star formation seems to be occurring most rapidly in the
   A. nucleus
   B. inner arms
   * C. intermediate and outer arms
   D. halo
   E. misleading: Little or no star formation is occurring.

9. The galaxies near us (say out to 1000 kiloparsecs) are called ___.
   * A. the Local Group
   B. the nearby crowd
   C. the near ones
   D. M33
   E. Orion

10. A spiral galaxy whose central region is a bright, bar like object is called a _____ galaxy.
    A. bright, bar like
* B. barred spiral
    C. giant elliptical
    D. barred irregular
    E. barrel

The following diagrams are for questions 11–15.

A   B   C   D   E

11. Which galaxy is an EO galaxy?
* A. A
    B. B
    C. C
    D. D
    E. E

12. An SO galaxy?
    A. A
    B. B
    C. C
* D. D
    E. E

13. Which galaxy is an Sc galaxy?
    A. A
    B. B
    C. C
    D. D
* E. E

14. Which galaxy is an Sa galaxy?
    A. A
* B. B
    C. C
    D. D
    E. E

15. Which galaxy is an SBb galaxy?
    A. A
    B. B
* C. C
    D. D
    E. E

16. The classification scheme for galaxies is called Hubble's _____.
    A. classification scheme
*   B. tuning fork diagram
    C. two-pronged classification
    D. diagram
    E. relation

17. Galaxies with amorphous appearance, no sharp nucleus, and some gas and dust and Population II stars are called _____.
    A. elliptical
    B. spiral
    C. irregular I
*   D. irregular II globular cluster
    E. intergalactic

18. Elliptical galaxies comprise about _____% of all galaxies (counting intergalactic globular elliptical).
*   A. 70
    B. 50
    C. 25
    D. 15
    E. 3

19. Spiral galaxies comprise about _____% of all galaxies.
    A. 70
    B. 50
    C. 25
*   D. 15
    E. 3

20. A galaxy's place in the "Hubble's tuning fork" is probably determined by its _____.
    A. age
*   B. initial conditions of mass, rotation, turbulence, and so on
    C. mass
    D. both A and B
    E. both A and C

21. Which of the following correctly sequences distance-measurement techniques in order of increasing distance of applicability?
    A. tape measure, H-R diagram, trigonometric parallax, Cepheids, Hubble relation
    B. tape measure, Hubble relation, H-R diagram, trigonometric parallax, Cepheids
    C. Hubble relation, trigonometric parallax, Cepheids, tape measure, H-R diagram
*   D. tape measure, trigonometric parallax, H-R diagram, Cepheids, Hubble relation
    E. H-R diagram, tape measure, Hubble relation, Cepheids, trigonometric parallax

22. We can get the distances to some of the nearby galaxies by using _____.
    A. binary stars
    B. parallax
*   C. variable stars
    D. radar
    E. Doppler shifts

Essay

1. Describe the differences and similarities of spiral, elliptical, and irregular galaxies.
2. Describe the Hubble tuning fork classification scheme. Draw the relevant diagram.
3. Describe the Local Group: types of members, distribution in space, and so on.
4. Summarize how our theory of stellar evolution is successful in describing how similar galaxies of great (equal?) age could have widely different populations of stars.
5. Discuss the importance of the Andromeda galaxy in stellar evolution theory.

Word Practice (* denotes other selected words from the chapter.)

1. The differences in galaxies probably are due solely to different __ __, not to evolutionary effects of ages.*
2. The _____ of galaxies can be determined by measuring Doppler shifts and applying Kepler's laws.*
3. ___ ___ galaxies are spiral galaxies whose central regions are bright and bar like.*
4. _____ _____ stars are the older stars in the galaxy.*
5. _____ _____ stars are the younger stars in the galaxy.*
6. Our galaxy is a member of a cluster of galaxies called the __ ___.
7. The Magellanic _____ is a bridge of hydrogen that may connect the two Magellanic clouds to our galaxy.*
8. _____ galaxies show little or no structure.
9. Our galaxy is a(n) _____ galaxy.
10. In a close encounter of two galaxies the _____ interaction may distort the shapes of the galaxies, even if they do not collide.
11. _____ galaxies resemble giant globular clusters.
12. ____ galaxies do not have direct stellar collisions, but the interactions can strongly influence galactic evolution.*
13. The ____ ____ measures the amount of mass required to produce the same amount of stellar radiation. It is high in ellipticals.
14. ___ ___ clusters may be small examples of elliptical galaxies.*
15. The _____ galaxy is the nearest spiral galaxy to the Milky Way.
16. The _____ _____ is another name for 30 Doradus.*
17. _____ galaxies are the most common type in our group.
18. Small dark objects between a distant star and us can produce gravitational ___ that will reveal the existence of the dark objects.
19. The _____ galaxy is similar to our galaxy except that it is more open and has blue globular clusters.*
20. The ___ ___ of a galaxy, or region of a galaxy, will depend upon the material left for star formation.*
21. __ ___ is believed to be the partially formed nucleus of the Large Magellanic cloud.*
22. The _____ _____ are the two satellite galaxies of the Milky Way.
23. A(n) _____ _____ galaxy is like our galaxy except that the nucleus is bar-shaped.*
24. _____ galaxies are like our galaxy without the disk and spiral arm structure.
25. The assumption of the _____ of nature is that the laws of physics are the same everywhere in the universe.*
26. The ____ ____ is the structured ordering of distances to astronomical objects.
27. A ___ ___ is said to occur if your unit of measurement is found to be incorrect.*
28. Neglecting dust obscuration when determining distances is an example of a(n) _____ error.*
29. The type of error that unavoidably arises in a single measurement is a(n) _____ error. Repeating the measurement many times can reduce this error.*
30. Classifying galaxies by their appearance is a classification of galactic _____.

31. The _____ galaxies have a prominent bulge but lack spiral arms.*
32. ___ galaxies do not fit into the Hubble galaxy classification scheme.*
33. The term ___ brightness measures how diffuse a galaxy appears and thus tells us how hard the galaxy will be to detect against the sky background.*
34. The ____ function is a graph of the relative number of galaxies with different luminosities and different Hubble types.*
35. If something is the same in all directions it is said to be ____.*
36. If a quantity is different in different directions it is said to be _____.*
37. The ___ ratio for a galaxy is the ratio of its mass (in M_o) to its luminosity (in L_o).
38. If the mass/luminosity ratio is large there must be a large amount of _____ matter.*
39. If we plot the velocity of different parts of a spiral galaxy, we can determine the mass distribution. This plot is called a(n) _____ curve.
40. If we measure the velocities of individual stars in dwarf galaxies, the velocity _____ can be used to find the mass of the galaxy.*
41. Objects whose intrinsic sizes or brightness's are well known are called _____ _____.
42. The _____ of galaxies can be initially understood in terms of the stellar populations/.
43. If a large and a small galaxy collide, the larger absorbs the smaller. This is called galactic _____.
44. The theory of galaxy _____ is not yet complete although a number of reasonable scenarios were discussed in the chapter.

Answers to Word Practice

1. initial conditions
2. masses
3. barred spiral
4. Population II
5. Population I
6. Local Group
7. stream
8. irregular
9. spiral
10. tidal
11. elliptical
12. colliding
13. mass/luminosity ratio
14. intergalactic globular
15. Andromeda
16. Tarantula nebula
17. elliptical
18. microlensing
19. Triangulum
20. stellar population
21. 30 Doradus
22. Magellanic clouds
23. barred spiral
24. elliptical
25. uniformity
26. distance scale
27. scale error
28. systematic
29. random
30. morphology
31. SO
32. peculiar
33. surface
34. luminosity
35. isotropic
36. anisotropic
37. mass/luminosity
38. dark
39. rotation
40. dispersion
41. standard candle
42. evolution
43. cannibalism
44. formation

Chapter 25
Galaxies and the Expanding Universe

Answers to Problems in the Text

1. 1 parsec = 3×10^{16} m, 1 megaparsec = 10^6 parsecs = 3×10^{22} m, 1 mile = 1.609 km = 1.609×10^3 m

    so

    $$1 \text{ megaparsec} = \frac{3 \times 10^{22} \text{ m}}{1.609 \times 10^3 \text{ m/mile}} = 1.9 \times 10^{19} \text{ miles}$$

    The teacher should demonstrate how the dimensions must check out and show how this helps in setting up the problem; that is, show that "meters" cancels "meters," leaving miles.

2. a. Red shift.
    b. Velocity is 6700 km/s, receding. The red shift could be expressed as $\frac{v}{c} = \frac{6700}{3 \times 10^5} = 2.2 \times 10^{-2}$; a shift of 2.2%.
    c. They would reach the same conclusion about us that we have reached about them: We are receding from them at 6700 km/s.

3. They have small, bright centers that produce large, varying amounts of energy. A Seyfert nucleus, seen from too far away for the arms to be resolved, would resemble a weak quasar.

4. These imply that red shift is not entirely cosmological, so there may be another explanation for the red shift of quasars. If there were another explanation, we could not determine quasar distances from their red shifts.

5. Our galaxy is a relatively weak radio emitter. Radio galaxies will emit hundreds to millions more units of energy at radio wavelengths.

6. The farther out we look, the farther into the past we see. We see distant galaxies as they were many billions of years ago since they are billions of light-years away. Some of the most distant are more than 10 billion light-years away, so their light shows them as they were when our galaxy was just forming.

7. Assume where galaxies appear in this question that clusters of galaxies is what is meant.
    a. To answer this question we will need to make some assumptions. Assume the distribution is uniform for both the red and the blue shifted galaxies. Then the universe consists of two populations of galaxies. One population is receding from us and the other is approaching us. Possibly, depending upon how the shifts depends upon distance, the universe has passed its maximum expansion and is now collapsing or it had a contracting state that has now changed into an expanding state.
    b. In this case we live is a universe that is collapsing, but at a slower rate now than in the past.
    c. One possibility is that the universe is static and we are moving rapidly through it. If this is the intended interpretation desired, the red shifts must, as we scan across the sky, decrease to zero and then increase as a blue shift with the maximum red and blue shifts diametrically opposed.

Advanced Problems

8. Normal automobile speeds are less than 100 km/hour, that is, less than 28 m/s; hence, $\frac{v}{c} =$

    $\frac{28\,m/s}{3\times10^8\,m/s} = 10^{-7}$.

    Thus, the wavelength shift is only 1 part in 10 million—too small to detect since the band of frequency covered by a single radio station is very wide compared to this.

9. a.   Shift = 3.4 × wavelength = 3.4 × 500 nm = 1700 nm = 1.7 microns = 1.7 μm.
    b.   Fainter.
    c.   It would be extremely hard to detect. Visible radiation would be very faint since all visible light is shifted to red. Apparent temperature is very cool: $T = \frac{0.0029}{17\times10^{-3}} = 1700$ K.

    Also, it would not be as intrinsically bright in radio as a quasar, so we would not find radio telescopes helpful.

10. $V = 5700$ km/s; $V = Hr \rightarrow r = V/H$. If $H = 57$ km/s/Mpc, $r = \dfrac{5700\ km/s}{57\ km/s/\,Mpc} = 100$ Mpc.

    If $H = 100$ km/s/Mpc, $r = \dfrac{5700\ km/s}{100\ km/s/\,Mpc} = 57$ Mpc.

11. $\alpha" = (d/D) \times 2.06 \times 10^5$ If $H = 57$, $\alpha" = \dfrac{30\times10^3\,pc}{10^2\times10^6\,pc} \times 2.06 \times 10^5 = 60" = 1'$.

    If $H = 100$, $\alpha" = 105" = 1.8'$.

Sample Test Questions

True-False

1.   One possible source of the red shift of quasars is a strong gravitational field. T
2.   All galaxies are red-shifted. F
3.   All distant clusters of galaxies are red-shifted. T
4.   The red shift in a cluster of galaxies is found to be directly proportional to the distance when this distance can be determined by other means. T
5.   The relationship between velocity of recession and distance for clusters of galaxies is called Hubble's relation. T
6.   Since distant galaxies are receding from us, we are at the center of the universe. F
7.   The only possible interpretation of the red shift of galaxies is that it is a Doppler shift. F
8.   At least some observed red shifts may be gravitational red shifts. T
9.   Our galaxy is a radio galaxy. F
10. The radio radiation of most radio galaxies is synchrotron radiation. T
11. There is no evidence that galaxies ever collide. F
12. *Quasar* stands for quasi-stellar radium source. F
13. Many quasars have large red shifts. T
14. If the red shift of quasars is cosmological, we have no difficulty explaining their energy generation. F
15. If a source brightens and dims regularly with a period of one day, its size must not be larger than one light-day. T
16. A Mpc is smaller than a ly. F

17. A Mpc is larger than a ly. T
18. When we can find the distance independently, we find the further away a galaxy is, the less the red shift. F
19. When we can find the distance independently, we find the further away a galaxy is, the larger the red shift. T
20. Although all distant galaxies are receding from us, we are not at the center of the universe. T
21. Few quasars have large red shifts. F
22. One possible source of the red shift of quasars is a strong gravitational field. T
23. The discrepancy in red shift among different galaxies that seem to be in a cluster supports the cosmological red shift theory. F

Multiple Choice

1. 1 megaparsec = _____ parsecs.
    A. 100
    B. 1000
 * C. 10^6
    D. 10^9
    E. 10^{21}

2. If a cluster of galaxies is receding from us at 15,000 km/s, its distance, by the Hubble relation, is (approximately) ____ megaparsecs. (Take $H = 65$ km/s/Mpc.)*
    A. 23
 * B. 231
    C. 285
    D. 975,000
    E. 1,125,000

3. If r represents the distance to a nearby cluster of galaxies and V represents the velocity of recession of the cluster, Hubble's relation states that $r = HV$, where H represents Hubble's constant.
    A. correct
    B. wrong: applies to individual galaxies, not clusters
 * C. wrong: relation is $V = Hr$
    D. wrong: both B and C
    E. wrong: but none of the above

4. The cosmological theory of red shifts proposes that the red shifts of galaxies are __.
 * A. Doppler shifts
    B. gravitational forces
    C. photons losing energy
    D. both A and B or either
    E. both B and C or either

5. In a non-cosmological theory of red shifts, the red shifts of galaxies are ___.
    A. Doppler shifts
    B. gravitational forces
    C. photons losing energy
    D. both A and B or either
 * E. both B and C or either

6. The radio-emitting regions of most optically visible radio galaxies are often ____.
   A. larger than the optically visible galaxy
   B. concentrated in two lobes in either side of the galaxy
   C. associated with ordinary spiral galaxies
   * D. both A and B
   E. all three, A, B, and C

7. When two galaxies collide ____.
   A. many stellar collisions occur, releasing energy
   * B. their gas clouds collide, emitting radio waves
   C. their total angular momentum is changed
   D. both A and B
   E. all three, A, B, and C

8. Other than a Doppler shift, what is another possible cause of red shifts in quasars?
   A. rotational
   B. temperature
   * C. gravitational
   D. magnetic
   E. no other interpretation

9. A Seyfert galaxy
   * A. is a spiral galaxy with a small, bright region in its nucleus that shows broad, bright emission lines
   B. is an elliptical galaxy with a small, bright, nearly stellar-appearing nucleus
   C. has a relatively small size and high surface brightness
   D. is a supergiant elliptical found near the center of a cluster of galaxies
   E. is a highly irregular galaxy, completely amorphous, without any resolved stars

10. Quasars appear as
    A. spiral galaxies with extended nuclei
    * B. strong radio sources of small sizes that are sometimes optically identified with a starlike object (unresolved) and often have large, red-shifted spectral lines
    C. strong ultraviolet and infrared sources
    D. X-ray sources
    E. spherical globes, reddish in color

11. The cosmological interpretation of quasars gives which of the following properties to quasars with large red shifts?
    A. great distance
    B. relative proximity
    C. large amount of energy
    * D. both A and C
    E. none of these

12. The ratio of the change in wavelength to the emitted wavelength for the spectral lines of a galaxy is 2. What is the velocity of recession as a fraction of the speed of light? (Hint: You must use the relativistic Doppler formula since the shift is large.)
    A. 0.5
    * B. 0.8
    C. 0.90
    D. not enough information
    E. 0.99

13. A quasar radio signal varies by a factor of 5, returning to its original brightness about every two months. Hence, the radio-emitting region is no more than _____ in size.
    A. 1/2 light-month (1.2×10^{-2} megaparsecs)
    B. 1 light-month (2.5×10^{-2} megaparsecs)
    * C. 2 light-months (5×10^{-2} megaparsecs)
    D. 1 light-year (0.3 megaparsec)
    E. not near any of these

14. The noncosmological interpretation of quasars gives which of the following properties to quasars with large red shifts?
    A. great distance
    * B. relative proximity
    C. large amounts of energy
    D. both A and C
    E. both B and C

15. One distance indicator for elliptical galaxies relates the size of the galaxy to the ___.
    A. Hubble parameter
    * B. stellar velocity dispersion
    C. rotation rate
    D. spiral arm size
    E. ellipness

Essay

1. Describe two possible causes of the red shift of distant galaxies.
2. What are some of the mysteries that still confront us about galactic nuclei?
3. What are two of the interpretations of quasars given in the text?
4. Compare how much we know about galaxies and remote galaxy like objects with how much we know about planets in our solar system.

Word Practice (* denotes other selected words from the chapter.)

1. The possible associations of clusters of galaxies are called _____.
2. Since light travels at a finite speed, we see distant galaxies as they were millions of years ago. This is called the _____ time.
3. The theory of _____ _____ _____ states that red shifts are due to the Doppler effect of recession.
4. _____ are radio sources that often have large red shifts. If the red shifts are cosmological, many of these are the brightest objects known.
5. Hubble's _____ is a proportionality between distance and recession velocity for clusters of galaxies.
6. The cosmological interpretation of red shift has the universe _____.
7. A _____ universe would have a Hubble parameter of zero.*
8. We cannot see the details of very distant galaxies, but we can use them to study the _____ _____ structure of the universe
9. Galaxies with evidence of explosions in their nuclei or with brighter than normal nuclei are called _____ galaxies.
10. The term standard candle often refers to light while a well defined size is termed a _____ _____ rod.
11. One million parsecs are one _____.
12. The _____ Supercluster, to which our galaxy belongs can be seen as a high concentration of galaxies nearly at right angles to the Milky Way..
13. The _____ relation is the relative number of different Hubble types as it depends upon the environmental density.
14. An example of one of the theories of _____ _____ _____ is photons losing energy over long distances.*
15. __ __ relates the recession velocity of a cluster of galaxies to its distance from us.
16. _____ _____ are galaxies with bright centers.
17. Galaxies that are strong radio emitters are called _____ _____.
18. Observationally, most galaxies show a(n) _____ in their spectral lines.
19. _____ are low-density regions almost empty of galaxies.
20. __ __ or the bending of light caused by matter can serve as a probe for dark matter.
21. In general, the radiation emitted by processes that are not in equilibrium with the surrounding gas is called ____ radiation.
22. _____ emission is non-thermal radiation requiring the presence of a magnetic field.*
23. A long strongly emitting radio region extending from the nucleus of a galaxy is called a radio ____.
24. A galaxy containing a quasar is called a(n) _____ galaxy.
25. The number of quasars in a volume of space as a function of their absolute magnitude is called the ___ ___ function.*
26. One possible model for a quasar is a(n) _____ black hole.
27. The reservoir of hot gas and dust that feeds the black hole in that quasar model is called a(n) ___ ___.
28. Clouds of gas within a parsec of a quasar are ionized producing ___ ___ clouds.
29. Radiation from a relativistic jet is focused in the direction of the jet. This is called ___.*
30. The finite velocity of light and relativistic motion near the line of sight causes an apparent _____ motion.
31. Radio sources with one sided jets and rapid optical variability are called _____.*
32. Galaxies are not usually along, they form _____ of galaxies.
33. Light from quasars contains many quasar _____ _____. These lines give us information about the matter between the quasar and us.

Answers to Word Practice

1. superclusters
2. look-back
3. cosmological red shifts
4. quasars
5. parameter
6. expanding
7. static
8. large scale
9. active
10. standard measuring
11. megaparsec
12. Local
13. morphology-density
14. non-cosmological red shifts
15. Hubble law
16. Seyfert galaxies
17. radio galaxies
18. red shift
19. Voids
20. gravitational lensing
21. non-thermal
22. Synchrotron
23. jet
24. host
25. quasar luminosity
26. supermassive
27. accretion disk
28. emission line
29. beaming
30. superluminal
31. blazer
32. measuring rod
33. cluster
34. absorption lines

Chapter 26
Size and Structure of the Universe

Answers to Problems in the Text

1. There is only one universe to observe; thus, it may not be susceptible to some kinds of scientific analysis.

2. Such a telescope could show us detailed structures of nearby galactic nuclei and of distant galaxies, the shapes of quasars, and so on. It could also help us tell which of the curves in Fig. 26-4 describes the universe.

3. The universe is expanding. Olbers' paradox can (or must) be explained, which the Newtonian model cannot do. The universe has clearly evolved—witness more quasars at large red shifts (z) than at small z.

4. The universe is expanding, so light from distant stars is red-shifted, and we do not believe the universe is old enough to be in thermal equilibrium.

5. No. When we look across large distances, we are looking back in time, so we see the universe at an earlier epoch. In fact, this quasar count is taken to support the big bang cosmologies against the steady state cosmology.

6. a. Cosmological red shifts; excess luminosity of distant galaxies (Fig. 26-9); distribution of quasars; darkness of the night sky.
   b. Distribution of quasars; lack of an explanation of 3-K isotropic blackbody radiation.

Advanced Problems

7. $W = 0.00290/T$; W is wavelength, T is temperature.
$$W = \frac{0.00290}{10^6} = 2.9 \times 10^{-9} \text{ m} = 2.9 \text{ nm}$$

   a. This wavelength is completely blocked by our atmosphere. A telescope in space would be needed to see it. This wavelength is soft X-ray.
   b. This extremely short wavelength is absorbed by the Earth's atmosphere. A space telescope would not have this problem.
   c. We want a red shift to change 2.9 nm to 500 nm. That is,
$$\frac{\text{change in wavelength}}{\text{wavelength}} = \frac{500 - 2.9}{2.9} = 171 \gg 1.$$

   This is a Doppler factor of $171 = z$, which is much larger than any known. Nor is it likely to be detected because of the 16-billion-year horizon.
   d. Use Stefan-Boltzmann law, $E = \sigma A T^4$. $\dfrac{E_*}{E_\odot} = \dfrac{\sigma A_* T_{*4}}{\sigma A_\odot \, T_\odot{}^4}$. We want to compare unit areas of each object.

   So, $\left(\dfrac{E_*}{E_\odot}\right)_{\text{unit area}} = \dfrac{T_{*4}}{T_\odot{}^4} = \left(\dfrac{10^6 \, K}{5.7 \times 10^3 \, K}\right)^4 = 5.4 \times 10^6$

   A unit surface radiates 5.4×10^6 times as much as the Sun.

8. 91 nm = 9.1×10^{-10} m

$\Delta\lambda/\lambda = [(1 + v/c)/(1 - v/c)]^{1/2} - 1 = 3.36$,

where the last equality follows from Chapter 25, problem 11a. Thus, $\Delta\lambda = 3.36 \times 9.1 \times 10^{-10}$ m = 3.06×10^{-9}, which is receding, so add $\lambda + \Delta\lambda = \lambda_{observed} = 3.97 \times 10^{-9}$ m. Shifted from the UV to the visible.

Sample Test Questions

True-False

1. The earliest cosmologies (BC.) made sense of the universe by using mathematics. F
2. The earliest cosmologies (BC.) could make no testable predictions. T
3. The Newtonian-Euclidean universe was static but evolving. T
4. Olbers' paradox deals with why the sky is blue. F
5. Olbers' paradox is resolved by noting that dust absorbs distant starlight. F
6. Any valid cosmological theory must be able to explain Olbers' paradox. T
7. Non-Euclidean geometries were developed in the late 1800s and applied to cosmology in 1917. T
8. In any geometry, a three-dimensional space must be infinite. F
9. Universes with infinite volumes are called closed universes. F
10. G. Lemaître first developed Big bang cosmologies. T
11. All big bang cosmologies propose a definite beginning time for the universe. F
12. Big bang theories are not able to explain why the initial fireball came into existence. T
13. The steady state cosmology assumes that space is the same everywhere and all the time. T
14. There is some indication that the real universe is uncurved, open, and Euclidean. T
15. According to present data, the universe is closed and finite in volume. F
16. Euclidean geometry describes curved space. F
17. In a curved space the angles of a triangle do not add up to 180 degrees. T
18. The surface of a sphere is curved. T
19. The Pythagorean theorem is correct for non-Euclidean geometry. F
20. The Pythagorean theorem is true only for flat space. T
21. Spaces with infinite volumes are called closed spaces. F

Multiple Choice

1. A study of the structure of the universe as a single, orderly system is
   A. history
 * B. cosmology
   C. cosmos
   D. cosmetology
   E. comic

2. Ancient models of cosmology can be essentially distinguished from others by the phrase
   A. a Euclidean geometry filled with particles obeying Newton's laws
 * B. consideration of the nonmaterial attributes or "essences" of things
   C. a static, curved universe
   D. a universe expanding from a point of maximum density
   E. a universe the same at all times

3. The Newtonian-Euclidean cosmology can be essentially distinguished from others by the phrase
*   A. a Euclidean geometry filled with particles obeying Newton's laws
     B. consideration of the non-material attributes or "essences" of things
     C. a static, curved universe
     D. a universe expanding from a point of maximum density
     E. a universe the same at all times

4. A big bang cosmology can be essentially distinguished from others by the phrase
     A. a Euclidean geometry filled with particles obeying Newton's laws
     B. consideration of the non-material attributes or "essences" of things
     C. a static, curved universe
*   D. a universe expanding from a point of maximum density
     E. a universe the same at all times

5. The steady state cosmology can be essentially distinguished from others by the phrase
     A. a Euclidean geometry filled with particles obeying Newton's laws
     B. consideration of the non-material attributes or "essences" of things
     C. a static, curved universe
     D. a universe expanding from a point of maximum density
*   E. a universe the same at all times

6. Inability to make testable predictions is a limitation of _____ cosmology(ies).
*   A. ancient
     B. Newtonian-Euclidean
     C. big bang
     D. steady state
     E. tired light

7. Inability to explain Olbers' paradox is a limitation of _____ cosmology(ies).
     A. ancient
*   B. Newtonian-Euclidean
     C. big bang
     D. steady state
     E. tired light

8. Inability to predict the radiation left from the primeval fireball is a limitation of _____ cosmology(ies).
     A. ancient
     B. Newtonian-Euclidean
     C. big bang
*   D. steady state
     E. tired light

9. If the universe is infinite and Newtonian, the sky should be uniformly bright; clearly it is not. The preceding is a statement of _____.
     A. the perfect cosmological principle
*   B. Olbers' paradox
     C. Einstein's postulate
     D. the cosmological principle
     E. Hubble's relation

10. The gravitational mass of an object is proportional to its ____.
    A. size
    B. distance from the Earth
  * C. weight
    D. density
    E. color

Refer to the following diagram for questions 11 and 12.

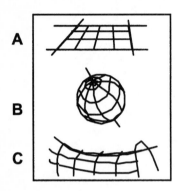

11. Which diagram of space, if continued, would be of finite extent?
    A. A
  * B. B
    C. C
    D. Both A and C
    E. none of these

12. Which diagram of space, if continued, would be of infinite extent?
    A. A
    B. B
    C. C
  * D. Both A and C
    E. none of these

13. Which of the following is(are) parts of the cosmological principle?
    A. The universe is homogeneous.
    B. The universe is isotropic.
    C. The universe is the same at all times.
  * D. Both A and B are parts.
    E. All three, A, B, and C, are parts.

14. Which of the following are parts of the cosmological principle used in the steady state cosmology?
    A. The universe is homogeneous.
    B. The universe is isotropic.
    C. The universe is the same at all times
    D. Both A and B are parts.
  * E. All three, A, B, and C, are parts.

15. The statement, "All observers, everywhere in space at one time, would view the same large picture of the universe" is called
   A. the cosmological paradox
* B. the cosmological principle
   C. the global principle
   D. the perfect cosmological assumption
   E. none of the above

Refer to the following diagram for questions 16-18.

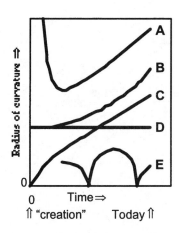

16. In the diagram, which is a universe that began contracting, reached a minimum, and is now expanding forever?
* A. A
   B. B
   C. C
   D. D
   E. E

17. In the diagram, which line represents a static universe?
   A. A
   B. B
   C. C
* D. D
   E. E

18. In the diagram, which line represents a periodically expanding and contracting universe?
   A. A
* B. B
   C. C
   D. D
   E. E

19 The idea that the universe was once infinitely dense is termed (the) ____.
   A. cosmic point
   B. cosmology
* C. cosmic singularity
   D. perfect principle
   E. small start

20. If matter is distributed uniformly on the large scale, then the universe is ___.
   A. Flat
   B. Open
   C. Anisotropic
   D. Isotropic
* E. Homogeneous

21. If the average density of matter over large volumes varies throughout the universe, then the universe is -not- ____.
   A. Flat
   B. Open
   C. Curved
   D. Isotropic
* E. Homogeneous

22. Cosmology is the study of the ____.
   A. Styling of hair
   B. Wavelength dependence of star light
* C. Size and structure of the universe
   D. Origin of the universe
   E. both B and C

23. Mythological cosmology associates the universe with ___.
   A. The power of reason
   B. Volcanic activity
* C. The spiritual life of humans
   D. The force of gravity
   E. Plate tectonics

24. Philosophical cosmology asserts that the force of gravity can provide a simple description of the structure of the universe. Isaac Newton was the forerunner in this cosmology. These statements are
   A. Correct
* B. Wrong—physical not philosophical cosmology
   C. Wrong—force of electrons, not gravity
   D. Wrong—Kepler not Newton
   E. wrong—both B and D corrections are needed

25. Physical cosmology asserts that the force of gravity can provide a simple description of the structure of the universe. Isaac Newton was the forerunner in this cosmology. These statements are ___.
* A. Correct
   B. Wrong—philosophical not physical cosmology
   C. Wrong—force of electrons, not gravity
   D. Wrong—Kepler not Newton
   E. wrong—both B and D corrections are needed

Essay

1. Describe the similarities and differences in big bang cosmologies and the steady state theory.
2. Explain by analogy how the universe may be expanding, have no edge, and yet be finite.
3. Describe the ideas in the tired light theory and the limitations of the theory.
4. Argue for or against the statement, "Modern astronomy has explained the universe better than ancient theologies."

Word Practice (* denotes other selected words from the chapter.)

1. The _____ comprises all matter and energy in existence anywhere.*
2. If something appears to be the same in all directions, it is said to be _____.
3. _____ _____ is used to find the distance to clusters of galaxies.*
4. By definition, the _____ mass of a body is proportional to its weight.
5. If the sum of all the internal angles in all triangles is 180°, and parallel lines never meet, the geometry is said to be Euclidean or _____.
6. Curved spaces were introduced into cosmology by _____.*
7. _____ _____ arises if we assume an infinite Euclidean universe.*
8. A flat space is a(n) _____ space.*
9. A(n) _____ _____ has an infinite volume
10. A(n) _____ universe has finite volume.
11. A(n) ____ universe means that the stars, galaxies, clusters, and so on are uniformly distributed on the large scale.*
12. _____ is the study of the structure of the universe.
13. The ____ mass of a body is a measure of the resistance it presents to a change of the body's motion.
14. The Newtonian cosmology is a(n) _____ universe.*
15. A _____ constant was proposed by Einstein to allow a static universe.
16. In the _____ _____ _____ , the universe is expanding from a past point of higher density.*
17. Euclidean geometry and Newton's laws were used to describe the _____ static cosmology.*
18. _____ _____ result when space is curved.*
19. The _____ _____ assumes that the universe is the same everywhere at one time.
20. If we have a(n) _____ space, then the Pythagorean theorem will not be satisfied.*
21. A space with a _____ curved geometry will be of finite size.*
22. The _____ _____ measures the rate of change of Hubble's parameter*.
23. A _____ curved geometry will extend forever.*
24. The _____ _____ is the ratio of the density of the universe to the density needed to just stop expansion.
25. Most of the helium in the universe was formed in _____ _____ soon after the big bang.*
26. The red shifted remnant of the big bang is called the cosmic _____ _____.*
27. A flat universe will occur when the university has the _____ _____ producing zero curvature.
28. The age of the universe estimated by taking the reciprocal of the Hubble expansion is called the Hubble _____.*
29. _____ uses radioactive isotopes to measure the age of the galaxy.*
30. Using H-R diagrams to arrive at age estimates is called _____ _____.*
31. Observed magnitudes of distant galaxies must have a(n) _____ correction before we can compare them with nearby galaxies.*
32. The recipical of the Hubble parameter is called the _____ ____ since it has the dimensions of time and roughly corresponds to the time since the big bang.
33. The _____ _____ provides the necessary mass to make the universe flat.

Answers to Word Practice

1. universe
2. isotropic
3. Hubble's relation
4. gravitational
5. flat
6. Einstein
7. Olbers' paradox
8. Euclidean
9. open universe
10. closed
11. homogeneous
12. cosmology
13. inertial
14. static
15. cosmological
16. big bang model
17. Newtonian
18. non-Euclidean geometries
19. cosmological principle
20. curved
21. positively
22. deceleration parameter
23. negatively
24. density parameter
25. cosmic nucleosynthesis
26. background radiation
27. critical density
28. time
29. nucleocosmo-chronology
30. isochrone fitting
31. evolutionary
32. Hubble time
33. dark matter

Chapter 27
Origin and Evolution of the Universe

Answers to Problems in the Text

1. a.

2. The big bang theories require the existence of this radiation, which was predicted before it was observed. Thus, the big bang theories had made a prediction rather than just describing what was already known. The text indicates isotropy, but a slight anisotropy has recently been reported. It seems to be due to the Earth's motion in the galaxy and the galaxy's motion in the local cluster.

3. Globular clusters are Population I stars—old—so the heavy elements (Si, Fe, O, and so on) that compose the Earth are very rare in them.

4. Identify spectral lines as red-shifted known lines. The lines would be absorption lines caused by processes in the galaxies; they would not correspond to individual stars. Take the red shift as cosmological and, hence, Doppler.

5. Just as a volume of gas cools as it expands (for example, there are devices on the market that chill and frost drinking glasses by means of expanding CO_2 gas), so has the universe. The radiation has been red-shifted from its high temperature to its present 3 K.

6. Each student's answer will be different. If your class is small or you can break up into groups, this would make an excellent discussion topic. Ask for explanations of answers to the second question. Do these answers apply only to astronomy or to other scientific research as well?

Advanced Problems

7. a. Since $V = Hr$, then $r = V/H$, where r is the distance of a galaxy from us and V is its speed. Compare this with the general equation for the distance traveled by a body, $r = vt$, where v is the velocity, t is the time of travel, and r is the distance traveled. By comparison, $t = 1/H$ (*note:* $1/H$ has the dimension of time) and $1/H$ is then a measure of the age of the universe. Of course, the universe's expansion must slow down (because of gravity), so today's value of H gives only an upper time limit.

   b. $H = 65$ km/s/megaparsec, $\dfrac{1}{H} = \dfrac{1 \text{ megaparsec}/s}{65 \text{km}}$ has dimensions of $\dfrac{\text{length} \times \text{time}}{\text{length}}$;

   that is, $1/H$ has dimensions of time.

   c. megaparsec $= 10^6$ parsecs $= 3 \times 10^{22}$ m

   $\dfrac{1}{H} = \dfrac{3 \times 10^{22} \text{m} \times \text{s}}{6.5 \times 10^4 \text{m}} = 4.6 \times 10^{17}$ s

   $= 4.6 \times 10^{17}$ s $\times \dfrac{1 \text{ year}}{\pi \times 10^7 \text{s}}$

   $= 1.5 \times 10^{10}$ years $= 15$ billion years

Sample Test Questions

True-False

1. Globular clusters are believed to be about 14 ± 4 billion years old. T
2. If *H* is Hubble's constant, then *H* can also be called the expansion age. F
3. The universe is believed to be between 12 and 16 billion years old. T
4. Uranium production models show that the universe must be no older than 7 billion years. F
5. The universe began, according to big bang theories, as a low-density, high-temperature object. F
6. When the universe began, it was composed of hydrogen. F
7. The first atoms to condense from the fireball were helium. F
8. At the end of the first hour, the universe was about 75% hydrogen by mass. T
9. The formation of galaxies began in the universe a few billion years after the big bang. F
10. The heavy elements are believed to have been made mostly inside massive stars. T
11. At present, we believe the universe will expand forever. T
12. Science can provide good answers as to why the universe exists. F
13. Science can provide good answers as to how the universe evolved. T
14. For all big bang models, the universe begins as a small hot object. F
15. Although the big-bang theory describes many observations, it is unable to predict the abundance of elements in Population II stars. F

Multiple Choice

1. The first atom to form as a fireball cooled was
* A. hydrogen
   B. helium
   C. deuterium
   D. uranium
   E. librium

2. The age of the universe based upon Hubble's constant is ____ years.
   A. 4.6 billion
   B. 7 ($\pm$3) billion
* C. 15 ($\pm$2) billion
   D. 1 million
   E. 20 billion

3. In the beginning, the universe was
   A. radiation
   B. subatomic particles
   C. atoms
* D. both A and B
   E. all three, A, B, and C

4. It is believed that at the end of the first hour of the universe the distribution was about _____%
   hydrogen, by mass, and _____ % helium-4, by mass.
   A. 25 / 75
 * B. 75 / 25
   C. 50 / 50
   D. 10 / 90
   E. 90 / 10

5. If c is the speed of light and G is Newton's gravitational constant, then the energy equivalent of a
   mass M is
   A. Mc
   B. $\dfrac{M}{c^2}$
   C. $\dfrac{GM}{c^2}$
 * D. Mc^2
   E. $\sqrt{\dfrac{Mc}{G}}$

6. It is believed that the primeval radiation of millions of degrees has been red-shifted to about _____ K.
   A. 273
   B. 20
   D. 2
 * C. 3
   E. 0.01

7. The heavy elements were first made
   A. in the primeval fireball
 * B. in the first massive stars
   C. when the density of the universe dropped enough for matter to form
   D. 0.001 second after creation
   E. misleading: never "first" made, always existed

8. The stars and galaxies formed when the universe was ___ of its present age.
   A. at the start
 * B. less than 10%
   C. between 30%-50%
   D. more than 50%
   E. about 25%

9. The creation of light elements in the universe took on the order of _____.
   A. seconds
 * B. minutes
   C. hours
   D. days
   E. years

10. The predicted amount of deuterium in the universe does not agree with Big Bang models since _____.
    A. the Big Bang is incorrect
    B. deuterium is a rare isotope
    C. deuterium is easily destroyed
 * D. both B and C
    E. none of these

11. As the universe expanded and cooled, the original thermal radiation became ____.
    A. shorter
    B. more energetic
 * C. red shifted
    D. blue shifted
    E. both A and C

12. The universe has its basic properties because we exist is a statement of the _____ principle.
    A. cosmological
    B. philosophical
 * C. anthropic
    D. Big Bang
    E. Hartmann

13. If the universe is closed it will ____.
    A. continue expanding
    B. continue collapsing
    C. stop expanding and become static
 * D. stop expanding and start collapsing.
    E. none of these

14. The SI unit of energy is the joule (J). Use the Einstein mass-energy equation to calculate the energy in 1 kg of matter.
    A. 2.06×10^5 J
    B. 3×10^8 J
 * C. 9×10^{18} J
    D. 9×10^{21} J
    E. 2.06×10^{23} J

Problem Involving Optional Mathematical Equation from Another Chapter

15. (Optional Equation IV) At what wavelength does the 3-K fireball radiation peak (approximately)?
    A. 0.03 m
 * B. 9.7×10^{-4}m
    C. 9.7×10^{-7} m
    D. 3×10^{-4} m
    E. 0.03 cm

Essay

1. Describe at least two astronomical observations consistent with our estimated age of the universe.
2. How are the heavy elements formed?
3. What existed before the big bang?
4. Do we know how, or if, the universe originated? Defend your answer.
5. Where did the carbon in our bodies originate?
6. Justify the statement, "We are but stardust."
7. Argue for or against the anthropic principle

Word Practice

1. The _____ diagram is a graphical way of showing the evolution of the universe in both time and space.*
2. At the time that it was too hot for nuclei to form, the universe was _____ dominated.
3. The creation of the light elements during the Big Bang is called cosmic _____.
4. When the universe cools sufficiently, it becomes _____ dominated.
5. The idea that the universe very rapidly expanded soon after the big bang is called the _____ universe model.
6. The measure of the disorder of a system is called _____.*
7. If the universe is closed, it must eventually change to contraction, leading to the eventual _____ __.*
8. The _____ principle assumes that the universe exists the way it does because life exists.*
9. As the universe cools, hydrogen suddenly forms in a process called _____.*
10. The time in the history of the universe when hydrogen forms is called the era of _____.
11. The coordinate frame in which the cosmic microwave background is isotropic is called the _____ reference frame.*
12. The cosmic microwave background _____ are believed to have been the starting points of galaxy formation
13. Any dark matter moving at relativistic velocities at the time of decoupling is called _____ _____ matter. This leads to a top-down structure formation.*
14. _____ has an atomic structure with negatively charged nuclei.
15. _____ is based upon the idea that all conservation laws reflect a simple underlying basis.
16. The weakest of the four fundamental forces is _____.*
17. Of the four fundamental forces, only gravity and _____ are long-range forces.
18. The _____ nuclear force governs the decay of the neutron.
19. Nuclei are held together by the _____ nuclear force.
20. In the bottom-up structure formation of galaxies, ___ dark matter particles are moving slowly.*
21. _____ constant relates the energy of the minimal unit of light and its frequency.
22. In the early universe and modern physics, particles can act like waves and waves can have particle aspects. This property is called the _____ duality.*
23. Matter can be converted to energy and energy to mass. This idea of Einstein is called the mass-energy _____.*
24. Scientists are searching for a _____, which will combine the four fundamental forces into a single force.
25. The low energies in our everyday world has led to a ___ symmetry leading us to see four fundamental forces when there is only one.*
26. The _____ theory unifies the electromagnetic and the weak nuclear forces.*
27. A _____ _____ theory would combine electromagnetic and the strong and weak nuclear forces.
28. In _____ theories, the fundamental entity is a tiny quantum singular string.*
29. The most distant observable objects in principle are said to be at the _____.*

30. The ____ _____ model of the universe starts the universe off as a high temperature object a finite time ago.
31. The discovery of the _____ _____ radiation, predicted by the big bang model is a strong support of its predictive powers.
32. Einstein's _____ equivalence explains the energy source for the stars and the universe.

Answers to Word Practice

1. space-time
2. radiation
3. nucleosynthesis
4. matter
5. inflationary
6. entropy
7. big crunch
8. anthropic
9. recombination
10. decoupling
11. absolute
12. fluctuations
13. hot dark
14. antimatter
15. symmetry
16. gravity
17. electromagnetism
18. weak
19. strong
20. cold dark
21. Planck's
22. wave-particle duality
23. equivalence
24. unification
25. broken
26. electroweak
27. grand unified
28. superstring
29. horizon
30. big bang
31. cosmic background
32. mass-energy

Chapter 28
Life in the Universe

Answers to Problems in the Text

1. Students need to look up the data for these stars. For example, what spectral type and population are they?

    Alpha Centauri is a binary system with G2 and K0 main-sequence stars of absolute magnitudes 4.4 and 5.7, respectively. γ Cephei is K1 sub giant of absolute magnitude 2.2. Sirius is another binary system consisting of an A1 main-sequence star and a white dwarf of absolute magnitudes 1.4 and 11.6, respectively.

    Of these stars, two (Alpha Centauri and Sirius) are binary stars, which reduces the chances of stable planetary orbits in the "habitable" zone. The companion of Sirius is a white dwarf that once must have been a giant, so if there is a planet upon which life existed, it probably would have been wiped out during that giant phase. Sirius itself is a large A1 star, so a near orbit to Sirius would be too hot (probably). There is a better chance for the Centauri system since both stars are relatively small and on the main sequence.

    γ Cephei is a single star and according to Table 28-1 may have a planetary companion of Jupiter's mass. However, γ Cephei is a subgiant probably in the process of evolving off the main sequence, so its "habitable" zone is changing. Life on a planet about γ Cephei would be in environmental trouble. In order of increasing probability of detecting signals, the choices are Alpha Centauri, Sirius, and γ Cephei, based solely upon distance. There is a good argument that Alpha Centauri, being a G2 star, has a greater probability of life than γ Cephei. The question is: Are Alpha Centauri A and B separated enough to allow good life-supporting orbits between?

2. Climatic changes have resulted from plate tectonics. "Outgassing" has altered atmospheric composition and has released some of our water supply. Some biologists attribute the extinction of some species to sudden climate changes, perhaps associated with continental drift and changing ocean currents.

3. As a star evolves, its total light output changes. Thus, over eons, the surface temperature will change dramatically. Even small solar changes may radically affect climates and life. As the star ages, it expands, heating the planet; later it cools, freezing the planet. If the planet's star explodes, all life is lost. Also, nearby stars might explode, bathing the planet in intense radiation that could affect existing life. Tidal forces can change spin rates. Orbital variations caused by perturbations change climate and may start ice ages.

4. Scenarios will vary—some possible examples:
    a. 1) International tensions build; nuclear war wipes out all life.
        2) Technology develops new bacterial weapons that get out of hand.
        3) Widespread use of new medicine. Long-term effects are genetic damage, killing all people.
        4) Industrial mistakes, such as widespread use of Freon, alter climate suddenly.
    b. Space travel developed. Materials and energy obtained from other planetary systems, enabling the human species to survive critical damage to the Earth. Population pressures reduced by emigration of excess population and the dissatisfied.

5. Answers will vary from student to student. At least two possible answers are given in each case. Of course, student answers should be much more detailed.
   a. 1) Panic; attempt made to destroy the aliens; war results.
      2) We go the way of the American Indians.
      3) They become our saviors; food and material problems solved.
   b. 1) Communication established; information exchange helps both cultures.
      2) Communication established; information causes one civilization to collapse.
      3) Only one nation controls communication on this planet; war starts over fear of unilateral control of the incoming information.
   c. 1) Space colonization as we expand.
      2) Space travel forgotten; people turn inward.
      3) Other possibilities (justify).

6. Summary of some key points:
   Political situation unstable, especially as fossil fuels and limited resources are used up. Technology has potential of both destruction and space travel. One or the other (or both, successively) should occur; might conclude that since we are a relatively young planet, this spread has already occurred in the galaxy.

7. Course 2 is safest.
   a. If others chose Course 1, we would hear a lot. If they also concluded 2 or 3 was best, we would not hear much; everybody would be listening to nothing.
   b. No. If all adopted Course 2 or 3, nothing would be heard. If we believe travel is ultimately impossible, then Course 1 is safe. After all, those in charge could keep secret what they learned (if social stability is desired).

Advanced Problems

8. Planet diameter $= 1.2 \times 10^7$ m, distance $= 3 \times 10^{16}$ m. (note: identical units)
   a. $\alpha'' = (d/D) \times 2.06 \times 10^5 = \dfrac{1.2 \times 2.06}{3} \times 10^{7-16+5} = 8.2 \times 10^{-5}$ seconds of arc
   b. No.
   c. $\alpha'' = \dfrac{1.5 \times 2.06}{3} \times 10^{11-16+5}; \alpha'' = 1''$
   d. Yes, in principle, but not in practice because the star will be so much brighter than the planet that to show the planet we would have to so overexpose the star that the effective resolution would be much worse than 1". (Most students may miss these latter comments.) General: Need to look for shifts in the star's position.

9. To solve this problem we must make a number of simplifying assumptions.
   a. Since we want free water somewhere on the planet's surface so the maximum temperature must be above 0°C = 273 K and the minimum surface temperature below 100°C = 373 K
   b. The energy per unit area at a distance r will be L divided by the area of a sphere of radius r, that is, $\dfrac{L}{4\pi r^2}$.
   c. Of this energy a fraction $100A$ is reflected and $100(1-A)$ is absorbed by the planet, so $100A\dfrac{L}{4\pi r^2}$ energy is added to the planet (per unit area).
   d. The planet is at a temperature T so it would emit an energy σT^4 per unit area if there were no atmosphere.

e. The atmosphere retains some of this energy (assuming the emissivity, e, is a %) so only $100e\sigma T^4$ per unit area is emitted.

f. For equilibrium, energy added = energy lost. Equate these and solve for r to get $r = \sqrt{\dfrac{1-A}{e\sigma}} \dfrac{\sqrt{L}}{T^2}$, so

$$r_{\text{inner}} = \sqrt{\frac{1-A}{e\sigma}} \frac{\sqrt{L}}{(373)^2} \quad \text{and} \quad r_{\text{outer}} = \sqrt{\frac{1-A}{e\sigma}} \frac{\sqrt{L}}{(273)^2}$$

Sample Test Questions

True-False

1. Life is a process. T
2. Most of your body weight is water. T
3. Proteins are composed of amino acids. T
4. The surface of the Earth is screened from ultraviolet rays by the ozone layer. T
5. The greater production of offspring by those individuals best adapted to the changing environment is called natural selection. T
6. The statistics of masses among binary and multiple stars suggest that few stars are likely to have companions. F
7. Massive stars spin more slowly than smaller stars. F
8. For life to evolve on a planet, the planet must be close enough to its star that water is a liquid but not so close that the water all evaporates. T
9. No Earth organisms could survive under any conditions found on other planets. F
10. Contact with an extraterrestrial civilization would pose no danger to humanity. F
11. Extraterrestrial intelligent life definitely exists in the solar system. F
12. There is the possibility of primitive life forms elsewhere in the solar system. T
13. Life, even intelligent life, is very probable elsewhere in the universe. T
14. The first radio message deliberately sent to the stars was sent toward M13 in 1974. T
15. The evolution of life is unaffected by astronomical processes. F
16. There is definitely extraterrestrial intelligent life in the solar system. F
17. No Earth organisms could survive under any conditions found on other planets. F
18. The current interpretation of all radio signals received, thus far, is that none have come from intelligent extraterrestrial life. T
19. The US government is currently sponsoring an extensive search for ETL. F
20. The first radio message deliberately sent to the stars was sent toward M13 in 1974. T
21. The only messages we have sent to possible extraterrestrial life near other stars are the radio signals we have transmitted both accidentally and deliberately. F
22. We have sent no messages to possible extraterrestrial recipients. F
23. Only living things can make organic molecules. F
24. By definition living things must be able to reproduce offspring; therefore a man with a vasectomy can not be considered to be living. F
25. A good analogy to life is a bucket of water into which water is flowing and at the same rate water is flowing out. T
26. A good analogy to life is a bucket of water. F
27. During star formation, it is likely that planets also form. T
28. The statistics of masses among binary and multiple stars suggest few stars are likely to have companions. F
29. The surface of the Earth is screened from ultraviolet rays by the ozone layer. T

30. Natural selection is -not- thought to have been responsible for the rapid phase of evolution in recent eras. F
31. Natural selection is thought to have been responsible for the rapid phase of evolution in recent eras. T
32. The greater survival rate of offspring produced by those individuals best adapted to the changing environment is called natural selection. T
33. Amino acids are composed of proteins. F
34. Amino acids are large molecules consisting of building blocks of smaller molecules called proteins. F

Multiple Choice

1. The chemistry of carbon compounds is termed
   A. cell chemistry
 * B. organic chemistry
   C. biochemistry
   D. a minor chemistry
   E. none of these

2. One of the first scientists to produce amino acids using electricity and a mixture that might approximate the primitive atmosphere was
   A. Oparin
   B. Fox
   C. Drake
   D. Shklovskii
 * E. Miller

3. Which of the following suggest(s) water was crucial to the development of life on Earth?
   A. People, animals, and plants are mostly water.
   B. Organisms without water quickly die.
   C. Iron is rusted by water.
 * D. Both A and B suggest water's importance.
   E. All three, A, B, and C, suggest its importance.

4. Which of the following is (are) evidence for planets near other stars?
 * A. Massive stars spin faster than smaller stars.
   B. Sirius is a binary star.
   C. The Sun is not special, so other stars have planets.
   D. Both A and C are evidence.
   E. All three, A, B, and C, are evidence.

5. It is unlikely that the oldest stars (Population II) have planets because
   A. they are too bright
   B. they are too big
   C. they contain too much of the heavy elements
 * D. they contain too little of the heavy elements
   E. they are too red

6. Binary stars are less likely to have habitable planets because
    A. most have widely differing masses
    B. the Lagrangian surface lies between them
 * C. many possible orbits suffer large perturbations, causing orbits to be highly elliptical if not parabolic
    D. both B and C
    E. all three, A, B, and C

7. Biologists concerned with possible life on other worlds are called
    A. crazy
    B. extraterrestrial biologists
 * C. exobiologists
    D. technocrats
    E. ecdysiasts

8. There is probably _____ intelligent life in the solar system, according to the text.
    A. no
 * B. no extraterrestrial
    C. permanent extraterrestrial
    D. visiting interstellar
    E. none of these

9. The spacecraft _____ flew by Jupiter in 1973 and will leave the solar system. It contains a plaque attempting to convey our appearance and location.
    A. Apollo 13
    B. Mariner 10
    C. Viking 2
    D. Pioneer 3
 * E. Pioneer 10

10. Why would we not expect native life on a planet orbiting a white dwarf?
    A. white dwarfs are young stars
 * B. the star is emitting much less light than it did in the past.
    C. the star is emitting much more light than it did in the past.
    D. white dwarfs are old stars
    E. none of these

11. Sudden changes in environment, which can affect evolution, include ___
    A. volcanic eruptions
    B. asteroid impacts
    C. planetary convection
    D. both A and B
 * E. all three (A, B, and C)

12. According to the text, what are the chances of any extraterrestrial life in the solar system?
    A. all the plants probably have life
    B. many planets in the solar system probably have life
 * C. a few locations such as Mars and Titian allow some possibility
    D. there is no possibility
    E. none of these

13. The organic compounds found in a few meteorites are probably non-terrestrial. They are believed to be produced abiologically since ___.
    A. they won't grow
  * B. they have equal numbers of right and left handed molecules
    C. they are almost all right handed molecules
    D. they are almost all left handed molecules
    E. misleading—no meteorites exist containing compounds that are believed to be extraterrestrial.

14. Amino acids found in some meteorites are known to have an extraterrestrial origin because _____.
    A. no fossils were found.
    B. the meteorites were carbonaceous chrondites.
  * C. they have a structure and symmetry different than those produced on Earth.
    D. meteorites have an extraterrestrial origin.
    E. meteorites come from the asteroid belt.

15. Organic molecules have been found in some meteorites, so there must be life elsewhere in the universe.
    A. correct
  * B. wrong—except for one Mars meteorite, the non-terrestrial cases were probably produced abiologically
    C. wrong—except for one Mars meteorite, all such cases are known to result from terrestrial contamination
    D. misleading—no organic molecules have been found in meteorites
    E. none of these

16. If we accept the text's plausible upper limit on the fraction of stars with planets having intelligent life, we get the distance to the nearest civilization as _____ light-years.
    A. 1.5×10^3
    B. 10^7
  * C. 15
    D. 30
    E. 150

17. If we take the most pessimistic, but plausible, lower limit to the fraction of stars and planets with intelligent life, then according to the Drake equation, how far away do we expect the nearest other intelligent life to be?
    A. near a star far away but in our galaxy.
    B. near a close-by star in our galaxy.
    C. in a different universe.
    D. on another planet of the solar system.
  * E. in a different galaxy.

18. Which of the following is -not- one of the factors considered in the Drake equation?
    A. number of stars in galaxy
    B. duration of civilization
  * C. age of the universe
    D. fraction of solar type stars
    E. fraction of planets with life

19. So far astronomers have not attempted to listen for radio signals from another planetary system.
    A. correct
  * B. wrong—they have listened but have received no signals yet
    C. wrong—they have listened and did receive intelligent signals from M13

20. What kind of messages have -not- been sent by us to extraterrestrials?
    A. accidental messages sent by our broadcasting leaking into space.
  * B. misleading—all three types (a, c, and e) have been sent
    C. intentional messages via radio waves.
    D. neither a nor c types of messages have been sent
    E. messages aboard spacecraft that have been sent out of the solar system.

Essay

1. What is the evidence for planets near other stars?
2. What astronomical processes could have affected biological evolution?
3. What are four conditions needed to make a planet habitable?
4. What evidence, and what statistical possibility, is there for alien life in the solar system? Intelligent life?

Word Practice (* denotes other selected words from the chapter.)

1. The basic structural unit of life on Earth is the _____.
2. The structural plans for life is contained in the _____ molecule.
3. The molecules formed of amino acids in cells are _____.
4. The _____ molecule is the "contractor" which communicates instructions to the cellular mechanisms.
5. The _____ layer screens the Earth's surface from ultraviolet radiation.
6. The _____ of DNA is essential for cell reproduction.
7. All life on Earth is _____ based.*
8. Life is a(n) _____ rather than a state.*
9. _____ _____ are the building blocks of proteins.
10. _____ is a process, not a state.
11. _____ communication is probably the best method of contact with alien civilizations.
12. The _____ _____ protects the Earth's surface from excessive ultraviolet radiation.
13. _____ _____ is the chemistry of carbon molecules.
14. The _____ is the chemical factory upon which life is based.
15. The _____ _____ produced amino acids under conditions believed to approximate the early Earth.
16. S. W. Fox created round cell-like objects called _____.
17. _____ is the process which green plants use to convert sunlight into chemical energy.
18. _____ selection affects evolution because those individuals best adapted to the changing environment are more likely to have offspring.
19. Natural _____ eliminates those species not suited to their environment.
20. Cells with nuclei are called _____.
21. The sudden loss of many species in a short time is called a _____ extinction.
22. The fossils called _____ are the oldest compelling evidence for life on Earth.
23. The idea that the current evolutionary status of life is the result of many branching points that were affected by external events is called _____.
24. The study of possible life outside the Earth's biosphere is called _____.
25. Molecules based on the carbon atom are called _____ molecules.

26. Some molecules can be either right-handed or left-handed. If a collection of molecules is mostly one or the other we have a _____ mixture.
27. Some molecules can be either right-handed or left-handed. If a collection of molecules is an equal mixture of the two it is called a _____ mixture.
28. H. G. Bungenberg de Jong produced cell-sized clusters of proteins called _____.
29. The _____ equation enables us to estimate the probable distance to another intelligent species.
30. We may not hear from other advanced civilizations since intelligent life may pass through only a short _____ interval during which it wants to contact other intelligent civilizations on other planets.

Answers to Word Practice

1. cell
2. DNA
3. proteins
4. RNA
5. ozone
6. replication
7. carbon
8. process
9. amino acids
10. life
11. radio
12. ozone layer
13. organic chemistry
14. cell
15. Miller experiments
16. proteinoids
17. photosynthesis
18. natural
19. selection
20. eukaryotes
21. mass
22. stromatolites
23. contingency
24. exobiology
25. organic
26. nonracemic
27. racemic
28. coacervates
29. Drake
30. explorative